Prentice Hall
LITERATURE
Timeless Voices, Timeless Themes

PRACTICE BOOK

Selection Support:
Skills Development

- **Build Vocabulary**

- **Build Spelling Skills**

- **Build Grammar Skills**

- **Reading Strategy**

- **Literary Focus**

S I L V E R

PRENTICE HALL
Upper Saddle River, New Jersey
Needham, Massachusetts

ISBN 0-13-436583-6

5 6 7 8 9 10   02 01

PRENTICE HALL

CONTENTS

UNIT 1: COMING OF AGE

UNIT 2: MEETING CHALLENGES

UNIT 4: FROM SEA TO SHINING SEA

UNIT 5: EXTRAORDINARY OCCURRENCES

UNIT 7: NONFICTION

UNIT 8: DRAMA

UNIT 9: POETRY

© Prentice-Hall, Inc.

UNIT 10: THE AMERICAN FOLK TRADITION

"The Drummer Boy of Shiloh" by Ray Bradbury (text page 5)

Build Vocabulary

Using the Word Part *bene-*

A. DIRECTIONS: The word part *bene-* means "well" or "good." The Word Bank word *benediction* means "an expression of good wishes, or a blessing." Apply what you know about the word part *bene-* and use context clues to match the underlined word to its definition. Write the letter of the definition on the line.

a. kindly   d. helpful
b. blessing   e. one who has helped others through gifts or kind acts
c. act of kindness   f. one who inherits money or property

_____ 1. The <u>benefactor</u> gave $1,000 to the scholarship fund.

_____ 2. The <u>benign</u> old man fed the birds in the park.

_____ 3. The warm climate was <u>beneficial</u> to Arthur's health.

_____ 4. As the priest gave a <u>benediction</u>, the people knelt.

_____ 5. Wendy thanked the generous contributor for her <u>benevolence</u>.

_____ 6. Carlos is the main <u>beneficiary</u> of his uncle's will.

Using the Word Bank

benediction	riveted	compounded	resolute

B. DIRECTIONS: Complete each of the following sentences with a word from the Word Bank.

1. The very youth of the soldiers was like a _____ because they seemed to be blessed with it.

2. It was obvious that Joby's attention was _____ on the general because he didn't take his eyes off the great man.

3. Patriotism _____ with courage would help get the soldiers through the battle.

4. The way the boy held his head up high showed he was _____ in his purpose.

Using Antonyms

DIRECTIONS: Each question below consists of a word in CAPITAL LETTERS, followed by four lettered words. Circle the letter of the word that is most opposite in meaning to the word in capital letters.

1. BENEDICTION   2. RIVETED   3. RESOLUTE
   a. blessing   a. distracted   a. unsolvable
   b. curse   b. staring   b. determined
   c. inheritance   c. drilled   c. jumpy
   d. scolding   d. focused   d. halfhearted

"The Drummer Boy of Shiloh" by Ray Bradbury (text page 5)

Build Spelling Skills: Adding *-ed* to a Two-Syllable Word

Spelling Strategy   When adding *-ed* to a two-syllable word, don't double the final consonant if the stress is on the first syllable.

riv'et + -ed = riveted

A. Practice: Add *-ed* to each word in parentheses. Write the new word on the line to complete the sentence.

1. (beckon) The guide _____ to the tourist, as if to say, "Follow me."

2. (darken) As the sun went down, the forest _____.

3. (offer) Dave _____ Dominic $10 for his pet lizard.

4. (favor) Anyone could see that the umpire _____ the home team.

5. (iron) Becky _____ her yellow blouse carefully.

B. Practice: Complete each sentence by adding *-ed* to one of the following words and writing the new word on the line.

strengthen	swallow	listen	flicker
whisper	murmur	open	happen

1. Joby _____ to his own heartbeat in the still night.

2. When he _____ his eyes, he saw his drum.

3. It seemed that the army _____ to itself in the dark.

4. Some of the men _____ to themselves.

5. Many of the young soldiers were _____ by thoughts of home.

6. Moths _____ about, drawn to the light of the fires.

7. What _____ at Shiloh was a terrible battle.

8. After the general left, Joby _____ and cleared his throat.

Challenge: One of the weapons mentioned in "The Drummer Boy of Shiloh" is the Minié ball, a bullet named after Claude Étienne Minié, a French army officer. Here is a list of other weapons named after people or places. In a dictionary that gives word histories, look up each word. Then, on the line, write the source for the word and a definition of it.

1. Gatling gun_____

2. bayonet _____

3. Mauser_____

4. shrapnel_____

5. Toledo_____

"The Drummer Boy of Shiloh" by Ray Bradbury (text page 5)

Build Grammar Skills: Nouns

Nouns are words that name persons, animals, places, things, or ideas. Here are some examples of each type of noun:

Persons: soldier, general
Animals: owl, butterfly
Places: field, country
Things: blossoms, band
Ideas: patriotism, bravery

A. Practice: Underline all of the nouns in each of the following sentences. On the line, write each noun and then write *person, animal, place, thing,* or *idea* to indicate what the noun names. The first one has been done for you.

1. He spoke to the boy about the importance of the rhythms.

   boy (person); importance (idea); rhythms (thing)

2. Forty thousand men lay on the ground, trying to sleep.

   _____

3. He wondered if his courage would fail him.

   _____

4. The general, smelling of sweat, leather, and earth, stopped to talk.

   _____

5. A terrible battle would be fought in the morning.

   _____

6. The boy understood, finally, his own significance.

   _____

B. Writing Application: Rewrite the following sentences, replacing each underlined word with a noun. You may have to add other words, such as *a, an,* or *the.*

1. As <u>he</u> listened to <u>him</u>, he began to feel important.

   _____

2. <u>He</u> began to lose his fear of <u>it</u>.

   _____

3. When <u>it</u> began in the morning, <u>he</u> would beat out a steady rhythm.

   _____

4. <u>It</u> would inspire <u>them</u> to fight with <u>it</u>.

   _____

5. <u>He</u> lay next to <u>it</u> as <u>they</u> fell from the tree on <u>it</u>.

   _____

Reading for Success: Literal Comprehension Strategies

Literal comprehension is an understanding of the writer's words and ideas on a basic level. The following reading strategies will help to increase your literal comprehension of a selection:

- **Break down long sentences.** Read long sentences in meaningful groups of words, not word by word. Punctuation will often guide you to words that work together as a unit. Read through the sentence quickly to find the subject—the person, place, thing, or idea that the sentence is discussing. Then decide what the sentence is saying about the subject.

- **Use context clues.** Use the context, or the surroundings, of an unfamiliar word to find clues to its meaning.

- **Reread or read ahead.** Reread confusing passages until you understand them. If rereading doesn't clarify a passage, read ahead. You may find the answer in the next few sentences or paragraphs.

- **Paraphrase.** Restate a sentence or paragraph in your own words to be sure you understand it.

DIRECTIONS: Read the following passage from "All You've Ever Wanted" by Joan Aiken, and use the reading strategies to increase your comprehension. In the margin, note where you break down sentences, use context clues, reread or read ahead, and paraphrase.

from *"All You've Ever Wanted"* by Joan Aiken

The following pasage is the opening of a story about a young girl's upbringing by six aunts.

Matilda, you will agree, was a most unfortunate child. Not only had she three names each worse than the other—Matilda, Eliza, and Agatha—but her father and mother died shortly after she was born, and she was brought up exclusively by her six aunts. These were all energetic, and so on Monday Matilda was taught algebra and arithmetic by her Aunt Aggie, on Tuesday biology by her Aunt Bettie, on Wednesday classics by her Aunt Cissie, on Thursday dancing and deportment by her Aunt Dorrie, on Friday essentials by her Aunt Effie, and on Saturday French by her Aunt Florrie. Friday was the most alarming day, as Matilda never knew beforehand what Aunt Effie would decide on as the day's essentials—sometimes it was cooking, or revolver practice, or washing, or boilermaking ("For you never know what a girl may need nowadays," as Aunt Effie rightly observed).

So that by Sunday, Matilda was often worn out, and thanked her stars that her seventh aunt, Gertie, had left for foreign parts many years before, and never threatened to come back and teach her geology or grammar on the only day when she was able to do as she liked.

However, poor Matilda was not entirely free from her Aunt Gertie, for on her seventh birthday, and each one after it, she received a little poem wishing her well, written on pink paper, decorated with silver flowers, and signed "Gertrude Isabel Jones, to her neice, with much affection." And the terrible disadvantage of the poems, pretty though they were, was that the wishes in them invariably came true. For instance, the one on her eighth birthday read:

Now you're eight Matilda dear

May shining gifts your place adorn

And each day through the coming year

Awake you with a rosy morn.

The shining gifts were all very well—they consisted of a torch, a luminous watch, pins, needles, a steel soapbox, and a useful little silver brooch which said "Matilda" in case she ever forgot her name—but the rosy morns were a great mistake. As you know, a red sky in the morning is the shepherd's warning, and the fatal results of Aunt Gertie's well-meaning verse were that it rained every day for the entire year.

Another one read:

Each morning make another friend

Who'll be with you till light doth end.

Cheery and frolicsome and gay,

To pass the sunny hours away.

For the rest of her life Matilda was overwhelmed by the number of friends she made in the course of that year—three hundred and sixty-five of them. Every morning she found another of them, anxious to cheer her and frolic with her, and her aunts complained that her lessons were being constantly interrupted. The worst of it was that she did not really like all the friends—some of them were so very cheery and frolicsome, and insisted on pillow fights when she had a toothache, or sometimes twenty-one of them would get together and make her play hockey, which she hated. She was not even consoled by the fact that all her hours were sunny, because she was so busy in passing them away that she had no time to enjoy them.

Long miles and weary though you stray

Your friends are never far away,

And every day though you may roam,

Yet night will find you back at home.

"The Drummer Boy of Shiloh" by Ray Bradbury (text page 5)

Literary Focus: Historical Setting

A story's **setting** is the time, place, and culture in which the story takes place. Setting is often an important element of a story. It can have significant influence on the ideas and actions of the characters. When a story has a **historical setting,** details about people, events, technology, the weather, and even clothing help bring that setting to life for the reader. Think about how the details of the historical setting are directly related to the emotions felt by the drummer boy, the general, and the other characters in "The Drummer Boy of Shiloh."

DIRECTIONS: As you read the story, pay particular attention to the specific details about the historical setting that the author provides. List some of these details, and then tell why they are important to the story.

Details that reflect the time of year:_____

_____

_____

Details that reflect the physical surroundings: _____

_____

_____

Details that reflect the technology of the time: _____

_____

_____

Details that reflect military customs of the time: _____

_____

_____

Importance of setting:_____

_____

_____

_____

_____

_____

_____

_____

_____

"**Charles**" by Shirley Jackson (text page 14)

Build Vocabulary

Using the Root -cred-

A. DIRECTIONS: The word root -cred- means "believe." The prefix in- makes what follows negative, so the Word Bank word *incredulously* means "with disbelief." Apply what you know about the word root -cred- and use context clues to define the underlined words.

1. Laurie gave a <u>credible</u> account of his first day of kindergarten.

   _____

2. The details in Laurie's stories gave <u>credence</u> to what he said about Charles.

   _____

3. Laurie's descriptions of Charles's behavior were almost <u>incredible</u>.

   _____

Using the Word Bank

renounced	insolently	elaborately	simultaneously	incredulously

B. DIRECTIONS: Match each word in the left column with its definition in the right column. Write the letter of the definition on the line next to the word it defines.

_____ 1. simultaneously   a. gave up

_____ 2. elaborately   b. with doubt or disbelief

_____ 3. renounced   c. boldly disrespectful in speech or behavior

_____ 4. incredulously   d. at the same time

_____ 5. insolently   e. painstakingly

Analogies

C. DIRECTIONS: Each question below consists of a pair of related words in CAPITAL LETTERS followed by four lettered pairs of words. Circle the letter of the pair that best expresses a relationship similar to that expressed in the pair in capital letters.

1. INSOLENTLY : DISRESPECTFULLY ::
   a. shyly : timidly
   b. calmly : energetically
   c. regularly : automatically
   d. courteously : rudely

2. ELABORATELY : PAINSTAKINGLY ::
   a. carefully : quickly
   b. lightly : heavily
   c. carefully : cautiously
   d. quickly : slowly

3. RENOUNCED : THRONE ::
   a. drove : highway
   b. threw : ball
   c. ran : pavement
   d. grew : tall

4. DOUBTFULLY : INCREDULOUSLY ::
   a. enormously : lovingly
   b. seriously : foolishly
   c. routinely : frighteningly
   d. intelligently : wisely

"**Charles**" by Shirley Jackson (text page 14)

Build Spelling Skills: Change Adjectives to Adverbs

Spelling Strategy You can change most adjectives to adverbs by adding *-ly*. When you add *-ly*, you usually do not change the spelling of the adjective.

Example: clear + *-ly* = clearly.

Exception: For words that end in *-ble*, drop the *-le* before adding *-ly*. For example, humble + *-ly* = humbly.

Another exception: For words that end in a consonant + *-y*, change the *y* to *i* before adding -ly. For example, ordinary + *-ly* = ordinarily.

A. Practice: Change each adjective to an adverb by adding *-ly*. Write the adverb on the line.

1. insolent _____
2. elaborate _____
3. simultaneous _____
4. awful _____

5. happy _____
6. joyful _____
7. comfortable _____
8. usual _____

B. Practice: Add *-ly* to the word in parentheses to form an adverb. Write the adverb on the line to complete the sentence.

1. (unusual) When Laurie got home from his first day of kindergarten, he was _____ rude to his family.

2. (thoughtful) Before telling his parents about Charles, Laurie paused _____.

3. (anxious) Laurie's mother fretted _____ about her son's behavior.

4. (reassuring) Laurie's father said, _____, that Laurie would be just fine.

5. (noisy) After school, Laurie _____ slammed the front door.

6. (solemn) As he told his stories, Laurie sat _____ in his chair.

7. (hearty) To show her interest, Laurie's mother spoke _____.

Challenge: The narrator in "Charles" meets her son's teacher at a PTA meeting. The familiar abbreviation PTA stands for "Parent-Teacher Association." An abbreviation is a shortened form of a word or phrase, made up of either lowercase letters or uppercase letters. In a dictionary, look up the meaning of each of the following abbreviations. Write the meaning on the line.

1. ETA _____
2. AMA _____
3. FDA _____
4. DNA _____
5. EKG _____

© Prentice-Hall, Inc.

"Charles" by Shirley Jackson (text page 14)

Build Grammar Skills: Common Nouns and Proper Nouns

Nouns may be common or proper. A **common noun** names any person, animal, place, thing, or idea. A **proper noun** names a particular person, animal, place, thing, or idea. Here are some examples:

Common nouns: student, cat, park, car, room, friendship,

Proper nouns: Laurie, Fluffy, Central Park, Mr. Fleming, Friday, Main Street

A proper noun is capitalized. A common noun is not capitalized unless it is the first word of a sentence.

A. Practice: Find at least four proper nouns and ten common nouns in the following paragraph. Write them in the correct columns in the chart below.

When Laurie started kindergarten, his personality seemed to change dramatically. He would slam the door when he got home. He would spill his baby sister's milk and speak insolently to his father. He told stories about what his teacher had said at school. He also told stories about a boy named Charles. After a few weeks of bad behavior, Charles suddenly started acting good. He handed out crayons and helped the teacher. The Monday after that, Charles started being naughty again. Laurie's mother and father looked forward to meeting Charles's mother. When they went to the PTA meeting and met Laurie's teacher, she had a little surprise for them.

Common Nouns	Proper Nouns

B. Writing Application: On the lines, write sentences following the directions.

1. Use a proper noun in a sentence Laurie's mother might say.

_____

2. Use a common noun in a sentence Laurie's teacher might say.

_____

3. Use a proper noun in a sentence one of the kindergarten students might say.

_____

4. Use a common noun in a sentence Laurie's father might say.

_____

"Charles" by Shirley Jackson (text page 14)

Reading Strategy: Break Down Long Sentences

Some stories have long or confusing sentences. By **breaking down these sentences** into their basic parts, you can make them easier to understand. After you've done that, you can reread the sentence to get the full picture.

You can use the natural breaks in the sentences to help in dividing them. These breaks might be signaled by punctuation. Then look for the main parts in each section, and then try to discover what each part is about. When you come to a long or confusing sentence as you read "Charles," use the chart below to help break each part of the sentence. Here is one example.

The day my son Laurie started kindergarten he renounced corduroy overalls with bibs and began wearing blue jeans with a belt . . .

What is the sentence or the sentence part about?	What does the sentence or sentence part say about the subject?
Laurie (he)	renounced overalls began wearing jeans

"Charles" by Shirley Jackson (text page 14)

Literary Focus: Point of View

The **point of view** of a story is the vantage point or perspective from which a story is told. What we learn about the characters and events of a story depends upon the point of view that a writer uses. For example, Shirley Jackson writes "Charles" from the point of view of Laurie's mother. Because Laurie's mother tells the story, we learn the details of her thoughts, feelings, and actions, but we don't learn all of the thoughts and feelings of her husband, the kindergarten teacher, or her son Laurie. If the story were written from another character's point of view, the story might be quite different. In fact, if the story were told from Laurie's teacher's point of view, the most important element of the story, its surprise ending, would be eliminated. We would learn the true identity of the kindergarten troublemaker early in the story.

DIRECTIONS: Following are characters from "Charles." On the lines provided, describe the role of each character in the story. Then explain how the reader's understanding of Laurie, his mother, his father, and his teacher would be different if the story were written from that character's point of view. Remember to explain what the reader would *not* learn as well as what the reader *would* learn

1. Laurie

    _____

    _____

    _____

    _____

2. Kindergarten Teacher

    _____

    _____

    _____

    _____

3. Laurie's Father

    _____

    _____

    _____

    _____

from I Know Why the Caged Bird Sings by Maya Angelou (text page 24)

Build Vocabulary

Using Forms of *tolerate*

A. DIRECTIONS: The verb tolerate, which means "to accept," forms the basis of many other words. Complete each sentence by writing one of these words in the blank: *intolerance, intolerable, tolerance, tolerant, tolerable.*

1. The boy was so _____ of his dog that he allowed him to bark all night.

2. Carol's _____ of weeds causes her to spend hours in the garden each day.

3. The hot weather is _____ if you wear light clothing.

4. Because of her high _____ for noise, Pat makes a good kinder- garten teacher.

5. Dean finds rainy weather _____, so he moved from Seattle.

fiscal	taut	benign	infuse	intolerant	couched

B. DIRECTIONS: Complete each of the following sentences with a Word Bank word.

1. Mrs. Flowers was able to _____ in young Marguerite an apprecia- tion of the printed word.

2. Mrs. Flowers, though thin, did not have the _____ skin that some thin people have.

3. Momma based the location of her first lunch counter on _____ concerns.

4. Mrs. Flowers _____ her ideas in words that were like music.

5. The _____ Mrs. Flowers was never anything but kind to Marguerite.

6. Mrs. Flowers advised Marguerite to be _____ of the ignorance in others but to be understanding of their illiteracy.

Synonyms

C. DIRECTIONS: Each question below consists of a word in CAPITAL LETTERS followed by four lettered words. Circle the letter of word or phrase that is most similar in meaning to the word in capital letters.

1. COUCHED
   a. served
   b. shouted
   c. whispered
   d. expressed

2. BENIGN
   a. cruel
   b. kindly
   c. belittle
   d. evil

3. FISCAL
   a. financial
   b. physical
   c. tight-fisted
   d. generous

from **I Know Why the Caged Bird Sings** by Maya Angelou (text page 24)

Build Spelling Skills: Silent *g* in *ign*

Spelling Strategy   In Maya Angelou's story, a character is described as "benign." A number of English words, such as benign have a silent *g* in *ign*.

A. Practice: Complete each of the defined words by adding *ign* in the blank. Then use the words to complete the sentences that follow. Write each word on the line.

al_____: to adjust or bring into a good working position, as parts of a machine

des_____: to work out and draw plans for

mal_____: to speak evil of; to slander

ass_____ment: something that is given as a task

ben_____: pleasant, friendly, or kind

1. The _____ for the costume called for a thousand sequins.

2. We will have to _____ the front end of this car soon.

3. No matter what Sid did, Hank would never _____ him.

4. The _____ for tomorrow is to read Chapter 32.

5. The _____ shopkeeper gave the child a sample of the trail mix.

B. Practice: Complete each of the following sentences with a word containing *ign*.

1. During the presidential _____, the candidates debated the issues on television.

2. The _____ of Queen Elizabeth II began in 1952.

3. We discovered a new No Parking _____ in front of the movie theater.

4. People who travel to other countries find it helpful to know one or more _____ languages.

Challenge: Maya Angelou lived for a time in Arkansas. The phonetic pronunciation of *Arkansas* given in a dictionary would show that the way the word is pronounced doesn't match the way it is spelled. Look up each of the following words in a dictionary. Then write the phonetic pronunciation on the line, and say each word out loud.

1. Arkansas _____

2. indict _____

3. hors d'oeuvre _____

4. alms _____

5. Des Moines _____

6. feign _____

Name _____ Date _____

from *I Know Why the Caged Bird Sings* by Maya Angelou (text page 24)

Build Grammar Skills: Plural and Possessive Nouns

A **plural noun** indicates more than one person, animal, place, thing, or idea. Most plural nouns end with -s. Here are some examples of plural nouns: *pies, points, years.*

A **possessive noun** shows ownership, belonging, or other close relationship. A possessive noun can be singular, ending in -'s, or plural, usually ending in -s'. Here are some examples of singular possessives: *man's* way of communicating, *Mrs. Flowers's* house. Here are some examples of plural possessives: the *customers'* visits, the *cookies'* sweetness. To form the possessive of a plural noun that does not end in s, add 's: *children's games.*

A. Practice: Draw a circle around the plural noun, and underline the possessive noun in each sentence. On the line, write whether the possessive noun is a singular possessive or a plural possessive.

1. To young Marguerite, her grandmother's store was full of treasures.

   _____

2. Marguerite was used to the customers' admiration of her measuring skills.

   _____

3. Next to her brother Bailey, Marguerite's favorite things were pineapples.

   _____

4. The teachers' reports on Marguerite were that she was a good but quiet student.

   _____

5. Mrs. Flowers's house smelled of freshly baked cookies.

   _____

6. Marguerite had read Charles Dickens's famous book, *A Tale of Two Cities.*

   _____

7. The words' sounds were like music when read by Mrs. Flowers.

   _____

B. Writing Application: Change each of the following nouns into a possessive form as indicated. Use each new word in a sentence about *I Know Why the Caged Bird Sings.*

1. shopper (singular possessive) _____

2. shopper (plural possessive)_____

3. poem (singular possessive) _____

4. poem (plural possessive) _____

5. teacher (singular possessive) _____

6. teacher (plural possessive) _____

7. woman (singular possessive) _____

8. woman (plural possessive)_____

Name _____ Date _____

from *I Know Why the Caged Bird Sings* by Maya Angelou (text page 24)

Reading Strategy: Reread or Read Ahead

If you just read something straight through, you may miss important details. It is often a good idea to **reread** or **read ahead** to clarify details and answer any questions you may have.

DIRECTIONS: Fill in the following chart as you read the excerpt from *I Know Why the Caged Bird Sings*. An example has been given.

READING Notes and Questions	READING Answers and Details	READING AHEAD Answers and Details
Maya Angelou writes "We lived with our grandmother and uncle . . ." Who is "we"?		Later, she refers to Bailey, and still later we learn that she is "Bailey's sister," so "we" must mean herself and her brother.

from *I Know Why the Caged Bird Sings* by Maya Angelou (text page 24)

Literary Focus: Memoir

When you read a **memoir**, you are reading a form of autobiography. A memoir deals with the writer's memories of a person or significant event in his or her life. In the excerpt from *I Know Why the Caged Bird Sings*, Maya Angelou remembers a special time in her life when she worked in her family's store and first met Mrs. Flowers.

DIRECTIONS: Use the following chart to record information given by Maya Angelou in her memoir.

Momma	The Store
Mrs. Flowers	**Mrs. Flowers's House**

Name _____ Date _____

"The Road Not Taken" by Robert Frost (text page 34)
"All But Blind" by Walter de la Mare (text page 36)
"The Choice" by Dorothy Parker (text page 37)

Build Vocabulary

Using the Word Root -verg-

A. DIRECTIONS: The word root -verg- means "to bend or turn." Knowing the meanings of prefixes like di-, from dis-, which means "apart" and con-, which means "with" or "together," you can figure out that the meaning of the word diverged is "moved apart or away from" and the meaning of converged is "came or moved together." Complete each sentence below with one of these words: divergent (moving away from one another), convergent (coming or moving together), divergence (a separating or moving apart), convergence (a coming or moving together).

1. Two _____ groups argued about the issues at the meeting.

2. Two _____ trails finally crossed in the foothills.

3. The town was built at the _____ of the two rivers, close to where they come together.

4. A strong _____ of opinion was causing the two groups to drift apart.

Using the Word Bank

diverged	blunders	smoldering	lilting

B. DIRECTIONS: Match each word in the left column with its definition in the right column.

____ 1. diverged   a. singing or speaking in a light, tripping manner

____ 2. lilting   b. burning or smoking without flame

____ 3. smoldering   c. moves clumsily or carelessly

____ 4. blunders   d. branched off

Analogies

C. DIRECTIONS: Each question below consists of a pair of related words in CAPITAL LETTERS followed by four lettered pairs of words. Circle the letter of the pair that best expresses a relationship similar to that expressed in the pair in capital letters.

1. DIVERGED : SEPARATED ::
   a. converged : split
   b. removed : extracted
   c. weighed : calculated
   d. dressed : appeared

2. BLUNDERS : GOOFS ::
   a. hates : likes
   b. skates : walks
   c. smiles : grins
   d. appears : vanishes

3. SMOLDERING : FIRE ::
   a. fizzing : soda
   b. growing : market
   c. stopping : acceleration
   d. pouring : choice

4. LILTING : GRACEFUL ::
   a. caring : wicked
   b. simple : difficult
   c. near : far
   d. dangerous : hazardous

"The Road Not Taken" by Robert Frost (text page34)
"All But Blind" by Walter de la Mare (text page 36)
"The Choice" by Dorothy Parker (text page 37)

Build Spelling Skills: Adding *-ing*

Spelling Strategy   To form the present participle of a verb that has more than one syllable and ends in a consonant preceded by a vowel, simply add *-ing* if the accent is <u>not</u> on the
last syllable: *rivet + -ing = riveting*. If the accent is on the last syllable, double the final consonant before adding *-ing*: *expel + -ing = expelling*.

A. Practice: Add *-ing* to each of the following verbs. Write the new word on the line. Hint: Say
each word out loud so you can hear where the accent falls.

1. smolder _____   6. answer _____

2. occur_____   7. garden _____

3. differ _____   8. program _____

4. vacuum _____   9. control _____

5. refer_____   10. swivel _____

B. Practice: Add *-ing* to each word in parentheses, and write the new word on the line to complete each sentence.

1. (label) Although Frost was born in California, we have no trouble _____
   him as a New England poet.

2. (recur) Frost's poems are notable for their _____ scenes of country
   life.

3. (develop) Frost studied Latin, which helped in his _____ word sense.

4. (travel) Twelve years after buying a house in New Hampshire, Frost was on a ship
   _____ to England.

5. (focus) He spent the next few years _____ on poetry and teaching.

6. (compel) When reading Frost's poetry aloud, you may find some of his images
   _____.

7. (refer) In "The Road Not Taken," the road "less traveled by" may be _____
   to Frost's career as a poet.

Challenge: Walter de la Mare's poetry has been described as having a sense of magic about it.
Here are some words often associated with magic, but they are scrambled. Use some of your
own magic to unscramble them.

1. reeei _____   2. eiwdr _____

3. prycee_____   4. seyomisrtu _____

"**The Road Not Taken**" by Robert Frost (text page34)
"**All But Blind**" by Walter de la Mare (text page 36)
"**The Choice**" by Dorothy Parker (text page 37)

Build Grammar Skills: General and Specific Nouns

Nouns name people, animals, places, things, or ideas. **General nouns,** like *gems* and *fabric,* convey broad information. **Specific nouns,** like *rubies* and *denim,* convey more precise information. Specific nouns give your writing greater clarity than general nouns do. They enable your readers to picture more precisely what you are describing.

Here are some examples. Notice that there are different degrees of specific nouns. Some are more specific than others.

General nouns	Specific nouns	More specific nouns
person	woman	Cousin Abby
animal	horse	mustang
building	house	cottage
food	fruit	banana
plant	flower	rose

A. Practice: Complete the chart by filling in columns two and three with examples of specific and more specific nouns.

General nouns	Specific nouns	More specific nouns
person		
animal		
relative		
building		
road		
rock		
writer		

B. Writing Application: Change each underlined general noun to a more specific noun. Write the new noun on the line.

1. They ate some <u>food</u> at the picnic. _____

2. The <u>car</u> ran out of gas. _____

3. The <u>holiday</u> fell on a Wednesday this year. _____

4. She gave her mom a <u>gift</u> for her birthday. _____

5. His <u>shoes</u> were very comfortable. _____

6. The <u>furniture</u> was in need of repair. _____

7. Terry spent an hour practicing his <u>sport</u>. _____

"The Road Not Taken" by Robert Frost (text page34)
"All But Blind" by Walter de la Mare (text page 36)
"The Choice" by Dorothy Parker (text page 37)

Reading Strategy: Paraphrase

The language in poetry is often not like everyday speech. For this reason, it is sometimes difficult to understand at first. One way to understand poetry more easily is to **paraphrase** the lines, or restate them in your own words.

DIRECTIONS: As you read these poems, fill out this chart. Choose lines that you find difficult and paraphrase them. One example has been given.

Poem Title	Original Lines	Paraphrased Lines
"The Road Not Taken"	as just as fair	just as nice
"The Choice"		
"All But Blind"		

"**The Road Not Taken**" by Robert Frost (text page34)
"**All But Blind**" by Walter de la Mare (text page 36)
"**The Choice**" by Dorothy Parker (text page 37)

Literary Focus: The Speaker in a Poem

The **speaker in a poem** is the voice taken on by the poet. Sometimes the speaker and the poet are the same. Other times, the speaker is a character the poet has created. The character does not have to be human. It can be an animal, a piece of furniture, or a cloud. Even if the poet uses the pronoun *I*, it does not necessarily mean that the poem's speaker is the author of the poem.

DIRECTIONS: As you read each poem, focus on the personality and attitude of the speaker. Then answer the following questions.

1. Suppose the speaker in "The Road Not Taken" had been walking with a companion when they got to the fork in the road. Write a conversation they might have had about which road to take.

_____

_____

_____

_____

_____

_____

2. Suppose the speaker in "All But Blind" is talking to someone about the place of human beings in the universe. Write the conversation they might have.

_____

_____

_____

_____

_____

_____

_____

3. Suppose the speaker in "The Choice" is talking to a friend about which of two suitors would be the better match. Write the conversation they might have.

_____

_____

_____

_____

_____

_____

_____

from "**E-Mail from Bill Gates**" by John Seabrook (text page 42)

Build Vocabulary

Using the Prefix *inter-*

A. DIRECTIONS: The prefix *inter-* means "between." Apply what you know about the prefix *inter-* to define the following words. Then use each word in a sentence that demonstrates the meaning. The first word is done for you.

1. international <u>between nations</u> _____
<u>The international soccer tournament featured a match between Brazil and Germany.</u>

2. interstate _____

_____

3. intercontinental _____

_____

4. interoffice _____

_____

Using the Word Bank

B. DIRECTIONS: Complete each of the following sentences to demonstrate your understanding of the underlined Word Bank words.

interaction	misinterpret	intimate	etiquette	spontaneously

1. Only your most <u>intimate</u> friends are likely to know about your _____

2. E-mail conversations do not move as <u>spontaneously</u> as normal conversations because

_____

3. One way to avoid having your friends <u>misinterpret</u> your messages is to

_____

4. One difference between the <u>etiquette</u> of regular mail and that of e-mail is that

_____

5. E-mail allows frequent <u>interaction</u> between people who are _____

C. DIRECTIONS: Each question below consists of a sentence beginning, followed by four lettered words or groups of words that could be endings. Circle the letter of the ending that best completes the sentence.

1. Etiquette demands that you
   a. sleep eight hours a night
   b. save money for college
   c. wear colorful clothing
   d. write thank-you notes for gifts

2. If you act spontaneously, you
   a. write a pro and con list first
   b. make mistakes
   c. act on your natural impulses
   d. act like a fool

Build Spelling Skills: Adding *-tion*

Spelling Strategy When adding the suffix *-tion*, you will probably have to drop the final letter or letters of the base word. For example: activate + *-tion* = activation.

A. Practice: Add the suffix *-tion* to each of the following words. Write the new word on the line.

1. interact_____

2. communicate _____

3. substitute _____

4. relate_____

5. contribute _____

6. attract_____

7. punctuate _____

8. affect_____

9. narrate _____

10. fascinate _____

B. Practice: Add *-tion* to the following words. Then write each new word in the blank where it makes the most sense.

pollute	communicate	aggravate	complete

The growth of the use of e-mail as a means of _____ has had an interesting effect on the lives of many people. The _____ of the hectic automobile commute has been replaced by the calm of the telecommute. Many workers receive work assignments over their computers, work at home to bring them to _____, and then send files of completed work as e-mail attachments. There is no doubt that such an arrangement can help cut down the air _____ caused by automobiles.

Challenge: John Seabrook says that Bill Gates would put an "&" at the end of an E-mail to say, "Write back." Here are some other symbols and abbreviations frequently used in E-mail. Find out what each one means. Write the meaning on the line.

1. :) _____

2. :(_____

3. ;) _____

4. lol_____

from *"E-Mail from Bill Gates"* by John Seabrook (text page 42)

Build Grammar Skills: Concrete and Abstract Nouns

Concrete nouns name places and things that you can perceive with your senses. For example, you can see a disk and you can touch a keyboard. An **abstract noun** names an idea, concept, belief, or quality—things that cannot be touched. When you write about ideas, you might use words like *clarity* and *difficulty*.

> **Concrete nouns:** letter, monitor, keyboard
> **Abstract nouns:** progress, future, enjoyment

One good way to judge whether a noun is concrete or abstract is to ask yourself if you can see, hear, smell, taste, or touch it. If you can, the noun is concrete. If you can't, it is abstract.

A. Practice: Underline all of the nouns in the following sentences. Then above each noun, write *C* if it is concrete and *A* if it is abstract.

1. If you have a computer and a telephone, you can send E-mail.

2. E-mail has been a useful advance in communication technology.

3. You can easily send messages to your friends.

4. You can use your computer to do research as well.

5. You can find information on many subjects on the Internet.

6. In some ways, E-mail can strengthen relationships.

7. Still, a face-to-face meeting is often the best way to communicate.

B. Writing Application: Write two sentences about each of the following subjects. In the first one, use a concrete noun and underline it. In the second one, use an abstract noun and underline it.

Subject: E-mail

1. (concrete)_____

2. (abstract) _____

Subject: communication

3. (concrete)_____

4. (abstract) _____

Subject: writing

5. (concrete)_____

6. (abstract) _____

Name _____ Date _____

from *"E-Mail from Bill Gates"* by John Seabrook (text page 42)

Reading Strategy: Context Clues

When you encounter unfamiliar words in your reading, you can use the **context clues** in the surrounding text to figure out their meaning.

DIRECTIONS: As you read the excerpt from "E-Mail from Bill Gates," complete this chart to record each unknown word you come across, any context clues to the meaning of each unknown word, and your guess at the meaning of the word. Later, consult a dictionary to see if each of your guesses was correct.

Word	Clue	Predicted Meaning
nevertheless	wasting money / logged on again	anyway / in spite of

from *"E-Mail from Bill Gates"* by John Seabrook (text page 42)

Literary Focus: Magazine Article

A **magazine article** is a short work of nonfiction that makes its first appearance in a periodical. Some magazine articles are human-interest stories about people and their accomplishments. Other articles might explain or investigate specific subjects, such as a new technology.

The magazine article by John Seabrook does both these things. It gives information about Bill Gates and his accomplishments. It also provides knowledge on how E-mail can be used as a communications tool.

DIRECTIONS: After you read this excerpt from "E-Mail from Bill Gates," answer the following questions.

1. Who is Bill Gates?

    _____

2. Why does John Seabrook decide to send an E-mail message to Bill Gates?

    _____

3. How much time passes between the time John Seabrook sends his first E-mail message and the time Bill Gates sends his first response?

    _____

4. What are two differences in appearance between an E-mail message and a regular letter?

    _____

5. According to the article, what are some advantages of E-mail over regular mail?

    _____

    _____

    _____

    _____

    _____

    _____

    _____

    _____

    _____

    _____

    _____

    _____

"The Girl Who Hunted Rabbits" Zuñi Legend (text page 49)

Build Vocabulary

A. DIRECTIONS: Match each word in the left column with its definition in the right column. Write the letter of the definition on the line next to the word it defines.

____ 1. mantle   a. ate greedily

____ 2. sinew   b. eager to eat large quantities of food

____ 3. bedraggled   c. sleeveless cloak or cape

____ 4. devoured   d. obtained by some effort

____ 5. procured   e. dirty and wet

____ 6. voracious   f. not usual

____ 7. unwonted   g. a tendon that connects muscles to bones

B. DIRECTIONS: Read each sentence. Complete the sentence with the best word from the list in the box. Use each word only once.

devoured	unwonted	mantle	voracious
bedraggled	sinew	procured	

1. Warm and excited by her _____ exercise, she did not heed a coming snowstorm . . .

2. . . . and so on until the poor maiden had thrown all the rabbits to the _____ old monster.

3. . . . the hunt was depended upon to supply the meat; or sometimes it was _____ by barter of the products of the fields to those who hunted mostly.

4. She threw the overshoes of deerskin, and these like the rabbits he speedily _____ .

5. . . . he moistened and carefully softened them, and cut out for the maiden long stockings, which he sewed up with _____ and the fiber of the yucca leaf.

6. . . . she had put on a warm, short-skirted dress, knotted a _____ over her shoulder and thrown another larger one over her back . . .

7. Then she threw off her snow-covered stockings of deerskin and the _____ mantles, and, building a fire, hung them up to dry.

"The Girl Who Hunted Rabbits" Zuñi Legend (text page 49)

Connecting Legend to Social Studies

From the legends told by different cultures, insights may be drawn about the people, their beliefs, and the way they live.

DIRECTIONS: In the following chart, read the details that have been taken from the legend "The Girl Who Hunted Rabbits." Then complete the chart by writing one insight you can draw from the evidence given in each set of details. The first one is done for you.

Details/Evidence	Insights
1. the maiden's brothers killed in war; the Zuñi believed in twin war-gods; the gods killed the demon with war clubs	1. The Zuñi people had fought wars against other people in the past.
2. axes made of deerskin; wild onions used to spice food; thread made from sinew and yucca leaf fiber; brush gathered for firewood	2.
3. when they hear the demon pounding in the distance, the war-gods know instantly that there is a maiden in danger and why; they rush to save the maiden; they sleep near the entrance of the cave; they tell and show the maiden many things she did not know; they counsel her	3.
4. the maiden's willingness to risk her life so that her parents will have heat; her unwillingness to marry and leave her parents	4.
5. the maiden has not accepted anyone's offer of marriage; the war-gods tell her she should not be fearful of marriage; they tell the maiden to return to her village; she thinks about what she has learned as she goes home	5.

"Christmas Day in the Morning" by Pearl S. Buck (text page 65)

Build Vocabulary

Forms of *finite*

The word *finite* is based on a Latin root *finis*, meaning "end" or "limit." With the prefix *in-*, meaning "not" or "without," the Word Bank word *infinite* means "without an end."

A. DIRECTIONS: All of the following words are based on the root *finis*. Use each of them in an original sentence that demonstrates the meaning of the word.

definite: certain

definitive: absolute; conclusive

unfinished: not completed

finish: end; complete

infinity: endlessness; eternity

infinitesimal: microscopic; tiny

1. _____

2. _____

3. _____

4. _____

5. _____

6. _____

Using the Word Bank

infinite	brisk	loitering	placidly	acquiescent

B. DIRECTIONS: Match each word in the left column with its definition in the right column.

_____ 1. infinite   a. lingering in an aimless way

_____ 2. brisk   b. extending beyond measure or comprehension

_____ 3. loitering   c. quick in manner

_____ 4. placidly   d. agreeing without protest

_____ 5. acquiescent   e. in a calm way

Using Verbal Analogies

C. DIRECTIONS: Each question below consists of a related pair of words in CAPITAL LETTERS followed by four lettered pairs of words. Circle the lettered pair that best expresses a relationship similar to that expressed by the pair in capital letters.

1. INFINITE : LIMITED::
   a. peaceful : calm
   b. rough : gentle
   c. genuine : real
   d. pink : red

2. BRISK : QUICK ::
   a. slow : fast
   b. light : dim
   c. enormous : huge
   d. young : elderly

3. PLACIDLY : FIERCELY ::
   a. tenderly : intelligently
   b. orderly : angrily
   c. honestly : truthfully
   d. silently : noisily

"Christmas Day in the Morning" by Pearl S. Buck (text page 65)

Build Spelling Skills: The *kw* sound spelled *qu*, as in *equal*

Spelling Strategy   The *kw* sound is often spelled *qu*, as in *equal*. Sometimes, as in the Word Bank word *acquiescent*, the sound is preceded by a silent *c*.

A. Practice: Complete each of the defined words by adding *qu* in the blank. Then use the words to complete the sentences that follow.

ac_____isitive: fond of getting things or ideas   in_____ire: ask

s_____irm: to turn and twist; to wriggle   s_____ander: spend foolishly

se_____ence: the coming of one thing after another

1. The sportcaster described the _____ of events at the games.

2. After receiving her inheritance, Ellie proceeded to _____ it.

3. Dorothy plans to _____ about the travel arrangements soon.

4. When the children _____, it makes Uncle John nervous.

5. Todd's _____ nature has contributed to the clutter in his house.

B. Practice: Use *qu* to complete each word below. Then use the words to complete the sentences that follow. Use each word once.

e_____ipment   _____iet   _____ilt

s_____atting   s_____are   _____art

1. Every _____ of milk in Robert's refrigerator came from his own cows.

2. Each morning he would milk the cows in the big _____ barn.

3. He sat on a three-legged stool—this was much easier than _____.

4. He had never bought modern milking _____.

5. He enjoyed the _____ mornings when he was the only one awake.

6. He found that as he got older, he would _____ think about the past.

Challenge: A descriptive word for cows is *bovine*, from the Latin *bovus*, meaning "ox." The adjectives below describe other animals often found on farms. In the blanks, write the the type of animal each word describes. Use a dictionary for help.

1. ovine _____   2. equine _____

3. porcine _____   4. canine _____

5. feline _____

"Christmas Day in the Morning" by Pearl S. Buck (text page 65)

Build Grammar Skills: Pronouns and Antecedents

A **pronoun** is a word that takes the place of a noun or a group of words functioning as a noun. An **antecedent** is the word or group of words that a pronoun replaces. The following are some common pronouns.

> *I, me, my, mine*   *we, us, our, ours,*
> *you, your, yours*   *they, them, their, their*
> *he, him, his, she, her, hers, it, its*

Example:

antecedent   antecedent   pronoun   pronoun
When **Alice** thought about **trimming the tree, she** decided to do **it** tomorrow.

A. Practice: Underline the pronoun or pronouns in each sentence, and draw a circle around the antecedent(s). The first one has been done for you.

1. When (Rob) was sleeping, his father hated to wake him.

2. When Rob heard his father speak, he knew that his father loved him.

3. There were chores to be done, and Rob did them.

4. Because their children were grown, Rob and Alice had a quiet Christmas alone.

5. Rob was grateful that he had learned how to love.

B. Writing Application: Rewrite each sentence, replacing the nouns with pronouns wherever appropriate. Not all nouns should be replaced.

1. Rob's mother reminded Rob's father that it was time Rob took Rob's turn at the chores around the farm.

   _____

   _____

2. Rob's father didn't like to wake Rob when Rob was sleeping so soundly.

   _____

3. Rob and Alice's grandchildren would open Rob and Alice's grandchildren's presents in the afternoon.

   _____

   _____

4. In the morning, Rob wrapped a gift for Rob's wife and wrote Rob's wife a love letter.

   _____

   _____

5. When Rob finished the letter, Rob sealed it and tied it on the tree where Alice would see it when Alice came into the room.

   _____

   _____

"Christmas Day in the Morning" by Pearl S. Buck (text page 65)

Reading Strategy: Identify Sequence of Events

The **sequence of events** in a story is the order in which things happen. Stories are not always written in the exact order of the events. Often, as in Pearl S. Buck's story, a character remembers something or looks forward to something. Authors use words like *first, before, later, than, after, shortly,* and *eventually* to let you know which things happen first, next, and last. In stories that shift backward and forward in time, these signal words are especially helpful.

DIRECTIONS: Keep track of the events in "Christmas Day in the Morning" on this timeline.

TIMELINE
[Present Time]

_____

_____

_____

_____

_____

_____

[Flashback]

_____

_____

_____

_____

_____

_____

[Present Time]

_____

_____

_____

_____

_____

_____

"Christmas Day in the Morning" by Pearl S. Buck (text page 65)

Literary Focus: Flashback

In any given day, you probably think back on events that happened in the past. These thoughts can affect the way you deal with events in the present. In much the same way, characters in a story often think back on events that happened before the opening of the story. If the story is then interrupted to provide greater detail about those past events, it is called a **flashback.** A flashback often makes a character's present motivations, attitudes, and actions easier to understand.

DIRECTIONS: Identify each of the following passages by writing *F* if it is an example of flashback or *P* if it is an example of present time within the story.

_____ 1. He had trained himself to turn over and go to sleep, but this morning, because it was Christmas, he did not try to sleep.

_____ 2. His childhood and youth were long past, and his own children had grown up and gone.

_____ 3. For it was a still night, a clear and starry night.

_____ 4. He was fifteen years old and still on his father's farm.

_____ 5. When he heard these words, something in him woke: his father loved him!

_____ 6. They were poor, and most of the excitement was in the turkey they had raised themselves and in the mince pies his mother made.

_____ 7. As usual he had gone to the ten-cent store and bought a tie.

_____ 8. He must have waked twenty times, scratching a match each time to look at his old watch—midnight, and half past one, and then two o'clock.

_____ 9. He finished, the two milk cans were full, and he covered them and closed the milkhouse door carefully, making sure of the latch.

_____ 10. In just a few minutes his father would know.

_____ 11. He found his father and clutched him in a great hug.

_____ 12. It was a little one—they had not had a big tree since the children went away—but he set it in the holder and put it in the middle of the long table under the window.

_____ 13. He tied the gift on the tree and then stood back.

_____ 14. It occurred to him suddenly that it was alive because long ago it had been born in him when he knew his father loved him.

_____ 15. He could write it down in a letter for her to read and keep forever.

"The Old Grandfather and His Little Grandson" by Leo Tolstoy (text page 74)
"Grandma" by Amy Ling (text page 75)
"Old Man" by Ricardo Sánchez (text page 76)

Build Vocabulary

Synonyms for *rivulets*

A. DIRECTIONS: Because English has so many words that come from other languages, it is a language rich in synonyms. Synonyms are words that mean about the same thing, but with slightly different shades of meaning. For example, *rivulets, streams, brooks, creeks,* and *rills* are all bodies of running water smaller than *rivers.* The word *brook* suggests a bubbly, lively body of water. Streams are larger than creeks, and creeks are larger than rivulets and brooks. Rills are the smallest of all, and they have the liveliness of brooks.

Underline the synonym that best completes each sentence. Explain your choice on the line.

1. The water of the [brook / creek] seemed to be dancing for joy as it bubbled over the rocks and fallen logs. _____

2. The girls were able to jump across the [stream / rill]._____

Using the Word Bank

| scolded | sturdy | rivulets | furrows | stoic | supple |

B. DIRECTIONS: Complete each of the following sentences to demonstrate your understanding of the Word Bank words.

1. The mother scolded her son because he _____

2. The furrows in the woman's face showed _____

3. If that ladder is not sturdy enough, _____

4. After our picnic near the rivulet, we _____

5. The dancer showed how supple she was by _____

6. Her stoic attitude showed when she _____

Using Antonyms

C. DIRECTIONS: Each question below consists of a word in CAPITAL LETTERS followed by four lettered words or phrases. Circle the letter of the word or phrase that is most opposite in meaning to the word in capital letters.

1. STURDY
   a. strong
   b. weak
   c. firm
   d. slippery

2. SCOLDED
   a. criticized
   b. nagged
   c. entertained
   d. praised

3. SUPPLE
   a. stiff
   b. flexible
   c. graceful
   d. simple

"The Old Grandfather and His Little Grandson" by Leo Tolstoy (text page 74)
"Grandma" by Amy Ling (text page 75)
"Old Man" by Ricardo Sánchez (text page 76)

Build Spelling Skills: Two-syllable words with a short vowel and a single consonant sound

Spelling Strategy When spelling most two-syllable words with a short vowel followed by a single consonant sound, double the consonant. If the vowel sound is long, do not double the consonant.

middle (short *i* sound followed by *d* sound)
bubble (short *u* sound followed by *b* sound)
Bible (long *i* sound followed by a *b* sound)

A. Practice: If the underlined word is spelled correctly, write C on the line. If it is spelled incorrectly, write it correctly.

1. Drinks come in three sizes: small, large, and <u>super</u>. _____

2. Dino served a salad and some poached salmon for <u>super</u>. _____

3. Apples and bananas were offered; Joni chose the <u>latter</u>. _____

4. Phil saved his dessert for <u>latter</u>. _____

5. The little kitten was very <u>fury</u>. _____

6. The <u>flurry</u> of the storm continued all night. _____

B. Practice: Choose the correct spelling of the word that completes each sentence. Write the word on the line.

1. The old man was (sitting, siting) on a mat. _____

2. The (little, litle) boy was playing on the floor. _____

3. The boy was (making, makking) a wooden bucket. _____

4. Tears began (filing, filling) the eyes of the parents. _____

5. The grandmother wore (slipers, slippers) on her feet. _____

Challenge: The Word Bank word *stoic* comes from the Greek word *stoikos*, which was the name for the porch from which the philosopher Zeno taught. In a dictionary that gives word origins, look up the meanings and origins of these words. Write the meaning and origin on the line.

1. stoa _____

2. stoicism _____

3. spartan _____

"The Old Grandfather and His Little Grandson" by Leo Tolstoy (text page 74)
"Grandma" by Amy Ling (text page 75)
"Old Man" by Ricardo Sánchez (text page 76)

Build Grammar Skills: Personal Pronouns

When you use pronouns to refer to individuals, you are using personal pronouns. Here are the personal pronouns:

First person: I, me, my, mine, we, us, our, ours
Second person: you, your, yours
Third person: he, him, his, she, her, hers, it, its, they, them, their, theirs

A. Practice: Underline each personal pronoun in these sentences.

1. He had become so old that his legs could not carry him.

2. He could not see well, nor could he hear.

3. When he ate, bits of food dropped out of his mouth.

4. She told him that he spoiled everything and broke their dishes.

5. She said that he would be fed from a wooden dish.

6. They later saw their son making something out of wood.

7. The boy told them that he was making a wooden bucket.

8. He would save it so he could feed them from it when they got old.

B. Writing Application: Revise the following sentences, replacing each italicized word or phrase part with an appropriate personal pronoun. The first one has been done for you.

1. The poet traveled to China to meet *Grandma*.

   The poet traveled to China to meet her. _____

2. In the grandmother's past, the poet saw *the poet's* own future.

   _____

3. The grandmother stretched out *the grandmother's* arms.

   _____

4. The poet's image stood before *the poet*.

   _____

5. As a child, the poet wanted to dig *that hole* to China, but *the poet* was not strong enough to dig *that hole*.

   _____

   _____

"The Old Grandfather and His Little Grandson" by Leo Tolstoy (text page 74)
"Grandma" by Amy Ling (text page 75)
"Old Man" by Ricardo Sánchez (text page 76)

Reading Strategy: Relate What You Know

One way to better understand what you read is to **relate it to what you know.** If you do so, you will have greater insight into how the characters might feel and what might be motivating them. As you read these poems, complete the following charts to relate the characters' experiences to your own. A sample entry is given.

"The Old Grandfather and His Little Grandson"	
Passage	**What I Know**
The grandfather had become very old. His legs would not carry him . . .	My grandfather recently fell and broke his hip.

"Grandma"	
Passage	**What I Know**

"Old Man"	
Passage	**What I Know**

"The Old Grandfather and His Little Grandson" by Leo Tolstoy (text page 74)
"Grandma" by Amy Ling (text page 75)
"Old Man" by Ricardo Sánchez (text page 76)

Literary Focus: Sensory Details

If you take note of the sensory details as you read, the images presented by the writer will be clearer and more enjoyable. As you read, imagine yourself actually seeing, smelling, hearing, tasting, or touching the things described by the writer. Put yourself at the scene mentally, and, picturing yourself there, experience the images in your mind's eye.

DIRECTIONS: Use this graphic organizer to help yourself focus on the sensory details, as you read these poems. From each poem, choose words that appeal to the senses. Write the words in the corresponding box or boxes. Remember that many images can be appreciated through more than one sense.

	See	Hear	Touch	Smell	Taste
"The Old Grandfather and His Little Grandson"					
"Grandma"					
"Old Man"					

Build Vocabulary

Prefix *extra-*

A. DIRECTIONS: The prefix *extra-* means "outside" or "beyond." In the Word Bank word *extravagance*, the prefix combines with the word root *vagant*, which means "to wander." Thus, an extravagance is something that wanders beyond what is normal. Apply what you know about the prefix *extra-*, and define the following words.

1. extraordinary _____

2. extracurricular _____

3. extrasensory _____

4. extraterrestrial _____

Using the Word Bank

horizon	extravagance	friction
constellation	descended	orbit

B. DIRECTIONS: Complete each of the following sentences with a Word Bank word.

1. Mercury's _____ around the sun is much smaller than Earth's because Mercury is so much closer to the sun.

2. In the evening, we looked toward the western _____ and saw a spectacular sunset.

3. If you rub two sticks together in a certain way, the _____ will eventually start a fire.

4. The Big Dipper is a _____ that is made up of seven stars.

5. The parachute opened, and Dan _____ to the grassy field below.

6. The _____ of Kurt's gift brought a look of shock to Cindy's face.

Using Synonyms

C. DIRECTIONS: Each question below consists of a word in CAPITAL LETTERS followed by four lettered words. Circle the letter of the word that is most similar in meaning to the word in capital letters.

1. EXTRAVAGANCE
   a. starvation
   b. poverty
   c. enthusiasm
   d. wastefulness

2. DESCENDED
   a. arose
   b. inherited
   c. dropped
   d. raised

3. FRICTION
   a. fraction
   b. rubbing
   c. smoothness
   d. sorrow

Build Spelling Skills: *s* sound spelled *sc,* as in *descended*

Spelling Strategy   The *s* sound is often spelled *sc*: *scent.* Notice that in the Word Bank word *descended*, the *s* sound is spelled *sc*.

A. PRACTICE: Complete each of the defined words by adding *sc* in the blank. Then use the words to complete the sentences that follow.

re_____ind: repeal, cancel   adole_____ent: a person between the ages of 12 and 20

_____ent: aroma, smell, odor   _____enery: the visible natural features of a landscape

_____imitar: a curved, short sword

1. The _____ was quite mature for someone her age.

2. The legislature met to _____ the unfair law.

3. The _____ of that perfume reminds me of my grandmother.

4. The _____ was part of a display of antique weapons in the museum.

5. The _____ in Yosemite can hardly be captured on film.

B. Practice: Complete each of the following words by writing *sc* in the blank. Then use each of the words in an original sentence.

1. _____intillate: sparkle   3. _____ientist: one who specializes in a science

2. _____ene: view; sight   4. _____enario: script; outline

1. _____

2. _____

3. _____

4. _____

Challenge: When describing his old clothes, Garrison Keillor mentions a panama hat, which is named after the country of Panama. Here is a list of other items or features of clothing that are named after places or people. In a dictionary, look up each one. Describe the item of clothing, and write the place or person for which it is named.

1. chesterfield _____

2. inverness _____

3. mackintosh _____

4. homburg _____

5. tuxedo _____

6. fez _____

"Shooting Stars" by Hal Borland (text page 82)
"Something From the Sixties" by Garrison Keillor (text page 84)

Build Grammar Skills: Indefinite Pronouns

An **indefinite pronoun** is one that refers to a person, place, or thing that is not specifically named.

> The park is open to *anyone* and *everyone*.

An indefinite pronoun can be singular or plural.

> Singular: *another, anyone, anything, each, either, everyone, everything, much, neither, nobody, no one, nothing, one, other, somebody, someone, something*
>
> Plural: *both, few, several, many*
>
> Singular or plural: *all, any, most, none, some, such*

Whether the indefinite pronoun is singular or plural depends on the meaning of the sentence.

> Singular: *Most* of this lettuce *is* spoiled.
>
> Plural: *Most* of these tomatoes *are* not ripe yet.

A. Practice: Circle the indefinite pronoun in each of the following sentences. On the line, write whether the pronoun is singular or plural.

1. Someone had invited Garrison Keillor's son to a sixties party. _____

2. His son was supposed to wear something from the sixties. _____

3. Garrison Keillor shows his son some of the clothes in the attic. _____

4. Everything, of course, looks like a costume. _____

5. Such is the pleasure at discovering old things. _____

6. Several of the hats are fairly unusual. _____

7. Many of the party guests wear bell bottoms. _____

8. Much of the fringe on the vest is tattered. _____

B. Writing Application: Use each of the following indefinite pronouns in a complete sentence about "Shooting Stars."

1. nobody _____

2. most _____

3. each _____

4. few _____

5. several _____

6. another _____

"Shooting Stars" by Hal Borland (text page 82)
"Something From the Sixties" by Garrison Keillor (text page 84)

Reading Strategy: Apply Word-Identification Strategies

When you encounter an unfamiliar word in your reading, you can **apply word-identification strategies** to figure out its meaning. Look for word parts that are familiar, such as word roots, prefixes, and suffixes. Break the word into these parts. Then try to arrive at the meaning of the word by defining each part and then putting the definitions together.

DIRECTIONS: Break the following words into word parts to arrive at a definition of each one. Then check your definitions in a dictionary.

Word	Word Parts	Definition
1. remarkable		
2. unusual		
3. fanciful		
4. downward		
5. notable		
6. countless		
7. overalls		
8. wonderful		

Name _____ Date _____

"Shooting Stars" by Hal Borland (text page 82)
"Something From the Sixties" by Garrison Keillor (text page 84)

Literary Focus: First-Person Narrative

A **first-person narrative** is a true story about a memorable experience, person, or period in the writer's life. The writer uses the personal pronouns *I, me,* and *we* throughout the narrative. Some first-person narratives focus mainly on external events, reporting them mostly in the style of a news report, but this style is not typical of first-person narratives. More often, a first-person narrative focuses on the writer's opinions, feelings, and insights, rather than focusing merely on external events.

DIRECTIONS: To understand the effect of a first-person narrative, readers can consider how it colors the telling of the story. To do so, it is sometimes useful to consider how a third-person point of view would have made the story different. Answer the following questions to analyze the point of view in "Shooting Stars" and "Something From the Sixties."

1. Hal Borland mixes third-person and first-person points of view in "Shooting Stars." Look at the fifth paragraph, the one that begins "I once watched . . ." Rewrite the paragraph from the third-person point of view. (Remember, the third-person point of view uses the pronouns *he, him, she, her, they,* and *them,* rather than *I, me, we,* and *us.*)

_____

_____

_____

_____

_____

_____

Then answer these questions: Which paragraph do you think is more interesting to read—the one written in the first person or the one you wrote in the third person? Why?

_____

_____

2. Garrison Keillor uses the first-person point of view in "Something From the Sixties." Look at the fifth paragraph, the one that begins "Then—presto!" Rewrite the paragraph from the third-person point of view.

_____

_____

_____

_____

_____

_____

Then answer these questions: Which paragraph do you think is more interesting to read—the one written in the first person or the one you wrote in the third person? Why?

_____

_____

"**Poets to Come**" by Walt Whitman (text page 90)
"**Winter Moon**" by Langston Hughes (text page 91)
"**Ring Out, Wild Bells**" by Alfred, Lord Tennyson (text page 92)

Build Vocabulary

Using the Suffix *-or*

A. DIRECTIONS: The suffix *-or* signals that a word means "a person or a thing that does something." In the Word Bank word *orators*, the suffix has the sense of "person who orates." Apply what you know about the suffix *-or*, and define the following words.

1. accelerator _____

2. instructor _____

3. incubator _____

4. conductor _____

Using the Word Bank

orators	indicative	sauntering	strife

B. DIRECTIONS: Complete each of the following sentences to demonstrate your understanding of the Word Bank words. Then use each word in a sentence of your own.

1. As each of the orators was introduced, the audience _____

_____

2. The young woman's high test scores were indicative of her _____

_____

3. The fact that Jake was sauntering along the road indicated that he _____

_____

4. The strife between the two friends was causing _____

_____

Using Verbal Analogies

C. DIRECTIONS: Each question below consists of a related pair of words in CAPITAL LETTERS followed by four lettered pairs of words. Circle the letter of the pair that best expresses a relationship similar to that expressed in the pair in capital letters.

1. ORATORS : SPEECHES ::
   a. bakers : rolls
   b. doctor : patient
   c. house : rooms
   d. baby : diapers

2. SAUNTERING : CONFIDENCE ::
   a. walking : intelligence
   b. running : kindness
   c. screaming : politeness
   d. smiling : happiness

3. STRIFE : PEACE ::
   a. imagination : creativity
   b. hopelessness : goodness
   c. agony : joy
   d. sympathy : reassurance

Name _____ Date _____

"Poets to Come" by Walt Whitman (text page 90)
"Winter Moon" by Langston Hughes (text page 91)
"Ring Out, Wild Bells" by Alfred, Lord Tennyson (text page 92)

Build Spelling Skills: Dropping the -e and adding *-or*, as in *creator*

Spelling Strategy   The silent e in a verb is dropped before adding the suffix *-or: create + -or = creator*. In Walt Whitman's poem, he refers to *orators* who may come in the future. Notice that the silent e in *orate* is dropped before adding the suffix *-or*.

A. Practice: Add *-or* to each of the following verbs in parentheses. Write the new word on the line. Then use the words to complete the sentences that follow.

1. (simulate) _____, a training device that duplicates conditions likely to be found in some operation, as in a spacecraft

   The pilot trained for flying a jeltliner in an aircraft _____.

2. (accelerate) _____, a pedal or lever that controls acceleration, or speed, of a vehicle

   To speed up, the driver pressed on the _____.

3. (escalate) _____, a moving staircase that allows people to escalate, or rise, and descend from one level of a building to another

   To get to the third floor of the department store, Stan took the _____.

4. (elevate) _____, a thing that raises or lifts up

   Robin took the [SWOL] to the fourth floor of the office building.

B. Practice: Add *-or* to each of the words in parentheses. Write the word on the line to complete each unfinished sentence below.

1. (indicate) The ringing of bells can be an _____ of a joyous occasion.

2. (captivate) The winter moon was a _____ of Hughes imagination.

3. (communicate) Walt Whitman is a great _____ to generations of poets that come after him.

4. (anticipate) Walt Whitman seems to have been an _____ of what would come later.

Challenge: Add *-or* to the following words and use each one in a sentence that demonstrates its meaning. You may have to refer to a dictionary.

1. emancipate _____

2. calculate _____

3. infiltrate _____

4. instigate _____

"Poets to Come" by Walt Whitman (text page 90)
"Winter Moon" by Langston Hughes (text page 91)
"Ring Out, Wild Bells" by Alfred, Lord Tennyson (text page 92)

Build Grammar Skills: Intensive Pronouns: -self and -selves

Intensive pronouns emphasize nouns or other pronouns.

Emphasizes a noun: The essay was written by Dennis *himself.*
Emphasizes another pronoun: She *herself* asked the question.

An intensive pronoun is used to emphasize a person or to indicate that a person acts alone.

Emphasizes a person: I *myself* walk the dog each afternoon.
Indicates that a person acts alone: I walk the dog *myself* each afternoon.

An intensive pronoun is formed by adding the suffix *-self* or *-selves* to a personal pronoun.

my + self = myself; our + selves = ourselves; your + self = yourself; your + selves = yourselves; her + self = herself; him + self = himself; it + self = itself; them + selves = themselves

Note: If a preposition—*to, by beside, about,* and so on—is used with a *-self* pronoun, the pronoun is *not* intensive, but **reflexive.**

They always talk *about themselves.*
She repeated the lines *to herself.*

A. Practice: Write an intensive pronoun on the line in each sentence below. Be sure that the pronoun agrees with the noun or pronoun to which it refers.

1. Walt Whitman _____ wrote these famous lines.

2. Later poets _____ were inspired by Whitman's works.

3. Whitman wrote, "I _____ but write one or two indicative words . . ."

4. You _____ were expecting great things from him.

5. Darryl _____ recited the poem by Langston Hughes.

6. Tennyson's poems _____ ring out the poet's greatness.

B. Writing Application: Use each of the following intensive pronouns in a complete sentence about "Poets to Come," "Winter Moon," or " Ring Out, Wild Bells."

1. myself _____

2. herself _____

3. ourselves _____

4. yourself _____

5. themselves _____

"Poets to Come" by Walt Whitman (text page 90)
"Winter Moon" by Langston Hughes (text page 91)
"Ring Out, Wild Bells" by Alfred, Lord Tennyson (text page 92)

Reading Strategy: Read Poetry According to Punctuation

If you **read poetry according to punctuation**—like any other text you read—the poetry will make more sense. Punctuation marks are like road signs that give you directions about how to continue. Just as you stop for a red light or a stop sign, you should stop when you come to some marks of punctuation. Just as you slow down at a flashing yellow light or a yield sign, you should slow down when you come to other marks of punctuation. In addition, some marks of punctuation require that you change your tone of voice.

Marks that require a stop: period (.), colon (:), semicolon (;)

> I but advance a moment only to wheel and hurry back in the darkness**.**

Mark that requires a pause: comma

> Ring out the want**,** the care**,** the sin**,**

Marks that require a change in tone and a stop: exclamation point (!), question mark (?)

> How thin and sharp is the moon tonight**!**

As you read poetry, take careful notice of the punctuation and adjust your reading speed or tone accordingly.

DIRECTIONS: Above each mark of punctuation, write *stop, pause,* or *change tone and stop.*

1. Poets to come! orators, singers, musicians to come!

   Not to-day is to justify me and answer what I am for,

   But you, a new brood, native, athletic, continental, greater than before known,

   Arouse! for you must justify me.

2. How thin and sharp and ghostly white

   Is the slim curved crook of the moon tonight!

3. Ring out, wild bells, to the wild sky,

   The flying cloud, the frosty light:

   The year is dying in the night;

   Ring out, wild bells, and let him die.

"Poets to Come" by Walt Whitman (text page 90)
"Winter Moon" by Langston Hughes (text page 91)
"Ring Out, Wild Bells" by Alfred, Lord Tennyson (text page 92)

Literary Focus: Repetition in Poetry

One reason that poetry reminds many people of music is the use of **repetition.** Poets often repeat a word or phrase, or reword the same idea. This repetition gives force and emphasis to what the poet is saying, and it makes the ideas clearer and easier to remember.

In addition to repeating words and phrases, poets use repetition in other ways. They repeat rhyming patterns, line length, and stanza form. Some poets, like Walt Whitman, do not use rhyme or regular meters in their poetry. Yet repetition of some kind is present in most poetry. It is this quality that makes poetry such a pleasure to read.

DIRECTIONS: Identify the repeated words, phrases, sounds or other elements in each of the following examples.

1. Poets to come! orators, singers, musicians to come!

   _____

2. How thin and sharp is the moon tonight!

   How thin and sharp and ghostly white

   Is the slim curved crook of the moon tonight!

   _____

   _____

3. Ring out the old, ring in the new,

   Ring, happy bells, across the snow:

   The year is going, let him go;

   Ring out the false, ring in the true.

   _____

   _____

4. Ring out a slowly dying cause,

   And ancient forms of party strife;

   Ring in the nobler modes of life,

   With sweeter manners, purer laws.

   _____

   _____

5. Ring out old shapes of foul disease;

   Ring out the narrowing lust of gold;

   Ring out the thousand wars of old,

   Ring in the thousand years of peace.

   _____

   _____

"Cub Pilot on the Mississippi" by Mark Twain (text page 109)

Build Vocabulary

Using Forms of *judge*

The word *judicious* is part of the family of words related to the verb *judge,* which means "to decide, especially in a court of law."

A. DIRECTIONS: In the following sentences, the words in italics are all part of the same word family as *judge.* Circle the letter of the choice that best completes each sentence.

1. The *judicial* branch of the federal government includes
   a. the President   b. Congress   c. the Supreme Court   d. ambassadors overseas

2. A *judicious* newspaper columnist probably expresses views that are
   a. ruled by emotions   c. extremely unfair
   b. carefully weighed and considered   d. inaccurate

3. "The *judiciary* is the safeguard of our liberty" is a sometimes quoted remark referring to
   a. America's court system   c. freedom of the press
   b. the United States military   d. freedom of speech

Using the Word Bank

furtive	pretext	intimation	judicious	indulgent	emancipated

B. DIRECTIONS: Read each definition, and fill in the word on the lines provided. When you are done, the letters in the shaded boxes, reading down, will spell out Mark Twain's real first name.

1. displaying good judgment   _ _ _ _ _ _ _ _ ▮ _

2. freed from someone else's control _ _ _ _ _ _ _ _ ▮ _ _

3. suggestion; hint   _ _ _ _ ▮ _ _ _ _ _

4. sneaky   _ _ ▮ _ _ _ _

5. pretended reason hiding the real reason _ _ ▮ _ _ _ _

6. lenient; not strict   _ _ _ _ ▮ _ _ _

Antonyms

C. DIRECTIONS: For each item, circle the letter of the word that is most nearly opposite in meaning to the word in capital letters.

1. INDULGENT: a. harsh   b. sweet   c. calm   d. clean

2. EMANCIPATED: a. organized   b. strengthened   c. hid   d. imprisoned

3. JUDICIOUS: a. illegal   b. unfair   c. enjoyable   d. serious

4. FURTIVE: a. open   b. rapid   c. silent   d. secretive

"Cub Pilot on the Mississippi" by Mark Twain (text page 109)

Build Spelling Skills: Spelling the *shus* Sound

Spelling Strategy   Many adjectives end in the *shus* sound, which has several spellings.

- If the adjective is formed from a word ending in *-tion*, the *shus* sound is spelled *-tious*.

  Examples: cau<u>tion</u> / cau<u>tious</u>   supersti<u>tion</u> / supersti<u>tious</u>

- If the *shus* sound immediately follows a *k* sound, the combination is generally spelled *-xious*.

  Examples: an<u>xious</u>   no<u>xious</u>   obno<u>xious</u>

- In most other cases, the *shus* sound is spelled *-cious*.

  Examples: judi<u>cious</u> atro<u>cious</u> deli<u>cious</u> fero<u>cious</u> pre<u>cious</u> mali<u>cious</u> vi<u>cious</u>

- **Exceptions:** ficti<u>tious</u>, ga<u>seous</u>, nau<u>seous</u>, preten<u>tious</u>, rambunc<u>tious</u>

A. Practice: Change each word into a related adjective that ends in the *shus* sound. Write the new word on the line provided.

1. judicial _____
2. gas _____
3. nutrition _____
4. flirtation _____
5. suspicion _____
6. pretension _____

B. Practice: Complete each sentence with an adjective formed from the word in parentheses. Write the adjective on the line provided.

1. (fiction) "Cub Pilot on the Mississippi" is not a _____ account.

2. (ambition) As a young man, Mark Twain was _____, but his dream was to be a riverboat pilot, not a writer.

3. (anxiety) Mr. Brown and the Mississippi itself both created some _____ moments.

4. (caution) Twain learned that a good riverboat pilot had to be very _____.

5. (grace) Sometimes the river seemed _____ and hospitable.

6. (ferocity) Sometimes it seemed violent and _____.

7. (nausea) The choppy waters would have made some people _____.

Challenge: The sound of the first syllable in *furtive* is not always spelled *fur*. It can also be spelled *fir*, as in *firm*, and *fer*, as in *refer*. From the clues below, think of other words that use these spellings. Write the words on the lines provided.

1. a type of tree that does not lose its leaves: _____

2. an animal's warm coat: _____

3. a basement appliance that can heat your house: _____

4. a word describing rich soil in which plants grow well: _____

"Cub Pilot on the Mississippi" by Mark Twain (text page 109)

Build Grammar Skills: Verbs and Verb Phrases

A **verb** is a word that expresses an action or the fact that something exists.

Action: An hour later, Henry <u>entered</u> the pilothouse.

Existence: He <u>was</u> a thoroughly inoffensive boy.

A **verb phrase** consists of a main verb and its helping verbs.

helping verb   main verb

Verb Phrases: One day we <u>were</u> <u>approaching</u> New Madrid.

helping verbs main verb

We <u>had been</u> <u>sailing</u> for many days.

Common Helping Verbs

be, been, am, are, is, was, were   do, does, did

have, has, had   can, could, will, would, may, might, shall, should, must

A. Practice: Read these sentences, and underline any one-word verbs. If the sentence contains a verb phrase, underline the main verb and circle any helping verbs.

1. I had experience of many kinds of steamboat pilots and many varieties of steamboats.

2. By this time he was picking his way among some dangerous "breaks."

3. After this there was a pause and another inspection.

4. By means of a dozen or so of pretty direct questions, he pumped my family history out of me.

5. Then he would jump from the bench.

6. I had committed the crime of crimes.

7. I do not know how long.

8. "So you have been fighting Mr. Brown?"

B. Writing Application: In the spaces provided, complete these sentences about a career that interests you. Use verbs that express actions or show existence, and include at least two verb phrases. When you are done, underline one-word verbs or main verbs and circle helping verbs.

1. Someday I may _____

_____

2. A career like that would _____

_____

3. Some of the qualifications _____

_____

Reading for Success: Literal Comprehension Strategies

Literal comprehension is a basic understanding of a writer's words and ideas. The following reading strategies will help to increase your literal comprehension of a selection:

- **Set a Purpose.** Decide what you want to get out of a piece of literature before you begin to read. Then look for details that help you achieve this purpose.
- **Use your prior knowledge.** Evaluate and criticize the works you read according to your own background and experience. Read to learn if the writer holds opinions or ideas that are different from your own.
- **Ask questions.** Do not blindly accept characters' actions and statements. Question their motives and judgement. Question why the character gives you certain information.
- **Respond.** Allow yourself to respond to characters and situations. Then examine why the characters and situations provoke a specific response from you.

DIRECTIONS: Read the following passage, and use the reading strategies to increase your comprehension. In the margins, note where you break down long sentences, apply word identification strategies, use context to determine meaning, and reread or read ahead. Finally, write your response to the selection on the lines provided.

"The House of Tiles" by Genevieve Barlow and William N. Stivers

In the eighteenth century, young don Luis, the second Count of Orizaba, lived with his wealthy and distinguished family in Mexico City. Luis was not a good son. He was lazy and selfish. He amused himself day and night and never thought of anything serious.

Luis's parents were very sad because of the bad conduct of their son. One day Luis's father said to lazy Luis, "You'll never be able to make a house of tiles."

"I don't care. I only want to have a good time," Luis answered, and left quickly to attend a party.

During the following days, Luis thought a lot about what his father had said and he decided to change his behavior.

Instead of amusing himself all the time, he would work long hours with great enthusiasm. At the end of a few years, he had amassed a fortune.

He bought a large two-story house not far from the cathedral. He and his workmen covered the house with beautiful white, yellow, and blue tiles. When all the work was finished, Luis lived in this elegant house. Afterwards, he spent a lot of time in Europe where he bought elegant and costly furniture.

Now Luis was ready to give a grand party in his magnificent house in honor of his parents. He invited all the wealthy and noble people of the capital.

During the party there were songs and dances. Shortly before midnight, Luis noticed that a very costly and ornate clock had disappeared from a table that was below some large windows. Luis thought that there was a thief among the guests. No doubt, the person hid the clock underneath his or her clothes. For that reason, the young man went to the center of the great room and announced aloud, "Ladies and gentlemen, I regret having to interrupt the music, but I am very sad. A valuable clock is no longer on the table below the large windows."

"How strange!" many people said.

"This clock, mounted with diamonds, is a gift from the king of Spain," Luis continued. "Now it is ten minutes to twelve. Soon the clock will play music before striking twelve. The doors of the house are all locked. No one can leave. Now we are going to turn out the lights of this room for a few minutes. In the dark, the person who has the clock can put it back on the table."

After a few moments the servants entered with the lights. Every eye was turned toward the table. There was the clock! It was one minute to twelve.

The people impatiently watched the tiny hands of the clock reach twelve and pass it, but the clock didn't play any music, nor did it strike the hour.

Luis, seeing the looks of surprise and curiosity on the faces of the people, said, "The truth of the matter is that the clock never plays any music or strikes the hour. Now we can go on with our party."

Thus ends the legend of Luis and the House of Tiles.

"Cub Pilot on the Mississippi" by Mark Twain (text page 109)

Literary Focus: Conflict Between Characters

Whether a story is true or fictional, it usually centers on a conflict, or struggle between opposing forces. Sometimes the conflict is between two characters with different ideas, personalities, and goals. In "Cub Pilot on the Mississippi," the plot centers on the conflict between the young Mark Twain and Mr. Brown. The struggle between the two characters builds and builds until it is finally resolved by the story's end.

DIRECTIONS: To help you understand the character differences at the root of the story's conflict, complete the following chart so that it lists the contrasting ideas, attitudes, personality traits, and motives of Mr. Brown and young Mark Twain. (For items 9 and 10, you will need to fill in details in both columns.)

Mr. Brown	young Mark Twain
1. experienced pilot	1.
2. middle-aged	2.
3. uneducated	3.
4. unhelpful	4.
5. nag, faultfinder	5.
6. bully	6.
7. dishonest	7.
8. self-important	8.
9.	9.
10.	10.

"The Secret" by Arthur C. Clarke (text page 122)

Build Vocabulary

Using the Word Part *micro-*

The word *microbe* contains the word part *micro-*, which means "small." A *microbe* is an extremely small organism. It is so small, in fact, that you can see it only with a *microscope*, an instrument (or "scope") for viewing small organisms.

A. DIRECTIONS: On the line before each sentence, write *T* if you think the statement is true. Write *F* if you think it is false.

_____ 1. In the metric system, a *micrometer* is smaller than a meter.

_____ 2. An executive who *micromanages* a company usually lets others take care of the details.

_____ 3. A *microcomputer* is a laptop computer, not a full-sized computer.

_____ 4. *Micronesia* is a vast continent in the Pacific Ocean.

Using the Word Bank

receding	microbes	radial	implications
competent	hemisphere	heedless	looming

B. DIRECTIONS: Match each word in the left column with its definition in the right column. Write the letter of the definition on the line next to the word it defines.

_____ 1. receding   a. hanging over in an awesome or ominous way

_____ 2. competent   b. half of a sphere or planet

_____ 3. microbes   c. moving back or away; shrinking

_____ 4. hemisphere   d. branching out from a common center

_____ 5. radial   e. likely meanings; conclusions you can draw

_____ 6. heedless   f. skillful; capable

_____ 7. implications   g. very tiny organisms

_____ 8. looming   h. paying no attention; careless

Sentence Completions

C. DIRECTIONS: Complete each sentence with the word from the Word Bank that makes the most sense.

1. From the moon, the huge sphere that is the planet Earth is a _____ presence.

2. When you see the Earth from the moon, you see only one _____ at a time.

3. On the moon, someone _____ of safety precautions will soon perish.

4. _____ and other small organisms found on Earth are not found on the moon.

"The Secret" by Arthur C. Clarke (text page 122)

Build Spelling Skills: Adding Suffixes to Words That End in Silent *e*

Spelling Strategy   Many English words end in a silent *e*, or an *e* that is not pronounced.

- When adding a suffix that begins with a vowel to a word that ends in silent *e*, generally drop the silent *e*. However, keep the *e* if the word ends in *ce* or *ge* or if the suffix starts with *a* or *o*.

  Examples: recede + -ing = receding   desire + -able = desirable
  notice + -able = noticeable   change + -able = changeable

  Exceptions: dying, hoeing, lying, mileage, shoeing, toeing, tying

- When adding a suffix that begins with a consonant to a word that ends in silent *e*, generally keep the silent *e*. However, drop the *e* if the word ends in -ble or -dge.

  Examples: nine + -ty = ninety   sure + -ly = surely
  incredible + ly = incredibly   judge + -ment = judgment

  Exceptions: argument, awful, duly, ninth, truly, wisdom

A. Practice: Make new words by adding as many of the suffixes as you can to the listed words. Write the new words on the lines provided. The first one is done for you as an example.

   Suffixes to use: -able -ed -ful -ing -less -ly -ment

1. time: timed, timing, timeless _____

2. recede: _____

3. care: _____

4. manage: _____

5. excite: _____

B. Practice: Add a suffix to the word in parentheses to form a word that completes the sentence in a way that makes sense. Suffixes you may use are *-able, -ed, -ful, -ing, -ly, -ment.*

1. (explore) Many parts of the moon still needed to be _____ .

2. (announce) The _____ was made in the three official languages of Earth.

3. (accurate) Cooper had always reported his news stories _____ .

Challenge: The *ph* spelling for the sound of *f* occurs in words that came originally from Greek. *Hemisphere*, for example, is made up of *hemi-*, from the Greek for "half," and *sphere*, from the Greek for "globe." Complete the following words, each containing one or more *f* sounds spelled *ph*. The information about the Greek origins should help provide clues to the words.

1. t e l ____ ____ ____ o n e: from the Greek for "sound over a distance"

2. ____ ____ ____ a s e: from the Greek for "speech" or "group of words"

3. ____ ____ o t o g r ____ ____ ____: from the Greek for "light + writing"

"**The Secret**" by Arthur C. Clarke (text page 122)

Build Grammar Skills: Action Verbs and Linking Verbs

An **action verb** expresses physical or mental action. A **linking verb** expresses a state of being; it links the subject of a sentence with a word or words that rename or describe the subject.

> **Action Verb:** The Inspector General <u>shook</u> his head.

> **Linking Verb:** His voice <u>was</u> unsteady, barely under control.

Though there are many action verbs, only a small number of verbs can serve as linking verbs. However, several of these can be either action or linking verbs, depending on their precise meaning. To determine whether a verb is an action verb or a linking verb, replace it with a form of *to be.* If the sentence still makes sense, the verb is a linking verb.

> **Action:** The tractor <u>turned</u> aside from the main road.

> **Linking:** The sky <u>turned</u> [*or* was] dark and dangerous during the meteor shower.

Common Linking Verbs

Forms of *to be:* be been am is are was were has been have been had been					
seem	stay	become	turn	feel	taste
appear	remain	grow	look	sound	smell

A. Practice: Read each sentence, and circle the verb. Then, on the line before the sentence, write *AV* if the verb is an action verb and *LV* if it is a linking verb.

_____ 1. Henry Cooper had been on the Moon for almost two weeks.

_____ 2. There still remained the wonder and mystery of a world as big as Africa.

_____ 3. Chandra would not lie.

_____ 4. There were three nervous breakdowns in the Medical Division last month.

_____ 5. The Moon did not appear glamorous to most people.

_____ 6. Their guide ushered them into a large circular chamber.

_____ 7. The short, gray-haired man looked very unhappy.

_____ 8. Cooper looked at the five-year-old hamster.

_____ 9. The Inspector General turned to his companion.

_____ 10. The span of human life will be at least two hundred years.

B. Writing Application: On the lines provided, write five sentences about space exploration today or in the future. Use the verbs indicated.

1. a form of *to be:* _____

2. *look* as an action verb: _____

3. *look* as a linking verb: _____

4. an action verb of your choice: _____

5. a linking verb of your choice: _____

"The Secret" by Arthur C. Clarke (text page 122)

Reading Strategy: Ask Questions

As you read a story, you'll probably understand it better if you **ask questions** about the characters, events, and other details and then keep reading to see if you figure out the answers. For example, consider this sentence from "The Secret" in which the reader first encounters Chandra Coomaraswamy:

> Presumably Chandra Coomaraswamy possessed a uniform, but Cooper had never seen him wearing it.

Here are some questions you might ask after reading the sentence:

Who is Chandra Coomaraswamy?

Is there any significance to his name? If so, what is it?

Why should it be presumed that he has a uniform?

How long has Cooper known him?

DIRECTIONS: Use this chart to record questions you ask as you read "The Secret" and answers to those questions. In answering the questions, include reasonable guesses as well as answers of which you are sure.

Questions:	Answers:
Who is Henry Cooper?	He's a journalist.
Why is he on the moon?	

"The Secret" by Arthur C. Clarke (text page 122)

Literary Focus: Science Fiction

Science fiction combines elements of fiction and fantasy with scientific fact. It usually offers imaginative speculations based on known scientific and other facts, in accordance with one of these basic formulas:

> Since *A* is true, then perhaps in the world of the future, or on another world, *B* will be true.

> Since *A* is true and *B* is true, then perhaps in the world of the future, or on another world, *C* will be true.

DIRECTIONS: Fill in the diagrams below to show how known facts lead to speculations in Arthur C. Clarke's story "The Secret." Then add two facts and speculations of your own.

1. Fact: People have settled new territories in the past.	+ Fact: Humanity has landed spacecraft on the moon.	> Speculation:
2. Fact: Many nations belong to the UN.	+ Fact: Many nations have been involved in exploring space.	> Speculation:
3. Fact: There are reporters on Earth.	+ Reporters go where there is news.	> Speculation:
4. Fact: The moon does not have a 24-hour day.	+ Humans are used to a 24-hour day.	> Speculation:
5. Fact: The moon's gravity is much weaker than Earth's.	+ Gravity takes its toll on living creatures.	> Speculation:
6.	+	>
7.	+	>

"Harriet Tubman: Guide to Freedom" by Ann Petry (text page 132)

Build Vocabulary

Using the Root *-fug-*

Fugitives, which means "people fleeing the law," contains the root *-fug-*, which means "to flee" or "to drive away." The root, from the Latin verb *fugere*, is sometimes spelled *-fuge-*.

A. DIRECTIONS: Circle the letter of the choice that best completes each sentence. Use your understanding of the root *-fug-* or *-fuge-* to help you figure out the answers.

1. A *fugitive* criminal is probably one who is
   a. behind bars   b. falsely accused   c. doing heavy labor in a prison camp   d. on the lam

2. A character full of *subterfuge* would be very
   a. sneaky   b. careful   c. kindhearted   d. flattering

3. The *refugees* of a war are the people who
   a. fight   c. leave their homelands
   b. die   d. organize antiwar protests

Using the Word Bank

fugitives	disheveled	mutinous	indomitable
incentive	guttural	cajoling	fastidious

B. DIRECTIONS: For each scrambled word in the left column, unscramble the letters to form a word from the Word Bank and write it on the line. Then match each word in the left column with its definition in the right column. Write the letter of the definition on the line next to the word it defines

____ 1. vitigufes   _____   a. rebelling against authority

____ 2. alttuurg   _____   b. full of spirit; not easily ruled

____ 3. mableiinodt   _____   c. reason to do something

____ 4. sodafistui   _____   d. overly

____ 5. sumunito   _____   e. messy; unkempt

____ 6. cieventni   _____   f. those fleeing the law

____ 7. eeevlddsih   _____   g. coaxing, talking into

____ 8. lingojac   _____   h. deep in the throat

Synonyms

C. DIRECTIONS: Circle the letter of the word that is most nearly the same in meaning as the word in CAPITAL LETTERS.

1. INCENTIVE: a. motive   b. relationship   c. payment   d. odor

2. MUTINOUS: a. silent   b. defective   c. rebellious   d. courageous

3. DISHEVELED: a. frightened   b. calm   c. unwise   d. untidy

"Harriet Tubman: Guide to Freedom" by Ann Petry (text page 132)

Build Spelling Skills: Using *c* to Spell the *s* Sound

Spelling Strategy   The sound of *s* has several different spellings in English. Sometimes it is spelled with a *c*.

- The sound of *s* spelled with a *c* almost always occurs before the letter *e, i,* or *y*.
  Examples: incentive conceal necessary success implicit city icy cycle
- The common suffixes -ance and -ence spell the sound of *s* with a *c*.
  Examples: guidance; existence

A. Practice: The italicized words below come from the selection, but many are misspelled. On the line after each sentence, write the correct spelling of the italicized word. If it is already spelled correctly, write *correct*.

1. The owl's cry was repeated four times in *succession* instead of three. _____

2. The man looked with *unconsealed* astonishment and fear at the runaways. _____

3. She told stories to the fugitive slaves as an *insentive* to keep going. _____

4. She told of Frederick Douglass and his *magnifissent* appearance. _____

5. She heard the sound of *pursuit*. _____

6. She had never used the gun *exsept* as a threat. _____

B. Practice: Complete each sentence by filling in a form of the word in parentheses.

1. (exist) At first many did not believe in the _____ of the person nicknamed "Moses."

2. (present) Once Tubman made her _____ known, word spread from cabin to cabin.

3. (vigilant) She spoke of William Still's _____ in guarding the freedom of former slaves.

4. (appear) Douglass also had an impressive physical _____.

5. (independent) She risked her own _____ each time she left Canada for another run.

Challenge: A **mnemonic device** (the *m* is silent) is a remark or saying that helps people remember something. Mnemonic devices can be very helpful when you want to remember how to spell words that give you trouble. For instance, suppose that instead of writing *principal* (the head of your school), you keep misspelling it *principle* (rule). The following mnemonic device could help you remember the correct spelling:

Principal ends in *pal*. The head of your school is your *pal*.

Try making up mnemonic devices for these frequently misspelled words:

1. *different*, not *diffrent* _____

2. *lightning* not *lightening* _____

"Harriet Tubman: Guide to Freedom" by Ann Petry (text page 132)

Build Grammar Skills: Transitive and Intransitive Verbs

A verb is **transitive** if it expresses action and passes that action to someone or something. The person or thing that receives the action of a transitive verb is called the **direct object** of the verb. A verb is **intransitive** if it does not pass an action to someone or something.

> **Transitive:** We <u>studied</u> abolitionism last month. [The direct object is *abolitionism*.]

> **Intransitive:** We <u>studied</u> hard for the test. [There is no direct object.]

Obviously, all linking verbs are intransitive (since they do not express action), but action verbs may be either transitive or intransitive. To determine whether an action verb is transitive or intransitive, look for a direct object. If the verb has a direct object, it is transitive. If it does not, it is intransitive.

A. Practice: Underline the verb in each sentence, and circle the direct object of the verb if it has one. On the line before the sentence, write *TV* if the verb is transitive or *IV* if it is intransitive.

_____ 1. In Maryland, rumors spread about a man named Moses.

_____ 2. At first the slavemasters were not convinced.

_____ 3. Then a group of slaves disappeared.

_____ 4. Bird calls signaled their flight.

_____ 5. Ironically, this Moses was a woman.

_____ 6. Like the biblical Moses, Harriet Tubman guided her people to freedom.

_____ 7. The dangerous journey took many days.

_____ 8. Tubman herself knew moments of doubt.

_____ 9. She told stories of her own first flight.

_____ 10. Finally, the group of fugitives arrived safely at its destination.

B. Writing Application: On the lines below, write five sentences about Harriet Tubman and her adventure. Use transitive or intransitive verbs, as indicated, and circle any direct objects.

1. admire (transitive): _____

_____

2. risk (transitive): _____

_____

3. conduct (transitive): _____

_____

4. arrived (intransitive): _____

_____

5. settle (intransitive): _____

_____

"Harriet Tubman: Guide to Freedom" by Ann Petry (text page 132)

Reading Strategy: Set a Purpose for Reading

People read for different reasons. For example, you may read a horror story to be entertained and a history of World War II to learn more about the subject that interests you. When you read, it is often helpful to **set a purpose for reading,** or determine what you'd like to get out of a piece of writing. To get an idea of that purpose, try asking yourself questions that begin with *who, what, when, where, why,* and *how.*

DIRECTIONS: Fill out the following diagram to help you set a purpose for reading "Harriet Tubman: Guide to Freedom." Finish each question; then supply a short answer.

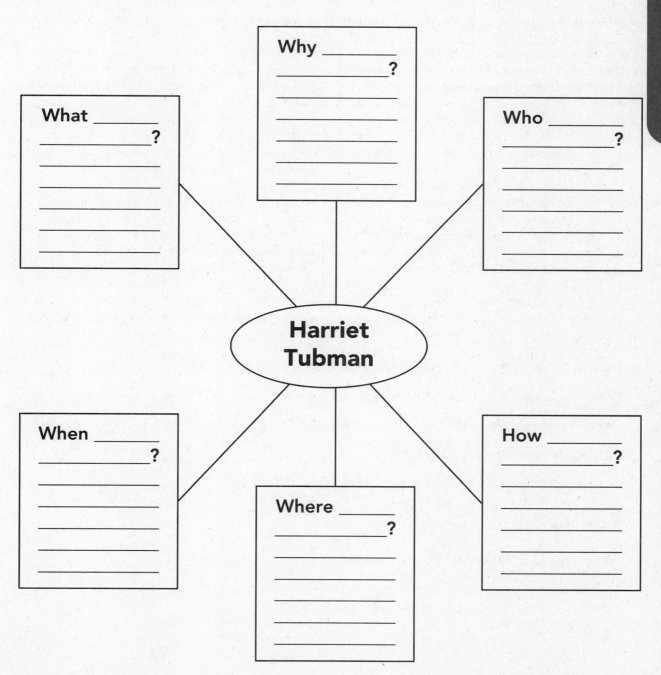

Unit 2: Meeting Challenges

"Harriet Tubman: Guide to Freedom" by Ann Petry (text page 132)

Literary Focus: Third-Person Narrative

A **narrative** is another term for a story; it may be true or fictional. A **third-person narrative** is one in which the storyteller, or **narrator,** stands outside the story and does not participate in the events. The third-person narrator refers to all the characters with third-person pronouns like *he* and *she.* Ann Petry's biography of Harriet Tubman is a third-person narrative.

In contrast, a **first-person narrative** is one in which the narrator participates in the story. The first-person narrator refers to himself or herself with first-person pronouns *I* and *me.* If Harriet Tubman had told her own story in an autobiography, it would have been a first-person narrative.

DIRECTIONS: Read the two passages below, and then answer the questions about them.

Passage A: Sometimes I felt like nothing but a voice speaking in the darkness, cajoling, urging, threatening. Sometimes I told the fugitives things to make them laugh. Sometimes I sang to them, and heard the eleven voices behind me blending softly with mine, and then I knew that for the moment all was well with them. I may have given an impression of mental strength, but underneath it all I lived in fear of what might happen next and of my little sleeping fits that I could not control, but I knew could spell disaster. One time I did fall asleep in the woods. The runaways, ragged, dirty, hungry, cold, did not steal the gun as they might have, and set off by themselves, or turn back. I'm not sure how long I was out, but when I awoke, they were sitting on the ground nearby, waiting patiently. I guess by then they had come to trust me.

Passage B: Sometimes she thought she had become nothing but a voice speaking in the darkness, cajoling, urging, threatening. Sometimes she told them things to make them laugh, sometimes she sang to them, and heard the eleven voices behind her blending softly with hers, and then she knew that for the moment all was well with them. She gave the impression of being a short, muscular, indomitable woman who could never be defeated. Yet at any moment she was liable to be seized by one of those curious fits of sleep, which might last for a few minutes or for hours. Even on this trip, she suddenly fell asleep in the woods. The runaways, ragged, dirty, hungry, cold, did not steal the gun as they might have, and set off by themselves, or turn back. They sat on the ground near her and waited patiently until she awakened. They had come to trust her implicitly, totally.

1. Which passage, *A* or *B*, is a third-person narrative? _____

2. Which passage, *A* or *B*, is a first-person narrative? _____

3. Who is the narrator of the first-person narrative? _____

4. Whose thoughts are revealed in Passage *A*? _____

5. Whose thoughts are revealed in Passage *B*? _____

6. Which passage did you find more immediate and exciting? Why? _____

_____

7. Which passage did you find more realistic, or true to life? Why? _____

_____

8. Which passage did you find more informative? Why? _____

_____

"Columbus" by Joaquin Miller (text page 146)
"The Other Pioneers" by Roberto Félix Salazar (text page 148)
"Western Wagons" by Stephen Vincent Benét (text page 150)

Build Vocabulary

Using Antonyms as Clues to Meaning

Antonyms are words with opposite, or nearly opposite, meanings. Sometimes an antonym can be a clue to the meaning of an unfamiliar word. For example, in the following sentence, the wording suggests that a contrast is being made and that *swarthy* and *wan* are antonyms. Therefore, if you know that *swarthy* means "dark," you can figure out that *wan* means "pale"; and if you know that *wan* means "pale," you can figure out that *swarthy* means "dark."

Though normally <u>swarthy</u> in complexion, the sailors now grew <u>wan</u> from sickness and lack of food.

A. DIRECTIONS: On the lines provided, write the meaning of each italicized word and the antonym that helped you determine the meaning.

1. On the *plains* we could see for miles, but when in the mountains our view was blocked.

   plains: _____   antonym: _____

2. Whereas the first candidate had *legions* of supporters, her opponent made very few.

   legions: _____   antonym: _____

3. Was your first night on stage a marvelous experience, or was it *ghastly*?

   ghastly: _____   antonym: _____

Using the Word Bank

mutinous	wan	swarthy	unfurled	stalwart

B. DIRECTIONS: Find and circle the Word Bank words in the puzzle. Then rewrite each word on the line next to its definition.

```
P S O U N I T U M E D
S W A N N R I M T P O
W A A D E F L J R Z Z
A R D X J Q U I A A V
W T E L N M F R W R W
Y H X K H G O A L P S
R Y T B V X C N A E C
B L E H C B D I T U D
K H D F J Q T X S A O
```

1. _____: rebelling against authority 4. _____: firm and loyal

2. _____: unwound 5. _____: dark in complexion

3. _____: pale; ashen

"**Columbus**" by Joaquin Miller (text page 146)
"**The Other Pioneers**" by Roberto Félix Salazar (text page 148)
"**Western Wagons**" by Stephen Vincent Benét (text page 150)

Build Spelling Skills: Adding *-ous* to Words That End in *y*

Spelling Strategy The suffix *-ous*, which turns nouns into adjectives, usually means "full of; possessing; having the qualities of." For example, a *dangerous* voyage is "full of danger."

- When adding the suffix *-ous* to a word that ends in a consonant + *y*, drop the *y* if the sound it represents disappears.

   Example: larceny + -ous = larcenous   complicity = -ous = complicitous

- When adding the suffix *-ous* to a word that ends in a consonant and *y*, change the *y* to *i* if the sound it represents remains.

   Examples: victory + -ous = victorious   envy + -ous = envious

   Exceptions: beauteous, piteous

- When adding the suffix *-ous* to a word that ends in a vowel and *y*, keep the *y*.

   Example: joy + -ous = joyous

A. Practice: Turn each noun into an adjective by adding the suffix *-ous*. Write the correctly spelled word on the line provided.

1. mutiny + -ous = _____

2. harmony + -ous = _____

3. industry + -ous = _____

4. melody + -ous = _____

5. villainy + -ous = _____

6. pity + -ous = _____

B. Practice: Complete each sentence with an adjective formed from the word in parentheses. Write the adjective on the line provided.

1. (mystery) Columbus and his crew set off for _____ lands.

2. (monotony) The long sea voyage was often _____.

3. (treachery) The waters were sometimes _____.

4. (mutiny) Faced with great suffering, the crew grew _____.

5. (joy) Their mood turned _____ when at last they sighted land.

6. (calamity) The _____ voyage finally ended on October 12, 1492.

Challenge: In *mutinous*, the sound of a long *u* is spelled with a *u*. The same sound has many other spellings, including *ew, ue, yoo, you,* and *yu.* On the lines below, list examples of words that illustrate these different spellings.

ew: _____   yoo: _____

u: _____   you: _____

ue: _____   yu: _____

"Columbus" by Joaquin Miller (text page 146)
"The Other Pioneers" by Roberto Félix Salazar (text page 148)
"Western Wagons" by Stephen Vincent Benét (text page 150)

Build Grammar Skills: Commonly Confused Verbs: *lie* and *lay*

Lay means "to put down; to place." *Lie* means "to be in a horizontal position" or "to be situated." *Lay* is a transitive verb, taking a direct object. *Lie* is intransitive, never taking a direct object. One reason *lay* and *lie* are so often confused is that the past tense of *lie* is *lay*.

Present: The ships often <u>lay</u> anchor in the harbor. (The direct object is anchor.)

Present: The ships usually <u>lie</u> in the harbor waiting for tugboats. (no direct object)

Past: Last Monday the ship <u>laid</u> anchor in the harbor. (The direct object is anchor.)

Past: Last Monday the ships lay in the harbor waiting for tugboats. (no direct object)

Basic Verb	Present Participle	Past Tense	Past Participle
lay	laying	laid	laid
lie	lying	lay	lain

A. Practice: Circle the form of the verb that correctly completes each sentence.

1. Here a wagon train once (laid, lay) like a snake in the hot sun.

2. A wide river (lied, lay) before the pioneers.

3. Several of the pioneers had (laid, lain) logs for a raft.

4. The pioneers (laid, lay) all their worldly goods on the raft.

5. Thank goodness the raft (laid, lay) on the river without sinking.

6. Now we are (laying, lying) a road to commemorate the event.

7. "Today our workers (lay, lie) a cobblestone road in honor of the pioneers," the governor says.

8. "Each stone will (lay, lie) here for future generations to see."

B. Writing Application: Write six sentences about explorers of the past, present, and/or future. Use the verbs indicated.

1. laid (past) _____

_____

2. lay (past) _____

_____

3. had, have, *or* has laid (past or present perfect) _____

_____

4. had, have, *or* has lain (past or present perfect) _____

_____

5. lay *or* lays (present) _____

_____

Unit 2: Meeting Challenges

"Columbus" by Joaquin Miller (text page 146)
"The Other Pioneers" by Roberto Félix Salazar (text page 148)
"Western Wagons" by Stephen Vincent Benét (text page 150)

Reading Strategy: Relate to What You Know

You'll gain a fuller appreciation of what you are reading if you **relate it to what you already know.** For example, when you read Benét's poem "Western Wagons," relating it to what you already know about America's western pioneers will give you a better appreciation of the hardships the pioneers faced and the feats they achieved.

A. DIRECTIONS: To gain a fuller appreciation of Salazar's poem "The Other Pioneers," answer these questions to see what you already know about its subject. If you don't know something, leave it blank. When you are done, share your answers with classmates.

1. What European country first colonized Texas and the rest of the Southwest? _____

2. Were there lots of Americans of English background there at the time? _____

3. What sort of terrain or landscape do you associate with most of the Southwest? _____

4. What is the Rio Grande and where is it located? _____

5. What language does "Rio Grande" come from? _____

6. What ethnic background do you associate with the last names Salinas, Sánchez, García, González, and Martínez? _____

B. DIRECTIONS: After sharing your answers above in 1–6 with classmates, explain how the information might help you understand or appreciate Salazar's poem "The Other Pioneers."

1. _____

_____

2. _____

_____

3. _____

_____

4. _____

_____

5. _____

_____

6. _____

_____

"Columbus" by Joaquin Miller (text page 146)
"The Other Pioneers" by Roberto Félix Salazar (text page 148)
"Western Wagons" by Stephen Vincent Benét (text page 150)

Literary Focus: Stanzas in Poetry

A **stanza** is a group of two or more lines of a poem. The stanzas of a poem are usually separated by spaces, and often they have matching lengths, rhythms, and rhyme schemes. For example, below are two stanzas from a famous poem that appears in Unit 1 in your textbook. Notice that each stanza has four lines, each line has four beats, and the first and fourth lines rhyme, as do the second and third. If you use letters to show the rhyme scheme, or pattern, you would say that the first stanza has an *abba* rhyme scheme. The second stanza has the same rhyme pattern but different rhyming sounds; it therefore has a *cddc* rhyme scheme.

Ring Out Wild Bells by Alfred, Lord Tennyson

Ring out, wild bells, to the wild sky,	a
The flying cloud, the frosty light;	b
The year is dying in the night;	b
Ring out, wild bells, and let him die.	a
Ring out the old, ring in the new,	c
Ring, happy bells, across the snow;	d
The year is going, let him go;	d
Ring out the false, ring in the true.	c

DIRECTIONS: Fill in the chart below for each poem in this grouping. If the number of lines, beats per line, or end rhymes do not form a pattern, or if there is no rhyme at all, be sure to indicate that in the appropriate column.

Poem	Number of Stanzas	Number of Lines in Each Stanza	Number of Beats in Each Line	Rhyme Scheme
"Columbus"				
"The Other Pioneers"				
"Western Wagons"				

"Up the Slide" by Jack London (text page 156)

Build Vocabulary

Using Forms of *exhaust*

As a verb, *exhaust* means "to tire or wear out; to use up; to drain away." As a noun, it refers to the waste products that drain away as vapor (from a car engine, for example). By adding prefixes and suffixes to the word exhaust, you can make several related words.

exhaust + -ed = exhausted, "tired or worn out; used up; drained away"

exhaust + -ive = exhaustive, "using up all options; thorough; complete"

in- + exhaust + -ible = inexhaustible, "not able to be worn out, used up, or drained away"

A. DIRECTIONS: Add these prefixes and suffixes to the word *exhaust* to create new words that complete the sentences below: *-ible   -ing   -ion   -ive.* You may use the prefixes and suffixes more than once and add more than one at a time, but do not make the same word more than once.

1. With all the mining we do, we are _____ many of the area's resources.

2. Even gold is an _____ resource that eventually runs out.

3. When we finally reached the tent, we collapsed in _____.

4. Despite our _____ search, we never found the lost gold mine.

Using the Word Bank

exhausted	thoroughly	manifestly	exertion
maneuver	ascent	descent	

B. DIRECTIONS: Use the clues below to help you complete this crossword puzzle with words from the Word Bank.

Across

1. great effort

2. fully

5. evidently

6. downward climb or path

Down

1. completely expended

3. planned move

4. upward climb or path

"**Up the Slide**" by Jack London (text page 156)

Build Spelling Skills: Spelling *ough* Correctly

Spelling Strategy   The letter combination *ough* has several different sounds in English.

- Sometimes *ough* spells the long *o* sound of *o* as in go: <u>dough</u>   <u>thorough</u>
- Sometimes *ough* spells the sound of *aw* as in paw: <u>bought</u>   <u>ought</u>
- Sometimes *ough* spells the sound of *awf* as in awful: <u>cough</u>   <u>trough</u>
- Sometimes *ough* spells the sound of *uff* as in bluff: <u>enough</u>   <u>rough</u>
- Sometimes *ough* spells the sound of *ow* as in how: <u>bough</u>   <u>drought</u>
- Sometimes *ough* spells the sound of *oo* as in too: <u>through</u>   <u>throughout</u>

A. Practice: On the lines provided, write the word described or defined.

1. the past tense of *bring:* _ _ _ _ _ _ _

2. the past tense of *seek:* _ _ _ _ _ _ _

3. a word that means "with careful regard to detail": _ _ _ _ _ _ _ _ _ _ _

4. a sweet round pastry with a hole: _ _ _ _ _ _ _ _ _

5. the past tense of *fight:* _ _ _ _ _ _ _

B. Practice: On the line provided, write a word that completes each rhyme so that the entire statement makes sense.

1. A few of the climbs made me huff and puff;

   Some were easy, but others were _____.

2. I left behind lots of gear I had brought.

   It turned out to weigh much more than I'd _____.

3. One of the climbers hollered, "Ow!"

   When she hit her head on a low tree _____.

4. Another thought he'd be riding a burro;

   Next time his plans better be more _____.

Challenge: The sound of *s* is sometimes spelled *sc*, as in *ascent* and *descent*. When it is, don't forget to include the *c*. On the line after each sentence below, write the correct spelling of the italicized word. If the word is already spelled correctly, write *correct*.

1. The *assending* escalator is in the shoe department. _____

2. Our *decent* into the cavern began at noon. _____

3. Biology is one branch of *science*. _____

4. Be careful when you hand someone a pair of *sissors*. _____

Selection Support   **71**

"**Up the Slide**" by Jack London (text page 156)

Build Grammar Skills: Active and Passive Voice

A verb is in the **active voice** when the subject performs the action. It is in the **passive** voice when the subject receives the action. Verbs in the passive voice use a form of the helping verb *be (is, are, was, were, have/has/had been)*.

Active Voice: He called aloud to the dogs.

Passive Voice: The dogs were reassured (by him).

A. Practice: On the line before each sentence, write *AV* if the sentence is in the active voice and *PV* if it is in the passive voice. Underline the verb or verb phrase in each sentence.

_____ 1. Clay Durham left the tent for firewood.

_____ 2. He expected a half-hour absence at most.

_____ 3. Swanson was surprised by Clay's assumptions.

_____ 4. Swanson knew the terrain's treacheries.

_____ 5. Difficulties were caused by the slippery ice.

_____ 6. Clay slid all over the place.

_____ 7. The tree was cut down with great difficulty.

_____ 8. Clay was nearly trapped on the trip back.

_____ 9. He studied the deadly cliff face.

_____ 10. Escape might be achieved in an upward climb.

B. Writing Application: In general, writing is more readable and exciting when you use the active voice. On the lines provided, rewrite these sentences in the active voice. One example is given.

1. Many young adventurers like Jack London were drawn to the area. The area drew many
   young adventurers like Jack London.

2. In the late 1890's, gold was discovered by miners in the Klondike region of the Yukon.

   _____

   _____

3. The Yukon Territory was visited by London in the winter of 1897. _____

   _____

4. No gold was found by him. _____

   _____

5. However, the experience was later "mined" by his stories and novels. _____

   _____

"Up the Slide" by Jack London (text page 156)

Reading Strategy: Predict

Good writers build suspense by making you wonder what will happen next and what will happen in the end. As you read, you try to **predict,** or make reasonable guesses, about future story events. Here are some guidelines for making predictions.

- Consider characters' personalities, attitudes, and interaction with other characters.

- Consider the events that have already occurred.

- Consider the setting and the events likely to occur in such a setting.

- Consider the themes or general messages about life that the writer is trying to convey.

- Take special notice of any **foreshadowing** in which the narrator makes statements that hint at what is going to happen.

- Take into account any outside knowledge you may have about similar human behavior and experiences in real life or in fictional works (books, films, plays, songs, and so on).

- Take into account any outside knowledge you may have about the author's life and works.

DIRECTIONS: Follow the guidelines as you use this chart to predict events in "Up the Slide," and then record whether your predictions come true.

Story Event or Clue	Prediction	Actual Outcome

Unit 2: Meeting Challenges

"Up the Slide" by Jack London (text page 156)

Literary Focus: Conflict

Most stories center on a **conflict** or struggle between opposing forces. In Jack London's stories of survival in the Yukon, the conflict is often between humans and nature.

DIRECTIONS: Among the related aspects of nature with which Clay struggles are the cold temperatures, the steep and hilly terrain, the icy surfaces, and the lack of vegetation, including trees. On the chart below, list story incidents that illustrate Clay's struggle with these aspects of nature.

Cold Temperatures	Steep, Hilly Terrain	Icy Surfaces	Lack of Vegetation

"The Pilgrims' Landing and First Winter" by William Bradford (text page 165)

Build Vocabulary

Using the Root -*marin*-

Mariner, which means "sailor," contains the root -*marin*-, which comes from the Latin word for the sea. If you speak Spanish, French, or Italian, you probably had no trouble figuring out that *mariner* has something to do with the sea. The Spanish word for "the sea" is mar, the French is *mer,* and the Italian is *mare.* All three also go back to *marinus,* the Latin word for the sea.

A. DIRECTIONS: Circle the letter of the choice that best completes each sentence. Use your understanding of the Latin *marinus* and the root -*marin*- to help you figure out the answers.

1. A *marina* is a place where you
   a. dock boats   b. grow flowers   c. repair cars   d. speak Latin

2. The United States *Marines* probably train to fight
   a. only on land   b. on sea as well as land   c. only at night   d. on horseback

3. The *Maritime* Provinces of Canada are probably
   a. interior provinces   c. western provinces
   b. coastal or island provinces   d. on the United States border

4. In French, *mal* means "bad." Someone with *mal de mer* is probably suffering from
   a. ignorance   b. headache   c. fear of horses   d. seasickness

Using Words from the Selection

When you come across an unfamiliar word in your reading, you can often determine its meaning by examining the **context,** or surroundings, in which the word appears.

B. DIRECTIONS: Read each of these selection passages, and use the context to help you determine the meaning of the word in italics. Circle the letter of the most likely definition.

1. Being thus arrived at Cape Cod the 11th of November, and necessity called them to look out a place for *habitation.* . .
   a. living; residing   c. sailing
   b. doing something over and over   d. enjoying a pastime

2. Whereupon a few of them *tendered* themselves to go by land and discover those nearest places. . .
   a. hardened   b. offered   c. paid   d. softened; made easier to chew

3. It was conceived there might be some danger in the attempt, yet seeing them *resolute,* they were permitted to go. . .
   a. wasted; decayed   b. frightened   c. firm of purpose   d. doubtful; questioning

4. . . . so as they could not come near them but followed them by the track of their feet *sundry* miles and saw that they had come the same way.
   a. bright   b. dark   c. holy; devout   d. various; many

5. . . . They had headed a great creek and so left the sands, and turned into the woods.
   . . . falling into such *thickets* as were ready to tear their clothes and armor in pieces.
   a. grassy meadows   b. areas of dense bushes   c. ponds; small lakes   d. heavy soups

"The Pilgrims' Landing and First Winter" by William Bradford (text page 165)

Connect Past and Present

People often study the past to get a better understanding of the present. Reading about the Puritans, for example, can teach us a lot about early Americans' qualities, many of which still exist today. It can also teach us how we have changed in certain ways.

DIRECTIONS: On the chart below, list the admirable and less admirable qualities that Bradford's account reveals about the Puritans. Also list examples of those qualities you still see in the United States today.

Quality	Admirable or Not, in Your Opinion?	Bradford's Detail(s) Showing This Quality	Example (if any) of Quality Today

"The Ninny" by Anton Chekhov (text page 176)
"The Governess" by Neil Simon (text page 178)

Build Vocabulary

Using the Suffix -ment

The noun *bafflement* contains the suffix -ment, which means "the action, process, or state of." *Bafflement* means "the state of being baffled." Usually the suffix is added to verbs to turn them into nouns.

Examples: baffle + -ment = bafflement   entertain + -ment = entertainment

A. DIRECTIONS: Complete each sentence with a noun formed from the verb in parentheses. Write the adjective on the line provided.

1. (govern) In 19th-century Russia, education was not provided by the _____.

2. (advance) The job of governess had little room for _____.

3. (assign) The governess gave the child a homework _____.

4. (baffle) The child was puzzled and looked at the governess in _____.

5. (encourage) With _____, the child will do better next time.

Using the Word Bank

bitter	inferior	discharged	bafflement
timidly	discrepancies	guileless	

B. DIRECTIONS: Circle the word that does not belong with the other two words because its meaning is different.

1. bitter, painful, sweet

2. timidly, strongly, shyly

3. inferior, classy, inadequate

4. discrepancies, differences, consistencies

5. guileless, crafty, clever

6. discharged, retained, dismissed

7. bafflement, understanding, puzzlement

Sentence Completions

C. DIRECTIONS: Complete each sentence with the word from the Word Bank that makes the most sense. Use each word only once.

1. As a hired servant, the governess's status was _____ to her employer's.

2. Knowing her lowly position, she always spoke _____.

3. Puzzled by her employee's lies, she wore a look of _____ on her face.

4. Though not deceitful herself, she was not entirely _____ either.

5. She recognized the _____ between the money she was owed and the money she was paid.

"The Ninny" by Anton Chekhov (text page 176)
"The Governess" by Neil Simon (text page 178)

Build Spelling Skills: Forming Plurals of Words That End in y

Spelling Strategy The **plural** form of nouns indicates that there is more than one. To form the plural of a noun that ends in a consonant and y, generally change the y to i and add es. For people's names and compounds with -by, just add s.

> **Examples:** ci<u>ty</u> / ci<u>ties</u>   fami<u>ly</u> / fami<u>lies</u>   opportuni<u>ty</u> / opportuni<u>ties</u>
>
> Bra<u>dy</u> / Bra<u>dys</u>   Murp<u>hy</u> / Murp<u>hys</u>   stand<u>by</u> / stand<u>bys</u>

- To form the plural of a noun that ends in a vowel and <u>y</u>, just add <u>s</u>.

> **Examples:** bo<u>y</u> / bo<u>ys</u>   monk<u>ey</u> / monk<u>eys</u>   Sund<u>ay</u> / Sund<u>ays</u>

A. Practice: On the lines provided, write the plural form of each noun.

1. discrepancy _____   5. Kennedy _____
2. Saturday _____   6. flyby _____
3. library _____   7. money _____
4. valley _____   8. ceremony _____

B. Practice: Complete each sentence with the plural form of the noun in parentheses. Write the plural form on the line provided.

1. (salary) A hundred years ago, the _____ of governesses were very low.

2. (Study) _____ show that governesses earned less than many other servants.

3. (Cheksky) One Russian family, the _____, paid nothing but room and board.

4. (curtsy) Governesses often made _____ as a sign of respect to employers.

5. (holiday) Most governesses had one day off a week, plus some _____.

6. (birthday) They usually had to work on their _____.

7. (ninny) Most governesses were not _____.

Challenge: When the spelling gu appears before a vowel, the u is not usually pronounced: *guileless*. From the clues below, think of other words that illustrate the silent u after a g and before another vowel. Write the words on the lines provided.

1. someone you invite to your home: __ __ __ __ __

2. a person who keeps watch over a building: __ __ __ __ __

3. a part of your mouth that helps you taste and swallow: __ __ __ __ __ __

4. a false appearance: __ __ __ __ __ __ __

5. a popular stringed musical instrument: __ __ __ __ __ __

Name _____ Date _____

"The Ninny" by Anton Chekhov (text page 176)
"The Governess" by Neil Simon (text page 178)

Build Grammar Skills: Principal Parts of Verbs

Every verb has four **principal parts,** or main forms.

Basic Form	Past	Present Participle	Past Participle
watch	watched	watching	watched
hire	hired	hiring	hired

• The **basic form** is used alone to show present action and also in combination with helping verbs such as *may, might, should, would, could*: Nannies <u>watch</u> small children.   Wealthy people also may <u>hire</u> governesses.

To make the basic form agree with a singular subject, you usually add *s.* If the verb ends in *s, ch, sh,* or *x,* add *es*: A wealthy person sometimes <u>hires</u> a governess.   A nanny <u>watches</u> small children.

• To form the **past,** you usually add *-ed* to the basic form. If the basic form already ends in *e,* drop the *e* before adding *-ed*: The nanny <u>watched</u> the small children.   The family <u>hired</u> a governess.

• The **present participle** is usually used after forms of the helping verb *be.* To form the present participle, add *-ing* to the basic form. If the verb ends in *e,* drop the *e* before adding *-ing*: The nanny was <u>watching</u> the children.   The family is <u>hiring</u> a governess.

• The **past participle** is most often used after forms of the helping verb *have.* To form the past participle, add *-ed* to the basic form. If the word already ends in *e,* drop the *e* before adding *-ed*: The nanny had <u>watched</u> the children for days.   The family has <u>hired</u> a governess.

A. Practice: Complete each sentence by providing the form of the verb indicated in parentheses.

1. (past participle of *invite)* The employer had _____ the governess into the room.

2. (present participle of *settle*) He was _____ the matter of her monthly salary.

3. (past participle of *agree*) According to him, they had _____ to thirty rubles.

4. (past of *whisper*) She _____ a correction to no avail.

5. (past of *deduct*) He _____ several sums for many ridiculous things.

6. (basic form of *take*) Even today, employers may _____ advantage of servants.

7. (basic form of *possess*) A servant with no contract _____ few rights.

B. Writing Application: Write four sentences to illustrate the principal parts of *employ.* Your sentences should be about jobs that teenagers often take in other people's homes.

1. employ:_____

_____

_____

_____

"The Ninny" by Anton Chekhov (text page 176)
"The Governess" by Neil Simon (text page 178)

Reading Strategy: Question Characters' Actions

One way you can better understand a story or play is to **question characters' actions**. For example, for a better understanding of the events in a story or a play, you might ask yourself "What is the character doing?" or "What will the character do next?" And each time you come across what seems to be an important or interesting bit of behavior on the part of the character, you might ask yourself, "Why did the character do that?" Then keep reading to see if you can answer your questions.

DIRECTIONS: As you read "The Ninny" and "The Governess," fill in the following table to help you question the characters' actions.

Character	What the Character Said or Did	Why?
"The Ninny"		
"The Governess"		

"The Ninny" by Anton Chekhov (text page 176)
"The Governess" by Neil Simon (text page 178)

Literary Focus: Characters' Motives

Characters' motives are the reasons that characters act or speak in a certain way. A particular action may have more than one motive. Sometimes a character's motives are directly stated within a selection. Often, however, the motives are unstated, and the readers must determine the motives for themselves. Even when the motives are unstated, they can be fairly obvious. For example, if someone does something wrong and then lies about it, you can figure out that the reason for the lie is probably embarrassment and/or fear of punishment. On the other hand, there are times when you cannot be certain about a character's motives. In "The Ninny" and Neil Simon's play based on it, the motives of the employer are not entirely clear, and exploring them is central to an appreciation of the two works.

- To determine a character's motives, you need to consider what you know about the character, what you know about other characters in the selection, and what you know about human nature in general.

- If it seems relevant, you should also consider what you may know about the times in which the selection takes place and what you may know about the author's experiences and concerns.

DIRECTIONS: On the lines provided, answer these questions about the selections.

1. How would you sum up the "trick" the employer plays on the governess? _____
   _____

2. What do you think is the main motive for the employer's behavior? _____
   _____

3. Which details in the selections lead you to that conclusion? _____
   _____
   _____

4. What outside knowledge about human nature leads you to that conclusion?_____
   _____
   _____

5. What other relevant outside knowledge, if any, leads you to that conclusion? _____
   _____
   _____

6. What other motives, if any, do you think the employer may have? _____
   _____
   _____

7. Which details from the selection and/or outside knowledge lead you to consider these other motives? _____
   _____

Build Vocabulary

Using the Suffix -able

The suffix -able means "capable of" or "tending to." It is usually added to verbs to turn them into adjectives. For example, the verb *disagree* means "to argue." When you add -able, you get the adjective *disagreeable*, "tending to argue."

A. DIRECTIONS: Complete each sentence with an adjective formed from the verb in parentheses. Write the adjective on the line provided.

1. (predict) Mrs. Jones's behavior was not very _____.

2. (understand) She thought Roger's crime was _____.

3. (manage) She thought that despite his crime he was still a _____ boy.

4. (present) She told Roger to comb his hair so he would look _____.

5. (work) Do you think her approach would be _____ in real-life situations?

Using the Word Bank

presentable	mistrusted	latching	barren	barely

B. DIRECTIONS: On the line before each statement, write *T* if the statement is probably true and *F* if it is probably false.

____ 1. Everyone else at a formal dinner will find you <u>presentable</u> if you go in T-shirts and shorts.

____ 2. In the month of November, the new year has <u>barely</u> begun.

____ 3. Compared to the Earth, the moon has a <u>barren</u> landscape.

____ 4. In football, <u>latching</u> on to another player may result in a holding penalty.

____ 5. If viewers <u>mistrusted</u> a TV commercial, they would rush out to buy the product.

Analogies

C. DIRECTIONS: For each related pair of words in CAPITAL LETTERS, choose the lettered pair that best expresses a *similar* relationship. Circle the letter of your choice.

1. BARELY : COMPLETELY ::
   a. somewhat : entirely   b. fully : substantially   c. reasonably : thoughtfully   d. naked : clothed

2. BARREN : DESERT ::
   a. dry : forest   b. cold : Arctic   c. hilly : flatland   d. fertile : soil

3. PRESENTABLE : DISGRACEFUL::
   a. polite : proper   b. gift : generous   c. absent : ill   d. right : wrong

4. TRUST : MISTRUSTED::
   a. flame : burnt   b. value : concerned   c. doubt : believed   d. puzzle : wondered

5. TOUCHING : LATCHING::
   a. nibbling : devouring   b. opening : closing   c. clasping : fastening   d. hugging : tapping

"Thank You, M'am" by Langston Hughes (text page 188)

Build Spelling Skills: Spelling Words with *mis-*

Spelling Strategy The prefix mis- means "bad; badly; wrong; wrongly." When adding *mis-* to a word, keep the original spelling of the word.

> **Examples:** mis- + spell = misspell   mis- + use = misuse
> mis- + manage = mismanage

A. Practice: For each item, add the prefix to the word and write the new word on the line provided.

1. mis- + trusted _____
2. mis- + spoken _____
3. mis- + pronounce _____
4. mis- + shapen _____

5. mis- + stated _____
6. mis- + trial _____
7. mis- + place _____
8. mis- + handle _____

B. Practice: Complete each sentence with a word formed by adding a prefix to the word in parentheses.

1. (deed) Roger performed a serious _____ when he took Mrs. Jones's purse.
2. (behavior) His _____ could have been severely punished.
3. (step) Taking Mrs. Jones's purse was more than a small _____ .
4. (understanding) It could have led to a serious _____ between them.
5. (trust) You might have expected her to _____ Roger after the incident.
6. (guided) Instead, she showed some sympathy for the _____ boy.

Challenge: In general, the suffix *-able* is added to words that are complete (*presentable*) or in which only a final *e* is dropped (*usable*), whereas *-ible* is added to roots that are not complete words (*terrible*). However, there are many exceptions to this general rule, so when you are in doubt, you'll need to check a dictionary. On the lines provided, add *-able* or *-ible* to the following words or roots. Then check the spellings in a dictionary, and correct any words you misspelled. Circle the words that do not follow the general rule.

1. comfort _____
2. predict _____
3. sens _____

4. incred _____
5. horr _____
6. poss _____

7. suggest _____
8. leg _____
9. mov _____

10. accept _____
11. deduct _____
12. invis _____

Selection Support **83**

Name _____ Date _____

Build Grammar Skills: Principal Parts of Irregular Verbs

An **irregular verb** is one in which the past or past-perfect form does not end in *ed*. Instead, the basic form of the verb either changes spelling or does not add any letters at all. Here is a list of some common irregular verbs.

Basic Form	Past	Past Participle	Basic Form	Past	Past Participle
be	was, were	been	lead	led	led
begin	began	begun	leave	left	left
bend	bent	bent	lose	lost	lost
break	broke	broken	make	made	made
buy	bought	bought	put	put	put
come	came	come	run	ran	run
cut	cut	cut	say	said	said
do	did	done	see	saw	seen
eat	ate	eaten	set	set	set
fall	fell	fallen	shake	shook	shaken
fly	flew	flown	shut	shut	shut
get	got	got or gotten	sit	sat	sat
give	gave	given	sling	slung	slung
go	went	gone	speak	spoke	spoken
have	had	had	take	took	taken
hear	heard	heard	teach	taught	taught
hold	held	held	tell	told	told
know	knew	known	think	thought	thought

A. Practice: Complete each sentence with the correct past-tense form of the verb in parentheses. Write the verb on the line provided.

1. (be) She _____ a large woman with a large purse.

2. (sling) She _____ it across her shoulder.

3. (have) She _____ everything in it but hammer and nails.

4. (run) A boy had _____ up behind her.

5. (give) He had _____ the strap a single tug.

6. (break) The strap had _____ .

7. (fall) He had then _____ from the weight of the purse.

8. (take) The woman _____ him home with her.

9. (make) She _____ him a meal.

10. (teach) She _____ him a lesson.

B. Writing Application: Using the indicated verb forms, write five sentences about Mrs. Luella Bates Washington Jones and Roger.

1. (past of *see*): _____

2. (past participle of *know*): _____

3. (past participle of *have*): _____

4. (past of *go*): _____

5. (past of *tell*): _____

"Thank You, M'am" by Langston Hughes (text page 188)

Reading Strategy: Respond to Characters' Actions

When you read a work of literature, you'll get more out of it if you **respond to characters' actions**, deciding what you think of the things characters do and say. Here are some questions you might ask yourself about a particular action.

- Do I understand the action? If so, what might be the motives behind it?

- Do I approve of the action? Why or why not?

- How would most others probably behave if they were in the same situation as the character?

- How would I probably behave if I were in the same situation as the character?

DIRECTIONS: Fill in the following chart to show your responses to characters' actions in "Thank You, M'am." Use the four questions listed above to help prompt your responses. Three actions are given.

Character's Action	Your Response
Roger tries to steal the purse.	
Roger is prevented from stealing the purse.	
Mrs. Jones takes Roger home.	

"Thank You, M'am" by Langston Hughes (text page 188)

Literary Focus: Theme

A **theme** is a general message about life or human nature that a writer conveys in a work of literature. A work may have more than one theme. Sometimes the theme is directly stated within the work. More often it is unstated, and readers themselves must determine the theme. To determine a story's theme, think about the story's characters, settings, and events. Then ask yourself, "What aspect of life does the author want me to think about?" and "What does the story seem to be saying about that aspect of life?"

DIRECTIONS: Create word webs listing details about the story's characters, settings, and events. Then answer the questions below the word webs.

Characters
— Roger _____
— Mrs. Jones _____

Settings
— Street/neighborhood _____
— Mrs. Jones's apartment _____

Events
— Purse snatching _____
— Taking Roger home _____

1. Based on the details you listed above, what aspects of life do you think the author is asking you to think about when you read this story? _____
_____
_____

2. Based on the details you listed above, what does the story seem to be saying about those aspects of life? _____
_____
_____
_____
_____
_____

"Prospective Immigrants Please Note" by Adrienne Rich (text page 194)
"Much Madness is divinest Sense—" by Emily Dickinson (text page 195)
"This We Know" by Chief Seattle (text page 196)
"Hard Questions" by Margaret Tsuda (text page 199)

Build Vocabulary

Using Forms of *evade*

The verb *evade* means "to avoid" or "to escape." It is related to several other words, including the following.

evasion: an instance of avoiding or escaping something; the act of avoiding or escaping

evasive: acting in a way that avoids or escapes; showing a tendency to avoid or escape

evasively: in a manner that attempts to avoid or escape

evasiveness: the quality of trying to avoid or escape; the tendency to try to avoid or escape

A. Directions: Complete each sentence by using one of the five words defined above—*evade, evasion, evasive, evasively, evasiveness.* Use each word only once.

1. Instead of stating ideas directly, some politicians show a certain _____.

2. Their _____ style causes voters to doubt the message.

3. Still, no politician wants to speak too _____.

4. They do not want to _____ their responsibility to the citizens they represent.

5. Each _____ puzzles voters, and too many might confuse them.

Using the Word Bank

worthily	evade	discerning	prevail	assent	ancestors

B. Directions: Read each definition, and fill in the word on the lines provided. When you are done, the letters in the shaded boxes, reading down, will spell out something Emily Dickinson is famous for creating.

1. to have one's views triumph and rule

2. past relatives from whom you descend

3. to escape something or someone

4. to say yes

5. showing sharp perception

6. in a valued or valuable manner

"Prospective Immigrants Please Note" by Adrienne Rich (text page 194)
"Much Madness is divinest Sense—" by Emily Dickinson (text page 195)
"This We Know" by Chief Seattle (text page 196)
"Hard Questions" by Margaret Tsuda (text page 199)

Build Spelling Skills: Using the Suffix *-or*

Spelling Strategy   The suffix *-or*, which creates nouns, indicates a person or thing that performs an action. Sometimes, as in *ancestor*, it is added to a root that cannot stand alone as an English word. More often, however, it is added to verbs to form nouns: *invent + -or = inventor*, "a person who invents."

• When adding *-or* to a verb that ends in *e*, drop the *e*.

   Examples: percolate + -or = percolator   operate + -or = operator

• When adding *-or* to a verb that ends in a consonant, no other changes are necessary.

   Examples: invent + -or = inventor   act + -or = actor

A. Practice: For each item, add the suffix to the verb and write the new noun on the line provided.

1. govern + -or _____

2. senate + -or _____

3. conquer + -or _____

4. protect + -or _____

5. narrate = -or _____

6. elevate + -or _____

7. accelerate + -or _____

8. direct + -or _____

B. Practice: Complete each sentence with a noun formed by adding *-or* to the verb in parentheses. Write the new word on the line provided.

1. (educate) Emily Dickinson's father worked for a college, though not as an

   _____ .

2. (visit) After 1862, Dickinson rarely welcomed a _____ to her home.

3. (contribute) Unlike most poets, Dickinson was not a _____ to magazines.

4. (edit) After Dickinson died, her relatives gave her poems to an _____.

Challenge: Many adjectives can be turned into adverbs of manner by adding the suffix *-ly*. When you add *-ly* to a word that ends in a consonant and *y*, change the *y* to *i: worthy + -ly = worthily*, "in a worthy manner." Add *-ly* to each of these adjectives to turn them into adverbs, and try using the adverbs in sentences. Write your sentences on the lines provided.

1. weary:_____

2. pretty:_____

3. dizzy:_____

"Prospective Immigrants Please Note" by Adrienne Rich (text page 194)
"Much Madness is divinest Sense—" by Emily Dickinson (text page 195)
"This We Know" by Chief Seattle (text page 196)
"Hard Questions" by Margaret Tsuda (text page 199)

Build Grammar Skills: Verb Tenses

Unlike other parts of speech, verbs can change form to show time. The different times that verbs show are called the tenses. The three main verb tenses are the **present,** the **past,** and the **future.** The chart below shows the verb forms of each tense when the verbs are **conjugated,** or arranged to agree with different possible subjects.

	Present Tense	Past Tense	Future Tense
First-person singular	I assent	I assented	I will (*or* shall) assent
Second-person singular	you assent	you assented	you will (*or* shall) assent
Third-person singular	he/she/it* assents	he/she/it assented	he/she/it will (*or* shall) assent
First-person plural	we assent	we assented	we will (*or* shall) assent
Second-person plural	you assent	you assented	you will (*or* shall) assent
Third-person plural	they** assent	they assented	they will (*or* shall) assent

*or any other singular subject   **or any other plural subject

A. Practice: On the line before each sentence, identify the tense of the verb in italics. Then, on the longer lines, rewrite the sentence using the verb form of the other two main tenses. For example, if the verb is in the present tense, rewrite the sentence using the past tense of the verb, and rewrite it again using the future tense.

_____ 1. The President *communicated* his plans to Chief Seattle.

_____

_____

_____ 2. The government *will purchase* the land.

_____

_____

_____ 3. Those in charge of it *share* in its bounty.

_____

_____

B. Writing Application: Using the indicated verb forms, write five sentences about the need to preserve nature.

1. (present of *need*) _____

2 (future of *preserve*) _____

3. (past of *move*) _____

4. (past of *slaughter*) _____

5. (future of *protect*) _____

Reading Strategy: Use Your Senses

Poetry and descriptive writing often appeal to one or more of the five senses: sight, sound, smell, taste, and touch. To appreciate such writing, it is valuable to **use your senses** as you read. Use the sensory, or sense-related, details that the writer provides to picture what is being described, and try to imagine what it sounds, feels, smells and perhaps even tastes like. For example, consider this line from Chief Seattle's "This We Know":

We love this earth as a newborn loves its mother's heartbeat.

If you use your senses as you read the line, you can try to picture, feel, and perhaps even smell the newborn baby nestled against its mother. You can also try to imagine hearing the heartbeat that the baby hears.

DIRECTIONS: Below are five more passages from "This We Know." On the lines provided, explain what you try to picture, feel, hear, smell, and/or taste as you read each passage.

1. Every part of this earth is sacred to my people. Every shining pine needle, every sandy shore, every mist in the dark woods, every meadow, every humming insect.

   _____

   _____

   _____

2. The perfumed flowers are our sisters. The bear, the deer, the great eagle, these are our brothers.

   _____

   _____

   _____

3. The rocky crests, the juices in the meadow, the body heat of the pony, and man, all belong to the same family.

   _____

   _____

   _____

4. The rivers are our brothers. They quench our thirst.

   _____

   _____

   _____

5. What will happen when the secret corners of the forest are heavy with the scent of many men and the view of the ripe hills is blotted by talking wires?

   _____

   _____

   _____

"Prospective Immigrants Please Note" by Adrienne Rich (text page 194)
"Much Madness is divinest Sense—" by Emily Dickinson (text page 195)
"This We Know" by Chief Seattle (text page 196)
"Hard Questions" by Margaret Tsuda (text page 199)

Literary Focus: Imagery

Imagery is the use of language that appeals to one or more of the five senses (sight, sound, smell, taste, and touch). Each instance or example of such language is called an **image.** This sentence from "This We Know," for instance, contains an image that appeals to the senses of both sight and smell:

The **perfumed flowers** are our sisters.

DIRECTIONS: The four selections in this grouping contain images that appeal to the different senses. Use the following chart to help you keep track of those images. If an image appeals to more than one of the five senses, list it in all appropriate columns.

Poem	Sight	Sound	Touch	Taste	Smell
"Prospective Immigrants"					
"Much Madness"					
"This We Know"					
"Hard Questions"					

"Flowers for Algernon" by Daniel Keyes (text page 204)

Build Vocabulary

Using the Word Root -psych-

Psychology is one of several words containing the Greek root *-psych-*, which has come to mean "mind" in English. In ancient Greece, the word more often meant "soul"; in fact, in Greek mythology, *Psyche* (si'ke) was the goddess of the soul.

A. DIRECTIONS: Circle the letter of the choice that best completes each sentence.

1. The word part *-logy* means "science" or "study." The science or study of the human mind is ____.
   a. psychology   b. sociology   c. anthropology   d. economics

2. If a jury agrees that a criminal is *psychotic*, the criminal's trial will probably end with ____.
   a. a guilty verdict   b. a mistrial   c. a verdict of not guilty by reason of insanity
   d. a plea bargain

3. If *-soma-* is the Greek root for body, a *psychosomatic* illness is probably one in which ____.
   a. your mind tells your body to be sick   c. your body goes crazy gaining weight
   b. your stomach aches painfully   d. you fail to recover

4. If you go to see a *psychodrama*, you should expect a play that contains ____.
   a. lots of laughs   b. romance   c. poetic language   d. efforts to explore characters'
                                                                    thoughts

Using the Word Bank

psychology	specter	vacuous	obscure	introspective
tangible	refute	illiteracy	syndromes	

B. DIRECTIONS: Circle the letter of the word or phrase that is most nearly the same in meaning as the word in CAPITAL LETTERS.

1. REFUTE: a. run away b. agree c. prove d. disprove

2. TANGIBLE: a. real b. tasty c. graceful d. breakable

3. INTROSPECTIVE: a. blind b. unwise c. thoughtful d. transparent

4. VACUOUS: a. coldhearted b. empty-headed c. noisy d. energetic

5. OBSCURE: a. reveal b. explain c. conceal d. heal

6. SYNDROMES: a. cures b. symptoms c. headaches d. dosages

7. PSYCHOLOGY: a. mind study b. counselor c. history study d. emotion

"Flowers for Algernon" by Daniel Keyes (text page 204)

Build Spelling Skills: Spelling the *s* Sound *ps* and the *k* Sound *ch*

Spelling Strategy   Many words from Greek use a *ps* to spell the sound of *s* and a *ch* to spell the sound of *k*.

- The sound of *s* spelled *ps* generally occurs at the beginning of a word.

   Examples: psychiatry   psychodrama   pseudoscience

- The sound of *k* spelled *ch* can occur in the beginning, middle, or end of a word.

   Examples: chorus   mechanism   monarch

A. Practice: On the lines provided, correctly complete the word being described or defined.

1. a group that sings in church: _ _ _ I R

2. a shiny gray metal: _ _ _ O M E

3. the study of the human mind: _ _ _ _ _ O L O G Y

4. a medical doctor who studies the human mind: _ _ _ _ _ _ I A T R I S T

5. a flower popular in corsages: _ _ _ _ S A N T H E M U M

6. December 25 holiday: _ _ _ _ _ _ M A S

7. a person who fixes machinery: M E _ _ _ _ I C

8. a substance used to keep pool water clean: _ _ _ O R I N E

B. Practice: On the line after each sentence, write the correct spelling of the italicized word. If the word is already spelled correctly, write *correct*.

1. Charlie was an interesting *karacter*. _____

2. He was the human guinea pig in a *sykiatric* experiment. _____

3. He kept a *kronological* report of the experiment's progress. _____

4. As he got smarter, he himself actually studied *sykology*. _____

5. I think he also studied biology, geology, and *kemistry*. _____

Challenge: Spelling plays a key role in "Flower for Algernon." Choose a report from early in the selection, and rewrite it with correct spellings. Circle the words you have corrected.

_____

_____

_____

_____

"Flowers for Algernon" by Daniel Keyes (text page 204)

Build Grammar Skills: Perfect Tenses

The **perfect tenses** go beyond the simple present, past, and future tenses to show relationships in time. You create the perfect tenses by using a form of the helping verb *have* before the past participle of the main verb.

- The **present perfect** shows an action or condition that began at some unspecified time in the past and may have continued into the present.

  Scientists have experimented with mice for many years now.

  They have conducted many valuable experiments.

- The **past perfect** shows a past action or condition that ended before another time in the past.

  That medical experiment had used mice before tests with humans started.

  They had also tested with rats before they switched to humans.

- The **future perfect** shows a future action or condition that will have ended before another time in the future.

  By next year, the lab will have completed all its tests.

  The scientists will have finished all their tests before they issue a report.

A. Practice: Using the verb tenses as clues, renumber these sentences to reflect their order in time. Write the new numbers on the lines before the sentences. On the line after each sentence, indicate whether the verb in italics is in the past, present, future, past perfect, present perfect, or future perfect tense.

_____ 1. Soon "Flowers for Algernon" *will have celebrated* its fortieth birthday. _____

_____ 2. Daniel Keyes *had first published* "Flowers for Algernon" as a short story. _____

_____ 3. The screen version, called Charly, *remains* a classic movie. _____

_____ 4. Keyes's story *will be* fifty years old in 2009. _____

_____ 5. The author then *expanded* the tale into a novel. _____

_____ 6. Keyes *has* never *penned* another work of equal fame. _____

B. Writing Application: On the lines provided, rewrite these sentences so that each sentence keeps one verb unchanged and uses the other verb in a perfect tense. Your revised sentences should reflect the correct time relationships in "Flowers for Algernon."

1. Charlie recorded his first progress report before the experiment started. _____

_____

2. Charlie never noticed Miss Kinnian's beauty until the day he commented on it. _____

_____

3. By the time he writes the report for April 30, his spelling and grammar improve. _____

_____

4. When he pens his April 30 progress report, he ends his job at Donnegan's. _____

_____

Name _____ Date _____

"Flowers for Algernon" by Daniel Keyes (text page 204)

Reading Strategy: Summarizing

When you **summarize,** you state in your own words the main ideas and details of a piece of writing. Pausing to summarize portions of a story will help you clarify events and remember them better. It may also help you predict the events to come.

DIRECTIONS: On the following chart, summarize each progress report in "Flowers for Algernon." The first one is done as an example.

Progress Report	Summary
Progress Report 1	Charlie begins keeping a journal.
Progress Report 2	
Progress Report 3	
Progress Report 4	
Progress Report 5	
Progress Report 6	
Progress Report 7	
Progress Report 8	
Progress Report 9	
Progress Report 10	
Progress Report 11	
Progress Report 12	
Progress Report 13	

Unit 2: Meeting Challenges

"Flowers for Algernon" by Daniel Keyes (text page 204)

Literary Focus: First-Person Point of View

Point of view refers to the vantage point from which a story is told. A story using **first-per-son point of view** is told by a character who appears in the story and refers to himself or her-self with first-person pronouns *I* and *me*. The first-person narrator, or storyteller, is often espe-cially sympathetic and can draw readers into a story and make it seem more realistic. On the other hand, the first-person point of view has strong limitations, for the first-person narrator can provide only his or her own thoughts, feelings, and experiences and can only guess at the thoughts, feelings, and experiences of other characters.

DIRECTIONS: Read these two passages, and then answer the questions about them.

A. Their going to use me! Im so exited I can hardly write. Dr Nemur and Dr Strauss had a argament about it first. Dr Nemur was in the office when Dr Strauss brot me in. Dr Nemur was worryed about using me but Dr Strauss told him Miss Kinnian rekemmended me the best from all the pepul who she was teaching. I like Miss Kinnian because shes a very smart teacher. And she said Charlie your going to have a second chance. If you volenteer for this experament you mite get smart. They don't know if it will be perminint but theirs a chance. Thats why I said ok even when I was scared because she said it was an operashun. she said dont be scared Char-lie you done so much with so little I think you deserv it most of all.

B. Charlie was so excited when he was chosen for the experiment. Doctors Nemur and Strauss had argued about using him, for Nemur had at first hoped for an intelligent subject that might be turned into someone of superhuman intelligence. But Strauss convinced Nemur that Char-lie's cooperative nature and deep desire to improve himself made him a deserving subject for the first experiment. Miss Kinnian actually had some doubts because she knew that the opera-tion might not prove permanent, but she pushed them aside, convincing herself that Charlie deserved a second chance at leading a meaningful life. She said much the same thing to Charlie himself, telling him not to worry about the operation and explaining, "If you volunteer for this experiment, you might get smart." Because of his respect for his teacher, Charlie was reassured by her words.

1. Which passage, *A* or *B*, is a first-person narrative? _____

2. Who is the narrator of the first-person narrative? _____

3. Whose thoughts and experiences are revealed in Passage *A*? _____

4. Whose thoughts and experiences are revealed in Passage *B*? _____

5. In which passage do you have more sympathy for Charlie Gordon? Why? _____

_____

_____

6. Which passage did you find more immediate and exciting? Why? _____

_____

_____

7. Which passage did you find more realistic, or true to life? Why? _____

_____

_____

"Brown vs. Board of Education" by Walter Dean Myers (text page 241)

Build Vocabulary

Using the Prefix *in-*

One meaning of the prefix *in-* is "not." For example, the word *tangible* means "able to be touched or defined." Something that is *intangible* is therefore *not* able to be touched or defined.

A. DIRECTIONS: Complete each sentence with an appropriate word formed by adding the prefix *in-* to one of the following four words. All the words come from "Brown vs. Board of Education."

ability   convenience   equality   frequent

1. In the early 1950's, there was still _____ between the races in America.

2. Educating blacks and whites together was _____ , even in the North.

3. African Americans protested their _____ to attend the best public schools.

4. Despite the _____, they were willing to travel to better schools if necessary.

Using the Word Bank

elusive	predominantly	diligent	intangible
unconstitutional	deliberating	oppressed	

B. DIRECTIONS: Read each sentence, and use the context to help you determine the meaning of the word in italics. Then circle the letter of the best definition from the choices given.

1. By the 1950's, freedom was an *elusive* thing that could not be captured in a physical sense.
   a. slippery   b. very weak   c. very powerful   d. requiring outside knowledge

2. In *predominantly* African American neighborhoods, most students were African American too.
   a. in a bossy manner   b. in a prejudiced manner   c. mainly   d. slightly

3. *Diligent* lawyers labored for years to overcome segregation in the public schools.
   a. hardworking   b. longwinded   c. sloppy; careless   d. greedy and dishonest

4. Some problems in education were measurable; others were *intangible.*
   a. unable to be defined   b. able to be captured   c. unforgettable   d. not serious

5. After *deliberating* for over a year, the Supreme Court reached a decision.
   a. purposely harming   b. accidentally harming   c. thinking and discussing   d. ignoring

6. The court declared segregation *unconstitutional* because it violated Americans' civil rights.
   a. unwise   b. unfair   c. untrue   d. illegal

7. After that civil rights landmark, others laws that *oppressed* African Americans began to fall.
   a. raised; uplifted   b. kept down by unjust use of power   c. hid one's true feelings   d. calmed

"Brown vs. Board of Education" by Walter Dean Myers (text page 241)

Build Spelling Skills: Adding *-ed* to Form the Past Tense

Spelling Strategy   You usually form the past tense of verbs by adding *-ed*.

- If the verb ends in silent *e*, drop the e before adding *-ed*.

   Examples: involve + -ed = involved   graduate + -ed = graduated

- If the verb ends in a consonant plus *y*, change the *y* to *i* before adding *-ed*.

   Examples: cry + -ed = cried   qualify + -ed = qualified

- In most other cases, just add *-ed* to the verb.

   Examples: attend + -ed = attended   delay + -ed = delayed

A. Practice: On the line provided, write the past tense of each verb.

1. oppress + -ed = _____

2. state + -ed = _____

3. try + -ed = _____

4. exist + -ed = _____

5. play + -ed = _____

6. separate + -ed = _____

7. deprive + -ed = _____

8. identify + -ed = _____

9. supervise + -ed = _____

10. deliberate + -ed = _____

B. Practice: Complete each sentence with the past tense of the verb in parentheses.

1. (segregate) In the early 1950's, many laws _____ public school students by race.

2. (rely) These laws _____ on an 1896 Supreme Court decision.

3. (deny) Segregation laws often _____ the best education to African Americans.

4. (live) Some African Americans _____ far from the only schools open to them.

5. (sue) Finally, thirteen families _____ the Board of Education in Topeka, Kansas.

6. (challenge) They _____ the segregation laws on constitutional grounds.

7. (struggle) Lawyers like Thurgood Marshall _____ to win the case.

8. (argue) They _____ that the separate schools were not equal.

9. (testify) Psychologists like Kenneth B. Clark _____ on their behalf.

10. (integrate) Because of their efforts, American communities _____ public schools.

"Brown vs. Board of Education" by Walter Dean Myers (text page 241)

Build Grammar Skills: Adjectives

An **adjective** is a word that modifies, or describes, a noun or a pronoun. In the sentences below, for example, the adjective *elusive* modifies the noun *thing*; the adjective *precious* modifies the pronoun *It*.

Freedom is an *elusive* thing. *It* is *precious*.

Adjectives make the nouns and pronouns they modify more vivid and precise. They answer questions such as *what kind? which one?* and *how many?* or *how much?* about those nouns and pronouns.

what kind? lovely thing   **which one?** this thing   **how many?** two things

A. Practice: Underline the adjective or adjectives in each sentence, and draw an arrow from every adjective to the noun or pronoun it modifies. Do not include the special adjectives *a, an,* or *the.*

1. Freedom was once a physical thing.

2. Then it became more elusive.

3. Even the strongest people could not grasp it.

4. There were no chains on black wrists, but there were dark shadows across black minds.

5. Segregation was different in different parts of the country.

6. In the South, actual laws kept African Americans in separate schools.

7. In northern states, custom or practice usually separated African American and white students.

8. Since the two groups generally lived in different neighborhoods, they attended different schools.

9. In the early 1950's legal cases challenged segregation.

10. One of the most famous was Brown vs. the Board of Education of Topeka.

B. Writing Application: Make the nouns and pronouns in these sentences more vivid and precise by adding adjectives that answer the questions in parentheses. Write each adjective on the line after the question.

1. The *(how much?)* _____ barriers to *(what kind?)* _____ freedom have changed over the *(which ones?)* _____ centuries.

2. Thurgood Marshall helped champion the *(what kind?)* _____ fight against segregation in *(what kind? or which ones?)* _____ public schools.

3. His *(what kind?)* _____ struggle led to a *(what kind?)* _____ Supreme Court decision.

4. Linda Brown remembers Brown vs. the Board of Education with *(what kind? or how much?)* _____ pride.

Reading for Success: Strategies for Constructing Meaning

To understand a work of literature fully—especially nonfiction—you must go beyond a simple scan of the page to put the writer's ideas together in your own mind. Use these strategies to help you construct meaning.

- **Make inferences.** Writers don't always tell you everything directly. You have to make inferences to arrive at ideas that writers suggest but don't say. You make an inference by considering the details that the writer includes or omits.

- **Determine cause and effect.** To understand information presented to you, look for relationships like cause and effect. A cause brings about a result, or an effect. Look for words and phrases that signal cause-and-effect relationships, such as *because, since, therefore, consequently*, and *as a result*.

- **Identify important ideas.** Ask the question, "What is the author's main point in this paragraph?" and identify the supporting details for each main idea.

- **Interpret what you read.** Interpret or explain the meaning or significance of what you read.

DIRECTIONS: Read the following excerpt from "When Does Education Stop?" by James Michener, and apply the reading strategies to increase your comprehension. In the margin, write notes showing where you make inferences, determine cause and effect, identify important ideas, and interpret what you read.

from **"When Does Education Stop?"** by James Michener

In this passage, Author James Michener shares with a student the key to success.

During the summer vacation a fine-looking young man, who was majoring in literature at a top university, asked for an interview, and before we had talked for five minutes, he launched into his complaint.

"Can you imagine," he lamented. "During vacation I have to write a three-thousand-word term paper about your books." He felt very sorry for himself.

His whimpering irritated me, and on the spur of the moment I shoved at him a card which had become famous in World War II. It was once used on me. It read: Young man, your sad story is truly heartbreaking. Excuse me while I fetch a crying towel.

My complaining visitor reacted as I had done twenty years earlier. He burst into laughter and asked, "Did I sound that bad?"

"Worse!" I snapped. Then I pointed to a novel of mine which he was using as the basis for his term paper. "You're bellyaching about a three-thousand-word paper which at most will occupy you for a month. When I started work on *Hawaii*,[1] I faced the prospect of a three-million-word term paper. And five years of work. Frankly, you sound silly."

This strong language encouraged an excellent discussion of the preparation it takes to write a major novel. Five years of research, months of character development, extensive work on plot and set-

[1] **Hawaii:** long novel by James Michener, published in 1959.

ting, endless speculation on psychology and concentrated work on historical backgrounds.

"When I was finally ready to write," I replied under questioning, "I holed up in a bare-wall, no-telephone Wakiki[2] room and stuck at my typewriter every morning for eighteen months. Seven days a week I wrestled with the words that would not come, with ideas that refused to jell. When I broke a tooth, I told the dentist I'd have to see him at night. When DeWitt Wallace, the editor of *Reader's Digest* and a man to whom I am much indebted, came to Hawaii on vacation, I wanted to hike with him but had to say, 'In the late afternoon. In the morning I work.'"

I explained to my caller that I write all my books slowly, with two fingers on an old typewriter, and the actual task of getting the words on paper is difficult. Nothing I write is good enough to be used in first draft, not even important personal letters, so I am required to rewrite everything at least twice. Important work, like a novel, must be written over and over again, up to six or seven times. For example, *Hawaii* went very slowly and needed constant revision. Since the final version contained about 500,000 words, and since I wrote it all many times, I had to type in my painstaking fashion about 3,000,000 words.

At this news, my visitor whistled and asked, "How many research books did you have to consult?"

"Several thousand. When I started the actual writing, there were about five hundred that I kept in my office."

"How many personal interviews?"

"About two hundred. Each two or three hours long."

"Did you write much that you weren't able to use?"

"I had to throw away about half a million words."

The young scholar looked again at the card and returned it reverently to my desk. "Would you have the energy to undertake such a task again?" he asked.

I would always like to be engaged in such tasks," I replied, and he turned to other questions.

Young people, especially those in college who should know better, frequently fail to realize that men and women who wish to accomplish anything must apply themselves to tasks of tremendous magnitude. A new vaccine may take years to perfect. A Broadway play is never written, cast and produced in a week. A foreign policy is never evolved in a brief time by diplomats relaxing in Washington, London, or Geneva.

The good work of the world is accomplished principally by people who dedicate themselves unstintingly to the big job at hand. Weeks, months, years pass, but the good workman knows that he is gambling on an ultimate achievement which cannot be measured in time spent. Responsible men and women leap to the challenge of jobs that require enormous dedication and years to fulfill, and are happiest when they are so involved.

---

[2]**Wakiki:** Famous beach and resort area in Honolulu, Hawaii.

"Brown vs. Board of Education" by Walter Dean Myers (text page 241)

Literary Focus: Informative Essay

An **informative essay** is a brief piece of nonfiction that explains a topic or gives information about it. In addition to providing statistics, examples, and other factual information on the topic, an informative essay may present the writer's view or opinion about it. However, the chief purpose of the informative essay is to inform or explain, not to persuade readers to share the writer's views.

A. Directions: List examples from Myers's essay on the chart below, placing factual information in the left column and the author's opinions in the right. One example is given.

Factual Information	Author's Views or Opinions
From the end of the Civil War in 1865 to the early 1950's, many public schools in both the North and South were segregated.	Slowly, surely, the meaning of freedom changed to an elusive thing that even the strongest people could not hold in their hands.

B. Directions: Use the information you listed on the chart above to prove that Myers's piece is an informative essay.

_____

_____

_____

_____

"A Retrieved Reformation" by O. Henry (text page 252)

Build Vocabulary

Using the Root -simul-

-Simul- is one form of the root -sim- (also spelled -sem-), which means "same." *Simultaneous* events happen at the same time, for example, and *similar* things have many of the same qualities.

A. DIRECTIONS: Circle the letter of the choice that best completes each sentence. Use your understanding of the root -simul- or -sim- to help you figure out the answers.

1. A *simulcast* is a radio broadcast _____ a TV broadcast.

   a. advertising   b. just before   c. that occurs at the same time as   d. that costs more than

2. A *simile* is a figure of speech stating that two things _____ .

   a. are alike   b. are different   c. lead to a third   d. are poetic

3. A computer *simulation* of an air disaster probably _____ a real disaster.

   a. reports on   b. imitates or re-enacts   c. interviews survivors of   d. claims more lives than

4. Members of the *simian* family, known for imitating, illustrate the saying _____.

   a. Curiosity killed the cat   b. It's a dog's life   c. You can lead a horse to water, but you can't make it drink   d. Monkey see, monkey do

Using the Word Bank

assiduously	virtuous	retribution	unobtrusively
simultaneously	anguish	rehabilitate	

B. DIRECTIONS: Match each word in the left column with its definition in the right column. Write the letter of the definition on the line before the word it defines.

____	1. anguish	a. showing great attention to detail
____	2. assiduously	b. having a good character; upstanding
____	3. rehabilitate	c. without being noticed
____	4. retribution	d. restore to a former condition
____	5. simultaneously	e. great pain or torment
____	6. unobtrusively	f. repayment with a just punishment
____	7. virtuous	g. at the same time

Sentence Completions

C. DIRECTIONS: Circle the letter of the word that best completes each sentence.

1. An effective thief sneaks into a building _____.

   a. virtuously   b. anguishedly   c. unobtrusively   d. simultaneously

2. A careful safecracker opens a safe _____.

   a. assiduously   b. virtuously   c. anguishedly   d. simultaneously

Unit 3: Quest for Justice

"A Retrieved Reformation" by O. Henry (text page 252)

Build Spelling Skills: Adding *-tion* to Words

Spelling Strategy   The suffix *-tion,* which forms nouns, usually means "the act, process, state, or condition of." Sometimes, as in *retribution,* it is added to a root that cannot stand alone as an English word. More often, however, it is added to verbs to form nouns.

- If the verb ends in *t,* generally drop the *t* before adding *-tion:*

   Examples: corrup<u>t</u> – <u>t</u> + <u>-tion</u> = corruption   subtrac<u>t</u> – <u>t</u> + <u>-tion</u> = subtraction

- If the verb ends in *te,* generally drop the *te* before adding *-tion.*

   Examples: crea<u>te</u> – <u>te</u> + <u>-tion</u> = creation   pollu<u>te</u> – <u>te</u> + <u>-tion</u> = pollution

A. Practice: On the line provided, write the noun formed by adding *-tion* to each verb.

1. complete + -tion = _____   6. hesitate + -tion = _____

2. elect + -tion = _____   7. disrupt + -tion = _____

3. locate + -tion = _____   8. aggravate + -tion = _____

4. promote + -tion = _____   9. select + -tion = _____

5. react + -tion = _____   10. simulate + -tion = _____

B. Practice: Complete each sentence by filling in a noun formed from the word in parentheses.

1. (erupt) There was an _____ of bank robberies in Jefferson City.

2. (investigate) When a bank was robbed, Ben Price conducted an _____.

3. (convict) Though guilty, Jimmy Valentine protested his innocence with _____.

4. (rehabilitate) He was sent to prison for _____.

5. (situate) As Ralph Spencer, Jimmy found a new _____ in life.

Challenge: The sound of long *e* before *-ous* may be spelled with an *e* or an *i: simultaneously, previous.* Complete each word by writing *e* or *i* —whichever is the correct spelling—on the line provided. Check your answers in a dictionary.

1. E N V ____ O U S   4. D E V ____ O U S   7. C O U R T ____ O U S

2. B E A U T ____ O U S   5. H I D ____ O U S   8. F U R ____ O U S

3. C U R ____ O U S   6. M Y S T E R ____ O U S   9. I G N ____ O U S

"A Retrieved Reformation" by O. Henry (text page 252)

Build Grammar Skills: Placement of Adjectives

Adjectives are words that modify, or describe, nouns and pronouns. Usually they tell *what kind, which one,* or *how many* about the nouns and pronouns they modify. Adjectives may occupy various positions in relation to the words they modify. Here are the most common positions.

Before the modified word: Annabel spied the handsome newcomer.

Right after the modified word: Jimmy, handsome as any actor, caught her eye.

After a linking verb, modifying the subject: He was very handsome.

A. Practice: Underline the adjective or adjectives in each sentence, and draw an arrow from every adjective to the noun or pronoun it modifies. Do not include the special adjectives *a, an,* or *the.*

1. The next morning, Jimmy put on a new suit.

2. His shoes, stiff and squeaky, were also new.

3. He had been a compulsory guest of the state, but now he was free.

4. He paid no attention to the green trees and the sweet music of birds.

5. The flowers, fragrant as honey, held little interest for him.

6. Instead, he tasted the first sweet joys of liberty in the form of a succulent dinner.

7. He then rode a train for three hours to a small town some distance away.

8. In a dusty suitcase in a secret shelf in his old lodgings, he found his professional tools.

9. He also donned a new suit that was much more tasteful that the cheap one from the prison.

10. Now he was really ready for a new life.

B. Writing Application: On the lines provided, write sentences about a bank robbery. Use adjectives as requested. Do not count the special adjectives *a, an,* or *the.*

1. a sentence with an adjective before each noun:

    _____

2. a sentence with two adjectives in a row, both before the same noun:

    _____

3. a sentence with two adjectives that are linked by *and* and come right after a noun:

    _____

4. a sentence with an adjective that comes after a linking verb and modifies a pronoun:

    _____

Unit 3: Quest for Justice

"**A Retrieved Reformation**" by O. Henry (text page 252)

Reading Strategy: Ask Questions

Usually you will better understand and remember a story if you ask questions as you read. Ask yourself questions about the events, characters, and other details in the story, and then keep reading to see if you can determine the answers to your questions. For example, consider this sentence from "A Retrieved Reformation," where the reader first encounters Jimmy Valentine:

> A guard came to the prison shoe-shop, where Jimmy Valentine was assiduously stitching uppers, and escorted him to the front office.

Here are some questions you might ask after reading this sentence:

> Who is Jimmy Valentine? Why is he in prison? Why is the guard escorting him to the office?

DIRECTIONS: Use this chart to record questions you ask as you read "A Retrieved Reformation" and answers to those questions. In answering the questions, include reasonable guesses as well as answers that become clear as you read. Three examples are given.

Questions	Answers
Who is Jimmy Valentine?	He's a professional safecracker now in prison.
Why is he in prison?	He was apparently convicted of burglary.
Why is the guard escorting him to the front office?	He has been pardoned by the governor and will be getting out of prison.

Literary Focus: Surprise Ending

O. Henry is famous for writing stories with surprise endings. A **surprise ending** is an unexpected twist that concludes the plot of a story. For a surprise ending to be effective, it must go unpredicted by readers but still be believable enough so that readers accept it. To make the ending believable, the writer usually provides some hints about it without giving it away. For example, in "A Retrieved Reformation," the title hints that Jimmy Valentine will try to reform his criminal past, have trouble doing so, but have his reformation successfully "retrieved" in the end.

A. DIRECTIONS: Fill out this chart listing other hints about the ending that O. Henry provides. One example is given.

Hint	What It Hints At
story title ("A Retrieved Reformation")	Jimmy Valentine will try to reform his criminal past, have trouble doing so, but be successful in the end.

B. DIRECTIONS: On the lines provided, evaluate the surprise ending of O. Henry's story. Were you surprised? Did you find the ending believable? Use the hints you listed on the chart above to help you explain your reaction.

_____

_____

_____

_____

from *Lincoln: A Photobiography* by Russell Freedman (text page 262)
"O Captain! My Captain!" by Walt Whitman (text page 266)

Build Vocabulary

Using the Suffix *-ate*

The suffix *-ate* is usually used to form verbs. Most often it is added to a root that cannot stand alone as an English word: *compensate, annihilate, emancipate.* Sometimes, however, it is added to a noun or an adjective: *vaccine + -ate = vaccinate, alien + -ate = alienate.*

A. DIRECTIONS: Complete each sentence with a verb formed from the word in parentheses. Write the verb on the line provided.

1. (captive) Abraham Lincoln could _____ an audience with his words.

2. (valid) They also helped _____ his political decisions.

3. (assassin) It is tragic that anyone would _____ such a great leader.

Using the Word Bank

alienate	compensate	shackles	peril
decisive	humiliating	exulting	tread

B. DIRECTIONS: Hidden in this puzzle are the eight words from the Word Bank. Their letters may read from right to left, from left to right, from top to bottom, from bottom to top, or diagonally. Find and circle the words. Then, below the puzzle, rewrite each word on the line next to its definition.

1. repay: _____

2. danger: _____

3. embarrassing: _____

4. step: _____

5. imprisoning chains: _____

6. vitally important: _____

7. to make unfriendly: _____

8. taking or showing joy in: _____

```
A  H  R  C  D  A  E  R  T  X  L  P
V  Z  U  O  E  M  B  D  Q  V  E  R
B  R  A  M  C  C  I  J  W  R  E  X
S  W  J  L  I  A  M  P  I  B  A  N
E  D  O  I  S  L  E  L  P  E  W  M
L  K  S  H  I  I  I  C  O  X  V  A
K  B  E  C  V  E  S  A  R  U  E  C
C  O  M  P  E  N  S  A  T  E  O  M
A  F  T  R  E  A  X  G  M  I  U  S
H  G  G  N  I  T  L  U  X  E  N  D
S  N  D  E  F  E  B  C  A  R  L  G
```

C. DIRECTIONS: For each related pair of words in capital letters, choose the lettered pair that best expresses a similar relationship. Circle the letter of your choice.

1. SAFETY : PERIL : :
   a. joy : happiness
   b. danger : warning
   c. risk : danger
   d. joy : grief

2. SHAME : HUMILIATING : :
   a. awe : amazing
   b. anger : exulting
   c. fame : bragging
   d. calm : exciting

3. METAL : SHACKLES : :
   a. wood : oak
   b. wood : furniture
   c. metal : iron
   d. mineral : vegetable

from _Lincoln: A Photobiography_ by Russell Freedman (text page 262)
"O Captain! My Captain!" by Walt Whitman (text page 266)

Build Spelling Skills: Using *ex* to Spell the Sound of *egz*

Spelling Strategy The *egz* sound is sometimes spelled *ex* at the beginning of words.

• If the opening *egz* is in an unstressed syllable, generally spell it *ex*.

Examples: exert   exhort   exult

• If the opening *egz* sound is in a stressed syllable, it may be spelled in various ways, including *ex*.

Examples: exit   eggs   eczema (a skin rash)

A. Practice: On the line after each sentence, write the correct spelling of the italicized word. If it is already spelled correctly, write *correct*.

1. "O Captain! My Captain!" is an *exsample* of a famous poem by Walt Whitman.

_____

2. In it, the speaker describes people *exulting* at the end of the Civil War. _____

3. He is sad and *egsassperated* that Lincoln cannot join the celebration. _____

4. He seems to *egzibit* great shock at the death of Lincoln. _____

5. It seems as if no American was *excempt* from the joy and sorrow. _____

B. Practice: On the lines provided in each item, write the letters of a word that begins with the sound *egz* and completes each sentence in a way that makes sense.

1. In "O Captain! My Captain!" the speaker tells the shores to ___ ___ ___ ___ ___ and the bells to ring.

2. The part of a car that releases waste fumes is called the ___ ___ ___ ___ ___ ___ ___ ___ pipe.

3. In addition to taking a written test, you may have to take an oral ___ ___ ___ ___.

4. When *CEO* refers to the head of a company, the *e* stands for ___ ___ ___ ___ ___ ___ ___ ___ ___.

5. An ___ ___ ___ ___ is the opposite of an entrance.

Challenge: Based on the following examples, what seem to be the spelling rules for adding the verb-forming suffix *-ate* to nouns and adjectives? On the lines below, one rule is provided. Write at least two more.

Examples: alien + -ate = alienate   formula + -ate = formulate   orchestra + -ate = orchestrate
captive + -ate = captivate   gravity + -ate = gravitate   origin + -ate = originate
facility + -ate = facilitate   motive + -ate = motivate   valid + -ate = validate

Rule 1: If the word ends in a consonant plus *y*, drop the *y* before adding *-ate*.

_____

_____

_____

Unit 3: Quest for Justice

from *Lincoln: A Photobiography* by Russell Freedman (text page 262)
"O Captain! My Captain!" by Walt Whitman (text page 266)

Build Grammar Skills: Adverbs

An **adverb** is a word that modifies, or describes, a verb, an adjective, or another adverb. In the sentence below, for example, the adverb *so* modifies the adjective *crucial*, the adverb *rather* modifies the adverb *carefully*, and the adverb *carefully* modifies the verb *studied*. Notice that most words that end in -*ly* are adverbs: *carefully, finally, completely, happily, loudly, softly, quickly, slowly, lately*, and so on. Common adverbs that don't end in -*ly* include *rather, very, almost, always, never, ever, here, there, then, now, still, only, once, twice, so, somehow, somewhat*.

With military victory <u>so</u> crucial, Lincoln studied the political situation <u>rather</u> <u>carefully</u>.

Though it is best to place an adverb as close as possible to the word it modifies, adverbs can often be moved in a sentence without changing the sentence's meaning.

He studied it <u>carefully</u>.   He <u>carefully</u> studied it.   <u>Carefully</u> he studied it.

Adverbs usually answer the questions *when? where? in what manner?* or *to what extent?*

when? studied <u>then</u>   **where?** studied <u>there</u>   **in what manner?** studied <u>carefully</u>
to what extent? studied very <u>carefully</u>

A. Practice: Underline the adverb or adverbs in each sentence, and draw an arrow from every adverb to the word it modifies.

1. During the Civil War, Lincoln considered his political options very cautiously.

2. Despite other concerns, he viewed restoration of the Union as the most important issue.

3. That goal clearly required a victory in the war itself.

4. To that end he worked quite tirelessly on both the political and the military fronts.

5. Border states generally had remained loyal to the Union.

6. Unfortunately those states' economies still relied on slavery.

7. Some people in those states openly sympathized with the South.

8. Lincoln eventually made his decision about slavery.

B. Writing Application: Make these sentences more vivid and precise by adding adverbs that answer the questions in parentheses. Write each adverb on the line after the question.

1. The Civil War *(when?)* _____ ended in April of 1865.

2. Many people identify the conclusion as the *(to what extent?)* _____
   famous surrender at Appomattox Court House in Virginia on April 9.

3. *(where?)* _____ Confederate General Robert E. Lee *(to what extent?)*
   _____ *(in what manner?)* _____ surrendered
   to Union General Ulysses S. Grant.

from *Lincoln: A Photobiography* by Russell Freedman (text page 262)
"O Captain! My Captain!" by Walt Whitman (text page 266)

Reading Strategy: Determine Cause and Effect

A **cause** is an event, an action, or a situation that produces a result; an **effect** is the result produced. You will often understand historical writing better if you focus on cause-and-effect relationships. For example, to understand this portion of *Lincoln: A Photobiography*, you need to focus on the events or situations that caused Lincoln to delay freeing the slaves and the events or situations that finally caused him to issue the Emancipation Proclamation.

DIRECTIONS: Use the following chart to detail the important cause-and-effect relationships discussed in the selection from *Lincoln: A Photobiography*. One example is given.

Cause(s)	Effect(s)
Border states loyal to the Union still have slavery.	Some people in border states are sympathetic to the South.

© Prentice-Hall, Inc.

Name _____ Date _____

from *Lincoln: A Photobiography* by Russell Freedman (text page 262)
"**O Captain! My Captain!**" by Walt Whitman (text page 266)

Literary Focus: Historical Context

The **historical context** is the time period of a literary work that describes or takes place in the past. Understanding the historical context can help you understand the work. For example, knowing the following details about the historical context of "O Captain! My Captain!" helps you understand the poem:

- Abraham Lincoln was the American president at the time of the Civil War.

- Lincoln fought the war, above all else, to preserve the Union.

- The war lasted for four long years and resulted in a Union victory.

- Celebration of that victory began with the surrender, on April 9, 1865, of Confederate General Robert E. Lee to Union General Ulysses S. Grant at Appomattox Court House in Virginia.

- Lincoln was assassinated five days later, on April 14, 1865

DIRECTIONS: On the lines below, list the historical information that helps you understand the selection from *Lincoln: A Photobiography*. Include information from the selection itself and, if you think it relevant, other information that you know or research about the American Civil War.

_____

_____

_____

_____

_____

_____

_____

_____

_____

_____

_____

_____

_____

_____

_____

_____

_____

"Gentleman of Río en Medio" by Juan A. A. Sedillo (text page 273)
"Saving the Wetlands" by Barbara A. Lewis (text page 276)

Build Vocabulary

Using the Root -num-

The root -num- is from the Latin word *numerus*, which means "number." *Innumerable* items are too many to be numbered, or counted.

A. DIRECTIONS: Use your understanding of the root -num- to help you determine if the following statements are probably either true or false. If the statement is probably true, write *T* on the line before the number. If the statement is probable false, write *F*.

_____ 1. A report with *numerous* problems most likely will get an A+.

_____ 2. If a list is called an *enumeration*, items on it are probably labeled *1, 2, 3*, and so on.

_____ 3. A Roman *numeral* is something you light and explode on the Fourth of July.

_____ 4. If *-logy* means "the study of," *numerology* probably involves the study of numbers.

Using the Word Bank

negotiation   gnarled   innumerable   broached   petition   wizened   brandishing

B. DIRECTIONS: For each item, fill in the letters of the word from the Word Bank that is being defined. Use each word from the Word Bank only once. When you are done, the letters in the shaded boxes, reading down, should spell out another word for a marsh.

1. dried up ▢ _ _ _ _ _ _

2. discussion to reach an agreement _ ▢ _ _ _ _ _ _ _ _

3. formal request _ _ ▢ _ _ _ _ _

4. twisted _ _ _ ▢ _ _ _

5. started discussing _ _ _ ▢ _ _ _

6. many, many _ ▢ _ _ _ _ _ _ _ _ _

7. waving in a challenging way _ _ _ _ ▢ _ _ _ _ _ _

Synonyms

C. DIRECTIONS: Circle the letter of the word that is closest in meaning to the word in CAPITAL LETTERS.

1. INNUMERABLE: a. few   b. free   c. foreign   d. countless

2. WIZENED: a. shriveled   b. leaned   c. clever   d. instructed

3. BROACHED: a. pinned   b. cooked   c. contained   d. proposed

4. GNARLED: a. knotted   b. plotted   c. bowed   d. yelled

5. PETITION: a. magazine   b. protest   c. request   d. ownership

"Gentleman of Río en Medio" by Juan A. A. Sedillo (text page 273)
"Saving the Wetlands" by Barbara A. Lewis (text page 276)

Build Spelling Skills: Silent *g* Before *n*

Spelling Strategy A silent *g* sometimes comes right before an *n*. Note that this *gn* spelling with a silent *g* can appear at the start, middle, or end of a word.

Examples: g̲narl   arrai̲g̲nment   si̲g̲n

A. Practice: On the lines provided, write the word described or defined. For each word, the silent *g* is given.

1. knotty and twisty: G __ __ __ __ __ __

2. STOP, YIELD, DEER CROSSING, and FALLEN ROCK ZONE: __ __ G __ __

3. king's or queen's rule: __ __ __ G __

4. a small two-winged fly that bites: G __ __ __

5. a creature similar to a dwarf: G __ __ __ __

6. a scent that one wears, like perfume: __ __ __ __ G __ __

7. in the navy, the rank below lieutenant: __ __ __ __ G __

B. Practice: On the line after each sentence, write the correct spelling of the italicized word. If it is already spelled correctly, write *correct*.

1. Don Anselmo's orchard was *knarled* and beautiful. _____

2. His coat was faded, and the tips of his gloves looked *nawed*. _____

3. Despite the new survey, he *signed* the deed without asking for more money. _____

4. The new owners could not *resine* themselves to having local children on the land. _____

5. I *ngashed* my teeth when Don Anselmo insisted he had not sold the orchard. _____

6. It took most of the following winter to complete the repurchasing *campain*. _____

7. Did Don Anselmo get the money innocently, or was it by *desine*? _____

Challenge: In addition to a silent *g*, an *n* can also be preceded by a silent *k*, *p*, or even *m*. For each item below, unscramble the letters to spell an English word, and write the word on the line.

1. neek: _____   4. nueaimpon: _____

2. gtnikh: _____   5. fenki: _____

3. elenk: _____   6. commenni: _____

Name _____ Date _____

Build Grammar Skills: Adverbs Modifying Adjectives and Adverbs

An **adverb** is a word that **modifies,** or describes, a verb, an adjective, or another adverb. Adverbs that modify adjectives or other adverbs generally answer the question *to what extent?* or *to what degree?* In the following sentence, for example, the adverb *very* modifies the adjective *proud* by telling us the extent of Don Anselmo's pride.

Don Anselmo was very proud of his large family.

Below are some words that are often used as adverbs to modify adjectives or other adverbs. Keep in mind that several of these words can also be used as adverbs modifying verbs and can even be used as other parts of speech, such as adjectives and pronouns.

absolutely	almost	barely	certainly	especially	greatly	hardly	indeed
less	least	more	most	much	partly	quite	rarely
rather	really	scarcely	so	surprisingly	too	usually	very

A. Practice: For each sentence, underline the adverb that modifies an adjective or another adverb, and draw an arrow from the adverb to the word it modifies. On the line before each sentence, write *ADJ* if the modified word is an adjective and *ADV* if the modified word is an adverb.

_____ 1. Andy campaigned very vigorously against development of local wetlands.

_____ 2. The drinking water in the area was already terrible, and now the development would destroy it.

_____ 3. Development most certainly would destroy rare wildflowers and animal habitats.

_____ 4. Quite often Andy carried his petition for an hour.

_____ 5. Almost everyone was really supportive.

_____ 6. One fairly elderly lady became a real activist.

_____ 7. The developer gave thirteen-year-old Andy's efforts too little respect.

_____ 8. The developer resented the surprisingly youthful activist.

_____ 9. As Andy predicted, a test hole filled almost immediately with water.

_____ 10. In spite of his age, Andy spearheaded the local effort rather effectively.

B. Writing Application: Clarify extent or degree by completing these sentences with adverbs that modify adjectives or other adverbs. Try to use a different adverb in each sentence. Write your adverbs on the lines provided.

1. Andy reads books about wildlife _____ often.

2. He _____ quietly observes nature from a rock or tree stump in the woods.

3. He also brings home wild animals with _____ grave injuries.

4. Once he _____ courageously rescued a skunk from a trap.

5. His mother was not _____ happy about that.

Unit 3: Quest for Justice

"Gentleman of Río en Medio" by Juan A. A. Sedillo (text page 273)
"Saving the Wetlands" by Barbara A. Lewis (text page 276)

Reading Strategy: Make Inferences

No writer can tell you every bit of information you need to know. Instead, good writers provide enough details to allow readers to make inferences about events, characters, settings, and themes or ideas. An **inference** is a reasonable conclusion that you draw from the details or clues that an author provides. An active reader is always "reading between the lines," **making inferences** as he or she reads. Consider these details about Don Anselmo:

> He lived up in Medio, where his people had been for hundreds of years. He tilled the same land they had tilled.

From these details you might infer, or figure out, the following:

- Don Anselmo is close to the land.
- Don Anselmo respects tradition.

DIRECTIONS: Choose one of the two selections in this grouping. Then, on the chart below, list details and the inferences you draw from them.

Selection Title:	
Details	Inferences

"Gentleman of Río en Medio" by Juan A. A. Sedillo (text page 273)
"Saving the Wetlands" by Barbara A. Lewis (text page 276)

Literary Focus: Resolution of a Conflict

A **conflict** is a struggle between two opposing forces. The **resolution** is the final outcome of the conflict For example, in a story about a woman trying to save her farm during a drought, the conflict is between the farm woman and nature in the form of a drought. The resolution might be (a) the farm is saved, (b) the farm is lost, or (c) something in between—realizing she is about to lose the farm, for instance, the woman sells it to developers who pay top dollar and make the woman rich enough to buy another farm somewhere else.

In most stories, the plot centers around a conflict that is resolved near the story's end. Non-fiction writing may also center around a conflict, especially if it recounts events or focuses on a social issue.

DIRECTIONS: Answer the questions on the lines provided.

1. What would you say is the main conflict in "Gentleman of Río en Medio"? How is it resolved?

   _____

   _____

2. How is the main conflict in "Gentleman of Río en Medio" resolved?

   _____

   _____

3. What would you say is the main conflict in "Saving the Wetlands"?

   _____

   _____

4. How is the main conflict in "Saving the Wetlands" resolved?

   _____

   _____

5. Contrast the resolutions of the two selections. Which seems more clear cut in terms of winners and losers? Cite details from the selections to explain your opinion.

   _____

   _____

   _____

Unit 3: Quest for Justice

"Raymond's Run" by Toni Cade Bambara (text page 293)

Build Vocabulary

Using the Word Part -scope

The word part -scope refers to an instrument or device for observing. It combines with the word part peri-, which means "around" or "near," to create periscope, the name for the instrument used for making observations from a submarine when the submarine is submerged.

A. DIRECTIONS: Complete each sentence with an appropriate word formed by adding -scope to one of the word parts below. Use each word part only once.

> **Word Parts:** kaleido-, meaning "beautiful form"   tele-, meaning "distant"
> micro-, meaning "small"   stetho-, meaning "chest"

1. Under a _____ you can see many things too tiny for the naked eye to see.

2. The lovely patterns in a _____ are created by mirrors and bits of colored glass.

3. Through the _____ the astronomer observed many distant stars.

4. A doctor uses a _____ to listen to a patient's heart and breathing.

Using the Word Bank

prodigy	signify	ventriloquist	periscope

B. DIRECTIONS: On the lines before each definition, write the word being defined.

1. _____: make known through words, gestures, etc.

2. _____: someone who projects his or her voice to make it seem as if a puppet or dummy is speaking

3. _____: a very talented person

4. _____: a submarine instrument used to see objects above the water

Analogies

C. DIRECTIONS: Circle the letter of the pair of words that expresses a relationship most like the relationship of the pair of words in CAPITAL LETTERS.

1. PRODIGY : TALENT : :
   a. genius : intelligent   b. skill : craft   c. clown : serious   d. politician : president

2. VENTRILOQUIST : DUMMY : :
   a. manipulate : marionette   b. puppeteer : puppet   c. clothing : model   d. teacher : pupil

3. PERISCOPE : SUBMARINE : :
   a. target : arrow   b. telescope : star   c. wave : ship   d. peephole : door

"Raymond's Run" by Toni Cade Bambara (text page 293)

Build Spelling Skills: Words Ending in *-gy*

Spelling Strategy Many English words end in a vowel followed by *gy*. In general, *ol* precedes *gy* and forms *-logy*, a common word part that means "the study, science, theory, or expression of":

Examples: anthropology   ecology   technology

Exceptions: elegy   effigy   prodigy   strategy

A. Practice: On the line after each sentence, write the correct spelling of the italicized word. If it is already spelled correctly, write *correct.*

1. A good runner needs a *strategy* for conserving energy. _____

2. *Psycholegy* also can play a role in winning races. _____

3. Squeaky offered an *apoligy* for stepping on the other runner's foot. _____

4. Squeaky was also called Mercury, a reference to Roman *mythology.* _____

5. According to Squeaky, Gretchen was a child *prodogy* on the piano. _____

6. She made an *analagy* comparing running to a dream. _____

B. Practice: Complete each definition with the word formed by adding *-logy* to the word part defined in parentheses.

1. (*bio-*, "life") The science that studies living things: _____

2. (*zoo-*, "animals") The branch of biology that studies animals: _____

3. (*socio-*, "society") The social science that studies society: _____

4. (*chrono-*, "time") A list that expresses events in time order: _____

5. (*astro-*, "star") The study of the stars to predict the future: _____

6. (*tri-*, "three") A group of three works expressing related subjects or themes: _____

Challenge: The suffix *-ify*, occasionally spelled *-efy*, is used to form verbs: *signify, solidify, liquefy.* Complete each sentence with a verb related to the word in parentheses. If you're not sure of a spelling, look in a dictionary.

1. (glory) Some movies almost _____ violence.

2. (horror) Scary movies often _____ young moviegoers.

3. (terror) Did that monster _____ the town?

4. (putrid) After the monster died, its flesh began to _____.

© Prentice-Hall, Inc.

Unit 3: Quest for Justice

"Raymond's Run" by Toni Cade Bambara (text page 293)

Build Grammar Skills: Prepositions

A **preposition** relates a noun or pronoun to another word in the sentence. The noun or pronoun is called the **object of the preposition.** It comes after the preposition, though it may not come right after it. In the sentences below, the preposition *around* relates the noun *house* to *help*, and the preposition *for* relates the pronoun *her* to *watch Raymond*.

Mom needs no help <u>around</u> the house, but I watch Raymond <u>for</u> her.

Below is a chart of common prepositions. Notice that some prepositions consist of more than one word (*according to, ahead of,* and so on).

about	because of	except	near	to
above	before	for	of	toward
according to	behind	from	off	under
across	below	in	on	until
after	beside	in front of	out	up
against	between	inside	outside	upon
along	by	instead of	over	with
among	down	into	past	without
around at	during	like	through	

A. Practice: In the following sentences, underline each preposition and circle its object. Some sentences may have more than one preposition.

1. I'm a small girl with a squeaky voice.

2. I'm fast, but I'm not really the fastest runner from the neighborhood.

3. My dad can beat me to the corner with his hands inside his pockets.

4. The information about him is private, though.

5. During music class, Gretchen always plays the piano for the rest of us.

6. I go past her house on my early morning trots around the block.

B. Writing Application: Complete these sentences with prepositions that show relationships based on the details in the story. Try to use at least ten different prepositions.

[1]_____ Squeaky, the beginning [2]_____ a track race was something [3]_____ a dream. Reality returned when she squatted down [4]_____ the starting mark and spread her fingers [5]_____ the dirt. Then the sound [6]_____ the gun sent her flying [7]_____ the track. [8]_____ the course, her brother Raymond ran his own race [9]_____ rather remarkable speed. Squeaky finished the race [10]_____ first place, [11]_____ Gretchen close behind. An even stronger feeling [12]_____ joy came when she thought [13]_____ Raymond's achievement and decided that she would help train Raymond [14]_____ a great runner [15]_____ the family tradition.

"Raymond's Run" by Toni Cade Bambara (text page 293)

Reading Strategy: Predict

To **predict** is to make an informed guess about what will happen. Active readers often try to predict what will happen next in a story and what will happen at the end. To make an informed guess, you need to pay close attention to the details that the author provides. Among the details you will want to consider are

- characters' personalities, attitudes, and interactions with other characters

- events that have already occurred

- the setting and the events likely to occur in such a setting

- the title and the clues it provides about the story's contents

- the themes, or general messages, that the author is trying to convey

- any direct statements that the narrator makes about what will happen

DIRECTIONS: Use this chart to predict events in "Raymond's Run" and then record whether your predictions come true.

Story Detail	Prediction	Actual Outcome

Unit 3: Quest for Justice

Name _____ Date _____

"**Raymond's Run**" by Toni Cade Bambara (text page 293)

Literary Focus: Major and Minor Characters

Characters are the people (or sometimes animals or other creatures) that appear in a work of literature. A **major**, or **main, character** is an important character whose personality is usually well developed and who often changes in the course of the work. A **minor character** is less important, though he or she still play a role in story events. Most short stories have only one or two major characters, but the number of minor characters varies a great deal from story to story.

DIRECTIONS: Complete this chart about the characters in "Raymond's Run."

Name of Character	Personality Trait(s)	Change or Growth (if any)	Major or Minor?

"Paul Revere's Ride" by Henry Wadsworth Longfellow (text page 307)
"Barbara Frietchie" by John Greenleaf Whittier (text page 311)
"Elizabeth Blackwell" by Eve Merriam (text page 314)

Build Vocabulary

Using the Root *-spect-*

The root *-spect-* means "observe, look, appear." A *specter* is a ghost or another disturbing image that appears suddenly. *Spectral*, the adjective formed from *specter*, means "ghostly."

A. DIRECTIONS: Circle the letter of the choice that best completes each sentence.

1. The *spectators* at a baseball game _____ the game.
   a. watch   b. play   c. sell food at   d. interview players after

2. People buy *spectacles* to improve their _____.
   a. hearing   b. vision   c. table manners   d. vocabulary

3. Many Americans consider _____ to be a great *spectacle*.
   a. a nicely kept lawn   b. an English textbook   c. a boring speech   d. the Super Bowl

Using the Word Bank

stealthy	somber	impetuous	spectral
tranquil	aghast	horde	

B. DIRECTIONS: Next to each definition below, write the word being defined. Then spell out the secret message by filling in the same letters on the lines with corresponding numbers.

Secret Message: __ __ __   __ __ __   __ __ __ __ __   __ __ __ __ __ __   __ __
                     1 2 3   4 5 6   7 4 8 1 2   9 2 10 8 9 2   11 7

__ __ __ __ __ __ __,   __ __ __ __ __ __ __ __   __ __ __ __ __
12 4 13 1 4 7   14 15 13 13 15 9 2 10   13 3 1 1 13

1. a large, moving group: __ __ __ __ __   5. serious; gloomy: __ __ __ __ __ __
                            2 4 8 6 3   13 4 14 12 3 8

2. reckless; rash: __ __ __ __ __ __ __ __ __   6. calm; serene: __ __ __ __ __ __ __ __
                   11 15 16 3 1 10 4 10 13   1 8 15 7 17 10 11 5

3. horrified; dismayed: __ __ __ __ __ __   7. ghostlike: __ __ __ __ __ __ __ __
                        15 19 2 15 13 1   13 16 3 9 1   8 15 5

4. cleverly secretive; sly: __ __ __ __ __ __ __ __
                            13 1 3 15 5 1 2 18

C. DIRECTIONS: Circle the letter of the word that is most nearly the opposite in meaning to the word in CAPITAL LETTERS.

1. SOMBER: a. grim   b. icy   c. colorless   d. carefree

2. TRANQUIL: a. noisy   b. motionless   c. dishonest   d. modest

3. SPECTRAL: a. shady   b. haunting   c. uncertain   d. solid

4. IMPETUOUS: a. cautious   b. cruel   c. daring   d. delightful

"Paul Revere's Ride" by Henry Wadsworth Longfellow (text page 307)
"Barbara Frietchie" by John Greenleaf Whittier (text page 311)
"Elizabeth Blackwell" by Eve Merriam (text page 314)

Build Spelling Skills: Using *gh* to Spell the Sound of Hard *g*

Spelling Strategy The sound of *g* as in *got* is called a hard *g*. That sound is sometimes spelled *gh*. Try to learn these words as you come across them in your reading.

Examples: ghetto   ghoul   Newburgh

A. Practice: On the lines provided, write the word being defined or described. The *g*'s are provided as clues. If you're unsure of the spelling of a word, look in a dictionary.

1. a common pasta served with meatballs: _ _ _ g _ _ _ _ _

2. an imaginary spectral being: g _ _ _ _

3. an African country whose capital is Accra: G _ _ _ _

4. the city that is home to baseball's Pirates: _ _ _ _ _ _ _ _ g _

5. a small cucumber (rhymes with her *kin*): g _ _ _ _ _ _

B. Practice: On the line after each sentence, write the correct spelling of the italicized word. If it is already spelled correctly, write *correct*.

1. The British man-of-war cast its *goulish* shadow in the harbor. _____

2. A *goastly* light shone from the Old North Church. _____

3. Revere rode like a *goast* through every Middlesex village and farm. _____

4. Many were *ahgast* to hear of the upcoming battle. _____

5. They knew the fighting would be *gastly*. _____

Challenge: Homophones are words with the same sound but different spellings. On the line after each word below, write a definition of the word. Then, on the next line, correctly spell and define a homophone for the word. The first one is done as an example.

1. horde: a large, moving group; a traveling tribe _____
   hoard: a hidden fund or treasure; to stash _____

2. horse: _____
   _____

3. pedal: _____
   _____

4. hall: _____
   _____

5. cord: _____
   _____

"Paul Revere's Ride" by Henry Wadsworth Longfellow (text page 307)
"Barbara Frietchie" by John Greenleaf Whittier (text page 311)
"Elizabeth Blackwell" by Eve Merriam (text page 314)

Build Grammar Skills: Prepositional Phrases

A **prepositional phrase** is a group of words that begins with a preposition and ends with a noun or pronoun that the preposition relates to another word in the sentence. That noun or pronoun is called the **object of the preposition.** Sometimes a prepositional phrase consists only of a preposition and its object; sometimes, intervening words modify the object of the preposition. For example, the prepositional phrase in the first sentence below consists only of the preposition *of* and its object, *April.* The prepositional phrase in the second sentence consists of the preposition *through;* its object, *village;* and the words *every* and *Middlesex,* which modify *village.*

It was the eighteenth *of* **April.** Paul Revere rode *through* every Middlesex **village.**

A. Practice: Circle the prepositional phrases in the following sentences. Some sentences may contain more than one prepositional phrase.

1. Revere's friend stationed himself at Boston's Old North Church.

2. With stealthy tread the friend climbed the wooden stairs to the church tower.

3. In the belfry, he startled the pigeons from their perch.

4. They had agreed beforehand on the signals about the movement of British troops.

5. One light would mean an invasion by land, and two would mean an invasion by sea.

6. Revere stood on the opposite shore.

7. When he saw the two lights, he jumped on his horse.

8. He rode through the countryside at midnight.

9. "The British are coming!" he warned the citizens of Massachusetts.

10. Soon the first battle of the American Revolution would take place in Lexington.

B. Writing Application: On the lines provided, write five sentences about Barbara Frietchie or Elizabeth Blackwell. Include at least one prepositional phrase in each sentence, and underline each prepositional phrase.

1. _____

2. _____

3. _____

4. _____

5. _____

Unit 3: Quest for Justice

"Paul Revere's Ride" by Henry Wadsworth Longfellow (text page 307)
"Barbara Frietchie" by John Greenleaf Whittier (text page 311)
"Elizabeth Blackwell" by Eve Merriam (text page 314)

Reading Strategy: Interpret the Meaning

Because poetry is a compact form of expression, poets do not always spell out all the ideas and feelings they hope to convey. You'll understand poetry better if you try to **interpret the meaning** behind the images that the poet does provide. For example, consider the images in the first three stanzas of "Barbara Frietchie" that describe Frederick, Maryland, and its surroundings. Using those images and your outside knowledge, you can figure out that Whittier is trying to suggest that Frederick and its surroundings is a fertile agricultural area.

DIRECTIONS: Complete the cluster diagrams below by filling in images that the poems provide about the person, place, or thing identified in the central circle. Then, on the line below each diagram, interpret what the images suggest about the person, place, or thing they help describe.

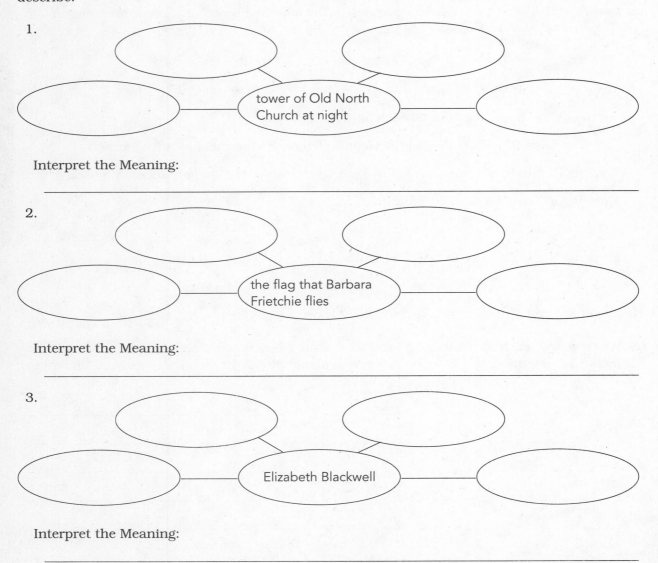

1.

tower of Old North Church at night

Interpret the Meaning:

_____

2.

the flag that Barbara Frietchie flies

Interpret the Meaning:

_____

3.

Elizabeth Blackwell

Interpret the Meaning:

_____

"Paul Revere's Ride" by Henry Wadsworth Longfellow (text page 307)
"Barbara Frietchie" by John Greenleaf Whittier (text page 311)
"Elizabeth Blackwell" by Eve Merriam (text page 314)

Literary Focus: Heroic Characters

A **heroic character** is one whose ideas are noble or inspiring in some way. Though heroic characters may have flaws, they nevertheless display many qualities that people admire and usually struggle to overcome obstacles or problems that stand in their way.

A. DIRECTIONS: Complete this chart for each of the title characters in this grouping of poetry.

Name of Character	Admirable Qualities	Obstacle(s) or Problem(s) Overcome
Paul Revere		
Barbara Frietchie		
Elizabeth Blackwell		

B. DIRECTIONS: On the lines provided, list at least one more heroic character from the poems, and explain what you find heroic about him or her.

_____

_____

_____

_____

© Prentice-Hall, Inc.

Unit 3: Quest for Justice

"Young Jefferson Gets Some Advice from Ben Franklin"
by Thomas Jefferson (text page 321)

Build Vocabulary

Using the Suffix *-ous*

The suffix *-ous* is used to turn nouns into adjectives. For example, a *tautology* is a statement that needlessly repeats the same information using different words. A *tautologous* statement is a redundant statement, or one that is characterized by this sort of needless repetition.

A. DIRECTIONS: Complete each sentence with an adjective formed from the word in parentheses. Write the adjective on the line provided.

1. (joy) The signing of the Declaration of Independence was a _____ event.

2. (thunder) However, there were some _____ arguments beforehand.

3. (humor) Ben Franklin's tale of the hatter is rather _____ .

4. (fame) At the time he told it, Franklin was much more _____ than Jefferson.

5. (ridicule) The hatter's experience with his sign was a bit _____.

6. (analogy) In what way was the hatter's experience _____ to Jefferson's?

Using Words from the Selection

B. DIRECTIONS: The following sentences contain words in italics which come from the selection. Show that you understand each word in italics by crossing out the other words in the sentence that might be omitted because they are tautologous. You may need to omit a few additional words to make the new sentence read smoothly. The first one is done as an example.

1. Thomas Jefferson wrote the famous document in which America declared its *independence* ~~as a nation separate and free~~ from Britain.

2. Jefferson's *declaration* was a statement that explained why the nation should be established.

3. Certain colleagues at congress found some of Jefferson's original language *offensive* and asked that he remove these nasty and upsetting words and phrases.

4. A remark about the Scotch, for example, aroused the *ire* of some members, filling them with anger.

5. Though a slaveholder himself, Jefferson's original draft also condemned a law allowing the *importation* of slaves so that they could be brought into the country.

6. Jefferson's original draft demanded a *repeal* that would result in the taking back of this law.

"Young Jefferson Gets Some Advice from Ben Franklin"
by Thomas Jefferson (text page 321)

Connecting a Firsthand Account to Social Studies

The letters, memoirs, and other firsthand accounts of famous people can give us many important insights about historical events and personalities. Reading Thomas Jefferson's account of Benjamin Franklin's advice at the First Continental Congress, for example, can teach us a great deal about Franklin, Jefferson, and other founding fathers and also about the discussions that took place before the Declaration of Independence was signed.

DIRECTIONS: On the chart below, jot down details from the selection that provide you with valuable insights about historical personalities and events. Also explain why each insight seems valuable to you. One example is given for you.

Detail	Insight Provided	Reason It Seems Valuable
". . . repeated repeals of the law which permitted the importation of slaves, were disapproved by some Southern gentlemen, whose reflections were not yet matured to the full abhorrence of that traffic."	Jefferson found slavery abhorrent.	Though a slaveholder himself, Jefferson found the institution abhorrent and was hoping to outlaw the slave trade at the time the nation was founded.

"Always to Remember: The Vision of Maya Ying Lin" by Brent Ashabranner
(text page 327)

Build Vocabulary

Using Foreign Plural Forms

Some nouns that come to English from Latin and Greek form their plurals as they did in their original languages. For example, those that end in *-on* or *-um* sometimes form their plurals by changing the *-on* or *-um* to an *-a: criterion—criteria.* Those that end in *-is* often form their plurals by changing the *i* to an *e: parenthesis—parentheses.* Those that end in *-us* sometimes form their plurals by changing the *-us* to an *i: stimulus—stimuli.*

A. DIRECTIONS: Complete each sentence by writing the plural of the word in parentheses. If necessary, check a dictionary to see if your answers are correct.

1. (alumnus) Three _____ of our local high school are in the TV news business.

2. (medium) Many people feel the news _____ have grown very irresponsible.

3. (crisis) The news shows prefer to cover crimes, scandals, and _____.

4. (datum) Reporters sometimes seem to draw conclusions with very little _____.

Using the Word Bank

criteria	registrants	anonymously	harmonious
eloquent	unanimous	prominent	

B. DIRECTIONS: On the lines provided, fill in the word from the Word Bank that is being defined. Use each word only once. When you are done, the letters in the shaded boxes, reading down, will spell out a famous artist.

1. standing out   _ _ _ _ ▓ _ _ _ _ _

2. standards   _ _ _ _ _ _ _ ▓ _

3. with one's name unknown to others   _ _ _ _ ▓ _ _ _ _ _ _

4. people who sign up   _ _ _ _ _ _ _ ▓ _ _ _

5. expressive   _ _ ▓ _ _ _ _ _ _

6. everybody in complete agreement   _ _ _ _ ▓ _ _ _ _

7. combined in a pleasant or tuneful manner   _ _ _ _ ▓ _ _ _ _

Artist:_ _ _ _ _ _ _

C. DIRECTIONS: Complete each sentence with the most appropriate word from the word bank.

1. What _____ did the teacher use in grading the term papers?

2. New _____ must sign up on the day before school starts.

3. The _____ speech deeply impressed the audience.

4. Opinion was _____; everyone agreed to the suggestion.

"Always to Remember: The Vision of Maya Ying Lin" by Brent Ashabranner
(text page 327)

Build Spelling Skills: Spelling *-ant* vs. *-ent*

Spelling Strategy   The related suffixes *-ant* and *-ent* are used to form nouns and adjectives. Sometimes they are added to roots that cannot stand alone as English words: conson<u>ant</u>, innoc<u>ent</u>. Sometimes they are added to verbs: consult + -ant = consultant, differ + -ent = different.

• If the verb ends in *-ate*, generally drop the *-ate* and add *-ant:*

Examples: stimul<u>ate</u> + <u>-ant</u> = stimul<u>ant</u>   toler<u>ate</u> + <u>-ant</u> = toler<u>ant</u>

• If the verb ends in silent *e*, drop the *e* before adding *-ant* or *-ent:*

Examples: ignor<u>e</u> + <u>-ant</u> = ignor<u>ant</u>   preced<u>e</u> + <u>-ent</u> = preced<u>ent</u>

• Since there are few rules governing when to use *-ant* and when to use *-ent*, you will need to memorize words with these spellings or to check them in a dictionary.

A. Practice: On the line after each verb, write the noun or adjective form that ends in *-ant* or *-ent*. If you are not sure which suffix to use, check the spelling in a dictionary.

1. inhabit _____

2. reside _____

3. account _____

4. depend _____

5. descend _____

6. revere _____

7. absorb _____

8. defend _____

B. Practice: On the lines provided, complete each word with *-ant* or *-ent*, whichever is correct. If you aren't sure, check the word in a dictionary.

1. The veteran gave an eloqu __ __ __ speech at the Vietnam Veterans Memorial.

2. The memorial was designed by the brilli __ __ __ young sculptor Maya Ying Lin.

3. At the time of the design contest, Lin was not at all promin __ __ __.

4. Lin's ancestors were immigr __ __ __ s from China.

5. Her design was chosen from those of over a thousand registr __ __ __ s.

6. Most people find the wall-like design simple but also eleg __ __ __ in its own way.

Challenge: The letter *y* has many different sounds in English. For example, in the word *anonymously*, the final y has the sound of long *e*, but the first y has the unstressed vowel sound represented by a schwa (ə), a sound similar to "uh." On the lines below, list additional examples that illustrate some of the different sounds of the letter *y*.

1. *y* sound: <u>you</u>

2. long *i* sound: <u>try</u>

3. long *e* sound: <u>silly</u>

4. short *i* sound: <u>symbolic</u>

Unit 3: Quest for Justice

"Always to Remember: The Vision of Maya Ying Lin" by Brent Ashabranner
(text page 327)

Build Grammar Skills: Prepositional Phrases as Adjectives and Adverbs

As you know, a **prepositional phrase** consists of a preposition, the noun or pronoun that is the object of the preposition, and any words that modify, or describe, the object of the preposition. The entire phrase serves as an adjective or an adverb. An **adjective phrase** is a prepositional phrase that modifies, or describes, a noun or a pronoun. In the following sentence, for example, the adjective phrase *for the monument* modifies the noun *designs* by telling the *kind* of designs.

The jury judged the designs <u>for the monument</u>.

An **adverb phrase** is a prepositional phrase that modifies, or describes, a verb, an adjective or an adverb. In this following sentence, the adverb phrase *on their merits* modifies the verb *judged* by telling *how* they judged.

They judged the designs anonymously <u>on their merits</u>.

A. Practice: Underline each prepositional phrase, and circle the word it modifies. On the line before the sentence, write *ADJ* if the phrase serves as an adjective and *ADV* if it serves as an adverb.

_____ 1. Jan Scruggs and his associates held a design competition open to all Americans.

_____ 2. They would build the Vietnam Veterans Memorial according to the winner's design.

_____ 3. The jury came from several different artistic fields.

_____ 4. It's members did not know the identities of the entrants.

_____ 5. The surprise winner was Maya Ying Lin, a twenty-one-year-old student at Yale.

_____ 6. Lin's design honored the memory of the war dead.

_____ 7. It displayed high artistic merit as a national monument.

_____ 8. It successfully harmonized with the surroundings.

B. Writing Application: Based on the information in the selection, add prepositional phrases to make these sentences more vivid or informative. Write your new sentences on the lines provided.

1. Congress passed a law authorizing the Vietnam Veterans Memorial.

_____

_____

2. The law indicated its location.

_____

_____

3. The law did not dictate its appearance.

_____

"Always to Remember: The Vision of Maya Ying Lin" by Brent Ashabranner
(text page 327)

Reading Strategy: Identify Important Facts

Biographical nonfiction works usually provide a wide assortment of ideas and details. Some of them are very important; others are less important. To get the most from your reading, you need to **identify the important facts.** To do so, you might ask yourself the following questions:

- Who is the subject of the selection?

- What was his or her main achievement or a famous event in his or her life?

- When did this achievement or event occur?

- Where did this achievement or event occur?

- Why did this achievement or event occur?

DIRECTIONS: Fill out the following diagram to help you identify the important information in "Always to Remember."

"Always to Remember: The Vision of Maya Ying Lin" by Brent Ashabranner
(text page 327)

Literary Focus: Biographical Profile

A **biography** is a nonfiction work that tells the full story of a person's life. A **biographical profile** is a shorter version, often focusing on one important event or achievement. "Always to Remember: The Vision of Maya Ying Lin" is a biographical profile of architect Maya Ying Lin that focuses on how she came to design the Vietnam Veterans Memorial in Washington, DC.

DIRECTIONS: In the space below, complete an outline of the details about Maya Lin that this biographical profile provides. Feel free to add several subsections under each main section.

Maya Ying Lin

I. Background and Education

   A. Background

      1.

      2.

      3.

   B. Education

II. The Vietnam Veterans Memorial Contest

III. The Vietnam Veterans Memorial

from *The People, Yes* by Carl Sandburg (text page 347)

Build Vocabulary

Using the Suffix *-eer*

The suffix *-eer* has two definitions. When it means "a person who makes or has to do with," it is added to nouns that are things to turn them into people: *mutiny + -eer = mutineer*, "*a person who makes a mutiny.*" When it means "to make or have to do with," it is added to nouns to turn them into verbs: *election + -eer = electioneer*, "*to have to do with an election.*"

A. DIRECTIONS: Complete each sentence with an appropriate word form by adding *-eer* to one of the words listed in italics. Use each word only once.

Words to Use: auction, command, mountain, pamphlet, puppet

1. The _____ distributed the little booklets all over town.

2. Who was the first _____ to climb the world's tallest peak, Mount Everest?

3. The admiral had to _____ the privately owned ships for emergency military use.

4. The _____ spoke with incredible speed as he sold off the different items.

5. The _____ put on an entertaining show on the miniature stage.

Using the Word Bank

mutineers	runt	mosquitoes	flue

B. DIRECTIONS: Write the word from the Word Bank that answers these questions.

1. Which word refers to members of a ship's crew that rebel against the officers? _____

2. Which word refers to a passage through which air or smoke flows? _____

3. Which word refers to a person or animal that is very small in size? _____

4. Which word refers to bloodsucking insects found in moist areas? _____

Analogies

C. DIRECTIONS: Circle the letter of the words that express a relationship most like the relationship of the words in capital letters.

1. MOSQUITOES : INSECTS ::
   a. beagles : dogs   b. dogs : cats   c. bite : mouth   d. bee : spider

2. RUNT : MONSTER ::
   a. animal : vegetable   b. mouse : elephant   c. shoe : foot   d. child : baby

3. MUTINEERS : REVOLT ::
   a. engineers : engine   b. profiteers : money   c. pioneers : west   d. mountaineers : climb

4. FLUE : SMOKE ::
   a. chimney : brick   b. pipe : water   c. cold : sneeze   d. blew : wind

Name _____ Date _____

Build Spelling Skills: Spelling Plurals of Nouns That End in *o*

Spelling Strategy   Here are some rules for forming plurals of nouns that end in *o*.

- To form the plural of a noun ending in a vowel and *o*, add just *s*:

    Examples: cam<u>eo</u> → cameo<u>s</u>   pat<u>io</u> → patio<u>s</u>   tab<u>oo</u> → taboo<u>s</u>

- To form the plural of musical terms, usually add just *s*:

    Examples: cello → cell<u>os</u>   soprano → soprano<u>s</u>   concerto → concerto<u>s</u>

- To form the plural of nouns ending in a consonant and o that are not musical terms, usually add *es:*

    Examples: pota<u>to</u> → potato<u>es</u>,   toma<u>to</u> → tomato<u>es</u>,   ech<u>o</u> → echo<u>es</u>

    Exceptions: arroyo<u>s</u>, burrito<u>s</u>, photo<u>s</u>, silo<u>s</u>, taco<u>s</u>

- A few words ending in a consonant and o have two acceptable plural forms:

    Examples: mosquito<u>es</u> or mosquito<u>s</u>,   tornado<u>es</u> or tornado<u>s</u>,   halo<u>es</u> or halo<u>s</u>

A. Practice: On the line after each word, write its plural form. Some of the words may have more than one acceptable plural form.

1. rodeo _____
2. tomato _____
3. halo _____
4. kangaroo _____
5. superhero _____

6. burrito _____
7. zero _____
8. solo _____
9. cargo _____
10. ratio _____

11. zoo _____
12. mosquito _____
13. photo _____
14. piano _____
15. banjo _____

B. Practice: Complete each sentence by filling in the plural form of the word in parentheses.

1. (hero) The _____ of tall tales perform some amazing feats.

2. (volcano) In one tale, the hero fights _____ and earthquakes.

3. (echo) In another, a heroine visits the land of lost _____.

4. (trio) Sometimes these amazing champions work in pairs or _____.

5. (duo) Which heroic _____ have you read about?

Challenge: Homophones are words that have the same sound but different spellings and meanings. On the line after each word below, write the definition of the word. Then, on the line below the word, write a homophone and *its* definition. The first one is done as an example.

1. flue: <u>smokestack, exhaust pipe</u>   <u>flew: traveled in air OR flu: the disease influenza</u>

2. sighed: _____

3. piece: _____

4. roll: _____

from *The People, Yes* by Carl Sandburg (text page 347)

Build Grammar Skills: Subordinating Conjunctions

A **conjunction** connects words or groups of words. A **subordinating conjunction** connects two clauses by making one subordinate to—or dependent on—the other, while at the same time showing how the two clauses are related. For example, in connecting the two clauses below, the subordinating conjunction *after* makes clear that the two clauses have a *time* relationship.

> **Clause 1:** The stock market crashed late in 1929.
>
> **Clause 2:** The Great Depression began.
>
> **Connected:** <u>After</u> the stock market crashed late in 1929, the Great Depression began.
>
> ***or*** The Great Depression began <u>after</u> the stock market crashed late in 1929.

Below is a list of common subordinating conjunctions, organized by the type of relationship they show. Note that some subordinating conjunctions are phrases rather than single words and that many of them can also be used as prepositions or other parts of speech.

Relationship	Subordinating Conjunction
Time	after, as, as long as, as soon as, before, since, so long as, until, when, whenever, while
Place	where, wherever
Contrast	although, even though, though, whereas, while
Cause or Reason	as, because, since
Effect or Purpose	in order that, so that
Manner	as, as if, as though, like
Condition	as long as, even if, even though, if, so long as, unless, whether, whether or not

A. Practice: Underline the subordinating conjunction in each of these sentences.

1. Sandburg wrote *The People, Yes* when the Great Depression ravaged America and the world.

2. Wherever you looked, there was poverty and high unemployment.

3. While it was a time of great economic hardship, Americans still retained dignity and pride.

4. Many viewed the future as if good times were just around the corner.

5. Others worked hard for social change since they wanted to improve the current conditions.

B. Writing Application: For each item, combine the two sentences by using a subordinating conjunction to show the relationship in parentheses. Write your new sentences on the lines provided.

1. (contrast) The Depression brought widespread poverty. Sandburg believed in a brighter

   future. _____

2. (cause/reason) He wanted to inspire Americans. He described many American folk heroes.

   _____

3. (place) Paul Bunyan traveled in the Midwest. He took his pet ox, Babe.

   _____

4. (time) Pecos Bill went to the West Coast. He traveled on a cyclone.

   _____

Unit 4: From Sea to Shining Sea

Reading for Success: Interactive Reading Strategies

Reading is an interactive process by which you get involved with the ideas, images, events, and information presented in the text. The more involved you are, the richer your understanding is. Apply the following strategies to interact with what you read.

- **Envision.** Use details that the author provides to help you picture in your own mind the places, people, and events in a piece of writing. Try to experience sounds, tastes, smells, and physical sensations as well.

- **Use your prior knowledge.** Your prior knowledge is what you already know. Apply this knowledge to make connections with what the author is saying.

- **Clarify.** When you read a passage you find difficult or confusing, take the time to pause to clarify the meaning. Try these strategies:

  Reread a section slowly to find out what the author is really saying.

  Ask questions to resolve the confusion.

  Look up a word in the dictionary or get information from another source.

- **Respond.** Get to your own reactions by asking yourself what the selection meant to you.

DIRECTIONS: Read the following excerpt from "Old Yeller" by Fred Gipson, and apply the reading strategies to increase your comprehension. In the margin, write notes showing where you envision, use your prior knowledge, clarify, and respond. Finally, write your response to the selection on the lines provided.

from *"Old Yeller and the Bear"* by Fred Gipson

Old Yeller is a stray dog that has been adopted by a pioneer family. This excerpt details how Old Yeller helps the youngest child Arliss do what he loves most—catch wild things.

That little Arliss! From the time he'd grown up big enough to get out of the cabin, he'd made a practice of trying to catch and keep every living thing that ran, flew, jumped, or crawled.

Every night before Mama let him go to bed, she'd make Arliss empty his pockets of whatever he'd captured during the day. Generally, it would be a tangled-up mess of grasshoppers and worms and praying bugs and little rusty tree lizards. One time he brought in a horned toad that got so mad he swelled out round and flat as a Mexican tortilla and bled at the eyes. Sometimes it was stuff like a young bird that had fallen out of its nest before it could fly, or a green-speckled spring frog, or a striped water snake. And once he turned out of his pocket a wadded-up baby copperhead that nearly threw Mama into spasms. We never did figure out why the snake hadn't bitten him, but Mama took no more chances on snakes. She switched Arliss hard for catching that snake.

Then, after the yeller dog came, Little Arliss started catching even bigger game. Like cottontail rabbits and chaparral birds and a baby possum that sulled[1] and lay like dead for the first several hours until he finally decided that Arliss wasn't going to hurt him.

[1] **sulled:** sulked

Of course, it was Old Yeller that was doing the catching. He'd run the game down and turn it over to Little Arliss. Then Little Arliss could come in and tell Mama a big fib about how he caught it himself.

I watched them one day when they caught a blue catfish out of Birdsong Creek. The fish had fed out into water so shallow that his top fin was sticking out. About the time I saw it, Old Yeller and Little Arliss did, too. They made a run at it. The fish went scooting away toward deeper water, only Yeller was too fast for him. He pounced on the fish and shut his big mouth down over it and went romping to the bank, where he dropped it down on the grass and let it flop. And here came Little Arliss to fall on it like I guess he'd been doing everything else. The minute he got his hands on it, the fish finned him and he went to crying.

But he wouldn't turn the fish loose. He just grabbed it up and went running and squawling[2] toward the house, Where he gave the fish to Mama. His hands were all bloody by then, where the fish had finned him. They swelled up and got mighty sore; not even a mesquite thorn hurts as bad as a sharp fish fin when it's run deep into your hand.

But as soon as Mama had wrapped his hands in a poultice of mashed-up prickly-pear root to draw out the poison, Little Arliss forgot all about his hurt. And that night when we ate the fish for supper, he told the biggest windy I ever heard about how he'd dived 'way down into a deep hole under the rocks and dragged that fish out and nearly got drowned before he could swim to the bank with it.

But when I tried to tell Mama what really happened, she wouldn't let me. "Now, this is Arliss' story," she said. "You let him tell it the way he wants to."

I told Mama then, I said: "Mama, that old yeller dog is going to make the biggest liar in Texas out of Little Arliss."

But Mama just laughed at me, like she always laughed at Little Arliss' big windies after she'd gotten off where he couldn't hear her. She said for me to let Little Arliss alone. She said that if he ever told a bigger whopper than the ones I used to tell, she had yet to hear it.

Well, I hushed then. If Mama wanted Little Arliss to grow up to be the biggest liar in Texas, I guessed it wasn't any of my business.

[2]**squawling:** crying

_____

_____

_____

_____

_____

_____

_____

_____

from *The People, Yes* by Carl Sandburg (text page 344)

Literary Focus: Oral Tradition

Although *The People, Yes* is a written composition, it pulls together many stories from American **oral tradition**, the body of stories, poems, and songs passed down by word of mouth from one generation to the next. The yarns and legends of oral tradition often contain exaggeration, magic, and other invented details. At the same time, they often have some basis in actual fact. Consider, for example, Sandburg's summary of a yarn about a corn crop:

They have yarns . . .
Of one corn crop in Missouri when the roots
Went so deep and drew off so much water
The Mississippi riverbed that year was dry.

Although no corn crop could cause the Mississippi riverbed to go dry, it is a fact that corn was grown in Missouri along the Mississippi River, and the yarn probably had its origins in a time when a Missouri drought followed a good corn crop.

DIRECTIONS: On the graphic organizer below, identify a yarn that Sandburg summarizes in this portion of *The People, Yes*. Then list the details about the yarn that you think are exaggeration and the details that you think are probably factual.

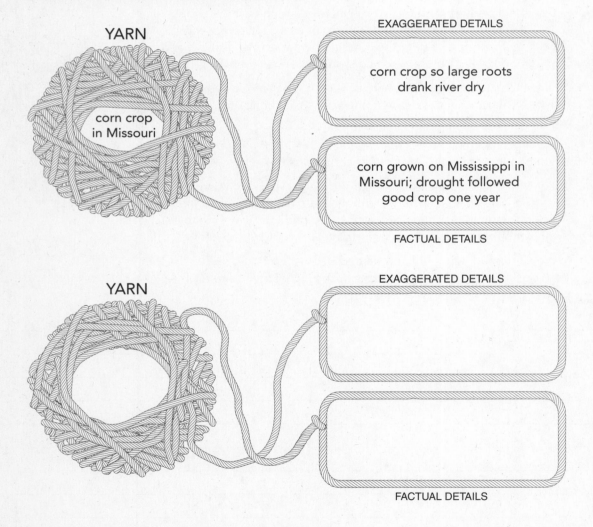

YARN

corn crop in Missouri

EXAGGERATED DETAILS

corn crop so large roots drank river dry

corn grown on Mississippi in Missouri; drought followed good crop one year

FACTUAL DETAILS

YARN

EXAGGERATED DETAILS

FACTUAL DETAILS

from *Travels with Charley* by John Steinbeck (text page 355)

Build Vocabulary

Using the Suffix -ic

When the suffix *-ic* is used to form adjectives, it generally means "like," "showing," or "having to do with." For example, *diagnostic* means "having to do with a diagnosis," or "a study of facts."

A. DIRECTIONS: Complete each definition on the lines provided. The first is done as an example.

1. diagnostic: having to do with a diagnosis, or a study of facts _____

2. energetic: showing _____, or _____

3. romantic: having to do with _____, or _____

4. atomic: having to do with _____, which are _____

5. titanic: like the _____, who were _____

Using the Word Bank

diagnostic	peripatetic	rigorous	maneuver
inquiry	inexplicable	celestial	

B. DIRECTIONS: Match each unscrambled word in the left column with its definition in the right column. First write the unscrambled word on the longer line just after it. Then write the letter of the definition on the short line before the word it defines.

____ 1. tailleecs _____   a. very harsh or strict

____ 2. pbelxeaciin _____   b. moving about; wandering

____ 3. ipetticaper _____   c. to handle or control effectively

____ 4. ruyiiqn _____   d. not easily explained

____ 5. nuveeram _____   e. testing a fact; providing a factual signal

____ 6. angidstoic _____   f. the act of asking questions

____ 7. urrigoos _____   g. heavenly

Recognizing Antonyms

C. DIRECTIONS: Circle the letter of the word that is most nearly opposite in meaning to the word in CAPITAL LETTERS.

1. PERIPATETIC: a. stationary b. temporary c. admirable d. weak

2. RIGOROUS: a. energetic b. cruel c. undemanding d. undesirable

3. INEXPLICABLE: a. stubborn b. educated c. unreasonable d. clear

4. CELESTIAL: a. starry b. earthly c. sparkling d. demanding

Unit 4: From Sea to Shining Sea

from *Travels with Charley* by John Steinbeck (text page 355)

Build Spelling Skills: Using *qu* to Spell the Sound of *kw*

Spelling Strategy   In general, use *qu* to spell the *kw* sound at the start of a word or syllable or as part of an *skw* sound at the start of a word or syllable:

Examples: ques•tion   quick   earth•quake   re•quire   squint   pip•squeak

• In compound words in which the *kw* sound is divided between two syllables, generally spell it *kw*, *ckw*, or, if it is preceded by a long vowel sound, *kew*, where the *e* is silent:

Examples: ink•well   back•woods   poke•weed (long *o*, silent *e*)

• In words containing the prefix *ac-*, meaning "toward" or "to," spell the *kw* sound *cqu*:

Examples: ac•quaint   ac•quiesce   ac•quisition   ac•quit

A. Practice: Complete each word by correctly spelling the *kw* sound on the line provided. Several of the words appear in the selection.

1. _____ ality   6. _____ alify   11. ba _____ ard

2. _____ arter   7. clo _____ ise   12. li _____ id

3. e _____ ip   8. es _____ ire   13. li _____ ise (two long *i* sounds)

4. in _____ iry   9. se _____ el   14. a _____ ittal

5. a _____ ire   10. s _____ eal   15. a _____ arium

B. Practice: On the line after each sentence, correctly spell the word in italics. If the word is already spelled correctly, write *correct*.

1. To Steinbeck, small towns had *kualities* that New York City lacked. _____

2. Steinbeck wished to *reaquaint* himself with the rest of America. _____

3. He had some *kwalms* about traveling alone. _____

4. He found he could make *inkquiries* without being recognized. _____

5. Apparently, even the *bookquorms* did not know what he looked like. _____

Challenge: Many English words from French have tricky spellings because of silent letters. For example, spelling *maneuver* is tricky because of the silent *e* before the *u*. To help you remember the *e*, you might use the saying, "A horse's *mane* in the rider's eyes can make the horse hard to **mane*uver*." For each of these English words from French, underline the part that you think is tricky. Then, on the line provided, make up a saying that might help you spell the word.

1. campaign_____

2. bureau _____

3. limousine_____

from *Travels with Charley* by John Steinbeck (text page 355)

Build Grammar Skills: Coordinating Conjunctions

A conjunction connects single words or groups of words. A **coordinating conjunction** connects words or groups of words of equal grammatical rank. For example, it might connect two or more adjectives, two or more predicates, two or more prepositional phrases, or two or more independent clauses.

Connecting Nouns: Before his trip, Steinbeck spent his time in *California* and *New York*.

Connecting Predicates: He **was** a famous writer but **traveled** anonymously.

Connected Prepositional Phrases: Should he travel *by himself* or *with someone*?

Connecting Independent Clauses: *He took a dog,* for *he wanted some kind of companion.*

The most common coordinating conjunctions appear in the box below. Note that some of these words can also be used as other parts of speech; for example, *for* is often a preposition.

and	but	or	nor	for	yet	so

A. Practice: Underline the coordinating conjunction in each sentence. Then, on the line, identify the parts of speech or grammatical structures that the conjunction connects.

1. My plan was clear, concise, and reasonable, I think. _____

2. In America, I live in New York or dip into Chicago. _____

3. I was working from memory, and the memory is at best faulty. _____

4. I wanted to smell the grass and trees and sewage. _____

5. I stopped where people stopped or gathered. _____

6. It arrived in August, a beautiful thing, powerful yet lithe. _____

7. I racked a shotgun, two rifles, and a couple of fishing rods in my truck. _____

8. I do not know how many people recognized the name, but no one ever asked about it.
_____

9. He is not a romantic nor a mystic. _____

10. It didn't snow, so naturally we forgot the whole thing. _____

B. Writing Application: On the lines below, write five sentences about travel in America. In each, use a coordinating conjunction to connect the parts of speech or grammatical structures in parentheses. Do not use the same conjunction twice.

1. (connect subjects)_____

2. (connect adverbs) _____

3. (connect prepositional phrases)_____

4. (connect adjectives) _____

Unit 4: From Sea to Shining Sea

from *Travels with Charley* by John Steinbeck (text page 355)

Reading Strategy: Clarify Details

When you are reading, you may sometimes come across a passage that you don't completely understand. If that happens, it's important to take time to **clarify the details,** or get them clear in your own mind. You might pause to think about the meaning of a puzzling detail. Or you might try reading backwards or forward for more information that can help you understand the detail. If that doesn't help, consider going outside the text for more information. For example, you might check with your teacher, another classmate, or in a reference work such as a dictionary or encyclopedia.

DIRECTIONS: Fill out the following chart to help you clarify details as you read.

Detail to Clarify	Meaning of Detail	Strategy Used: Pause, Read Ahead, Read Back, Use Other Source

from *Travels with Charley* by John Steinbeck (text page 355)

Literary Focus: Travel Essay

An **essay** is a short nonfiction work about a particular subject. A **travel essay** focuses on a trip or a journey that the author has made. Usually it presents factual information along with the author's personal thoughts and impressions. For example, notice the combination of factual information and personal impressions in this passage from Steinbeck's essay:

> Once I traveled about in an old bakery wagon, double-doored rattler with a mattress on its floor. I stopped where people stopped or gathered, I listened and looked and felt, and in the process had a picture of my country the accuracy of which was impaired only by my own shortcomings.

DIRECTIONS: On the diagram below, list the factual information and personal impressions that Steinbeck combines to portray North Dakota in the last three pages of his essay.

Factual Information		**Personal Impressions**
_____		_____
_____		_____
_____		_____
_____		_____
_____	**Place: North Dakota**	_____
_____		_____
_____		_____
_____		_____
_____		_____
_____		_____
_____		_____
_____		_____
_____		_____
_____		_____
_____		_____
_____		_____
_____		_____

© Prentice-Hall, Inc.

Unit 4: From Sea to Shining Sea

"The New Colossus" by Emma Lazarus (text page 366)
"Ellis Island" by Joseph Bruchac (text page 367)
"Achieving the American Dream" by Mario Cuomo (text page 368)
"Choice: A Tribute to Dr. Martin Luther King, Jr." by Alice Walker (text page 370)

Build Vocabulary

Using Forms of *migrate*

The word *immigrate* is part of the family of words related to the verb *migrate*, which means "to move from one place to another." Other words in the same family include *emigrate, emigrant, emigration, immigrant, immigration, migrant, migration,* and *migratory.*

A. DIRECTIONS: Circle the letter of the choice that best completes each sentence.

1. *Migrant* laborers are workers who ___.

a. earn high salaries   b. retire early   c. travel to find seasonal work   d. are often late to work

2. Calling the monarch butterfly *migratory* refers to its ___.

a. beauty   b. caterpillar stage   c. shrinking population   d. habit of flying south as summer ends

3. The French word for *emigrant* is *emigré.* Russian-born *emigrés* probably live in ___.

a. Paris   b. Moscow   c. spacious apartments   d. poverty

Using the Word Bank

immigrate	apprehension	immersed	ancestral
colossal	conscience	literally	

B. DIRECTIONS: Hidden in this puzzle are the seven words from the Word Bank. Their letters may read from right to left, from left to right, from top to bottom, from bottom to top, or diagonally. Find and circle the words. Then, alongside the puzzle, rewrite each word on the line next to its definition.

T F U I N O Z E D N A Y
B E M L A S S O L O C L
S C L K C D E J A E K L
N O I S N E H E R P P A
X N T M I E R R T S B R
W S S M M N Y D S R H E
V C L G M I N A E O A T
A I N L E M G T C F C I
Q E T R R A T R N I U L
P N N C S L L H A V N Z
F C E F E X C B V T I L
V E S B D Q U D H F E B

1. related to one's forefathers: _____

2. to move to a new country: _____

3. word for word; actually: _____

4. deeply involved in: _____

5. amazingly large: _____

6. fear; anxiety: _____

7. inner morality: _____

"The New Colossus" by Emma Lazarus (text page 366)
"Ellis Island" by Joseph Bruchac (text page 367)
"Achieving the American Dream" by Mario Cuomo (text page 368)
"Choice: A Tribute to Dr. Martin Luther King, Jr." by Alice Walker (text page 370)

Build Spelling Skills: Using Words Within Words to Remember Spellings

Spelling Strategy There are many devices you can use to remember unusual spellings.

- One way to remember the spelling of a word is to remember a smaller word it contains:

Examples: con<u>science</u>   appre<u>hens</u>ion   <u>literal</u>ly

- You may find that you remember the spelling even better if you make up a sentence that highlights the hard-to-spell word along with the smaller word it contains.

Example: She cheated on a SCIENCE test and now has a guilty CONSCIENCE.

A. Practice: For each word below, underline a smaller word that might help you spell it.

1. admittance
2. adolescent
3. cellophane
4. colossal
5. courtesy
6. defendant
7. environment
8. fourteen
9. government
10. guarantee
11. installment
12. literature
13. miscellaneous
14. nuclear
15. permanent
16. privilege
17. pollution
18. satellite
19. secretary
20. tournament

B. Practice: For each hard-to-spell word below, underline a smaller word that might help you spell it. Then, on the line that follows, write an easy-to-remember sentence that highlights both words.

Example: con<u>science</u>: <u>She cheated on a SCIENCE test and now has a guilty CONSCIENCE.</u>

1. apologize:_____

2. awkward:_____

3. canister:_____

4. colossal:_____

5. handkerchief:_____

Challenge: The letters *sc* can spell more than one sound in English. For example, in *science*, the *sc* spells the *s* sound; in *conscience*, it spells the *sh* sound; and in *script*, it spells the *sk* sound. On the lines below, list additional examples of the different sounds that *sc* can spell.

1. the s sound: *science,* _____

2. the sh sound: *conscience,* _____

3. the sk sound: *script,* _____

Unit 4: From Sea to Shining Sea

"The New Colossus" by Emma Lazarus (text page 366)
"Ellis Island" by Joseph Bruchac (text page 367)
"Achieving the American Dream" by Mario Cuomo (text page 368)
"Choice: A Tribute to Dr. Martin Luther King, Jr." by Alice Walker (text page 370)

Build Grammar Skills: Correlative Conjunctions

Correlative conjunctions work in pairs to link words or groups of words.

<u>Both</u> the Statue of Liberty <u>and</u> Ellis Island are located in New York Harbor.

<u>Not only</u> do they have historic importance, <u>but</u> they <u>also</u> represent important American ideals.

These are some common correlative conjunctions:

both . . . and   just as . . . so too   not only (or not just) . . . but also

either . . . or   neither . . . nor

A. Practice: Underline the correlative conjunctions in the following sentences.

1. Both Ellis Island and the Statue of Liberty are now part of the same national monument.

2. You can catch a ferry to them from either New York or New Jersey.

3. A few decades ago, Ellis Island was not only abandoned but also crumbling.

4. Then came proposals for either a housing development or a hospital there.

5. Not just historians but also many descendants of immigrants demanded a memorial instead.

6. They felt that neither the statue nor Ellis Island should ever be forgotten.

7. Just as the statue symbolized freedom, so too does Ellis Island symbolize freedom's doorway.

B. Writing Application: On the lines below, write five sentences about your own ancestors or those of someone you know. Use the correlative conjunctions in parentheses.

1. (both . . . and) _____

_____

2. (neither . . . nor) _____

_____

3. (not only . . . but also) _____

_____

4. (just as . . . so too) _____

_____

5. (either . . . or) _____

_____

"The New Colossus" by Emma Lazarus (text page 366)
"Ellis Island" by Joseph Bruchac (text page 367)
"Achieving the American Dream" by Mario Cuomo (text page 368)
"Choice: A Tribute to Dr. Martin Luther King, Jr." by Alice Walker (text page 370)

Reading Strategy: Summarize

A good way to understand and remember what you read is to summarize it. When you **summarize,** you restate in your own words the main points and key details in a passage or piece of writing. For example, consider this passage from Alice Walker's address:

> He was The One, The Hero, The One Fearless Person for whom we had waited. I hadn't even realized before that we had been waiting for Martin Luther King, Jr., but we had. And I knew it for sure when my mother added his name to the list of people she prayed for every night.

In focusing on only main points and key details, you might summarize the passage as follows:

> Martin Luther King, Jr., was a heroic leader of African Americans. Both the heroine and her mother deeply admired him.

DIRECTIONS: On the chart below, summarize Mario Cuomo's essay by writing a one- or two-sentence summary of each paragraph.

Summary
Paragraph 1
Paragraph 2
Paragraph 3
Paragraph 4
Paragraph 5
Paragraph 6
Paragraph 7
Paragraph 8
Paragraph 9
Paragraph 10

Unit 4: From Sea to Shining Sea

"The New Colossus" by Emma Lazarus (text page 366)
"Ellis Island" by Joseph Bruchac (text page 367)
"Achieving the American Dream" by Mario Cuomo (text page 368)
"Choice: A Tribute to Dr. Martin Luther King, Jr." by Alice Walker (text page 370)

Literary Focus: Epithet

An **epithet** is a phrase that points out a characteristic of a person, place, or thing. Some epithets are temporary creations; others are used again and again, like nicknames. For example, blues singer Bessie Smith is often called "the Empress of the Blues," and New Orleans is widely known as "the Big Easy." Epithets may be used alongside or in place of the person, place, or thing it describes, as the following examples illustrate.

Famous recordings by Bessie Smith, Empress of the Blues, are now available on CD.

Many jazz musicians got their start in the Big Easy.

A. DIRECTIONS: Underline the epithets in these sentences.

1. Many people take in the Statue of Liberty when they visit the Big Apple.

2. They also see a Broadway show on the Great White Way, where lights shine into the wee hours.

3. A baseball game by the Bronx Bombers, or New York Yankees, is another possibility.

4. New York has certainly changed since the days of Mayor Fiorello La Guardia, the Little Flower.

B. DIRECTIONS: Using information that you learned in the selections, create your own epithets for the famous people and places listed in parentheses below. Then, on the lines provided, write complete sentences using your epithets.

1. (the Statue of Liberty) _____

_____

_____

_____

2. (Ellis Island) _____

_____

_____

_____

3. (Mario Cuomo) _____

_____

_____

4. (Dr. Martin Luther King, Jr.) _____

_____

_____

"The Man Without a Country" by Edward Everett Hale (text page 377)

Build Vocabulary

Using the Root *-journ-*

From the French word *jour*, which means "day," comes the English root *-journ-*, which has the same meaning. When old Morgan says "The court is *adjourned*," he means that the court session is suspended for the day.

A. DIRECTIONS: Match the word on the left with its likely original meaning on the right. Write the letter of the meaning on the line before the word.

____ 1. adjournment   a. a day's travel

____ 2. journal   b. a day's writing

____ 3. journey   c. a worker who does a day's work

____ 4. journeyman   d. someone who makes daily stops in his or her travels

____ 5. sojourner   e. suspending for the day

Using the Word Bank

availed	stilted	swagger	blunders

B. DIRECTIONS: Circle the letter of the choice that best answers each question.

1. Of the following people, which one would be most likely to have a *stilted* conversation?
   a. a practiced politician meeting with contributors   c. an auctioneer selling an item
   b. a teenager on his or her first date   d. a talented actress reciting her lines

2. Of the following people, which one would you most expect to *swagger*?
   a. a bold pirate   c. an embarrassed sinner
   b. a shy librarian   d. an absent-minded professor

3. What would you expect from a research report that is full of *blunders*?
   a. It contains a great deal of accurate information.   c. It will get a very high grade.
   b. It contains sloppy research.   d. It will be too short.

4. What would you expect if the report's writer *availed* himself or herself of all possible resources?
   a. He or she used only recent information.   c. He or she used only eyewitness accounts.
   b. He or she ignored most resources.   d. He or she used all information available.

Recognizing Synonyms

C. DIRECTIONS: Circle the letter of the word that is most nearly the same in meaning as the word in CAPITAL LETTERS.

1. SWAGGER:
   a. wash
   b. fight
   c. boast
   d. tease

2. BLUNDERS:
   a. shades
   b. remarks
   c. mistakes
   d. mysteries

3. AVAILED:
   a. covered
   b. displayed
   c. complained
   d. used

4. STILTED:
   a. awkward
   b. tall
   c. short
   d. spoiled

Unit 4: From Sea to Shining Sea

"The Man Without a Country" by Edward Everett Hale (text page 377)

Connecting Historical Fiction to Social Studies

Historical fiction is writing that sets invented characters and their actions amid the events of real history. Although not every detail in historical fiction is factual, a work of historical fiction can still provide a great deal of information that is factually true. It can also give readers a general sense of people's attitudes and of the social, political, and economic conditions of the times in which it is set. The best historical fiction portrays its setting as accurately and realistically as possible. Clearly, "The Man Without a Country" is a realistic historical fiction—so realistic that many who first read it believed they were reading historical fact.

DIRECTIONS: Answer these questions on the lines provided. Use the textbook information preceding the story as well as the footnotes that accompany it to help you with your answers.

1. List five story details that seem to be historical fact.

   _____

   _____

   _____

   _____

   _____

   _____

   _____

2. List five story details that you think are probably fiction.

   _____

   _____

   _____

   _____

   _____

   _____

   _____

   _____

3. What does the story reveal about American attitudes and conditions at the time it was published?

   _____

   _____

   _____

   _____

   _____

   _____

   _____

"Sancho" by J. Frank Dobie (text page 400)
"The Closing of the Rodeo" by William Jay Smith (text page 405)

Build Vocabulary

Using the Word Endings *-ent* and *-ant*

The endings *-ent* or *-ant* are often used to turn verbs into adjectives: *absorb + -ent = absorbent; expect + -ant = expectant.*

A. DIRECTIONS: Complete each sentence with an adjective formed from the verb in parentheses.

1. (differ) Sancho was _____ from typical dogie calves.

2. (insist) The cowhands were _____ about driving Sancho north with the others.

3. (accept) Sancho, however, was not _____ of his new home.

4. (persist) After _____ efforts, he returned to Texas.

5. (excel) There he remained an _____ family pet. (*Hint:* Double the *l.*]

Using the Word Bank

| orphan | vigorous | consumption | yearling | disposition | persistent | accustomed |

B. DIRECTIONS: Read each definition, and fill in the word on the lines provided. When you are done, the letters in the shaded boxes, reading down, will spell out a kind of animal.

1. the act of eating   _ _ _ _ _ _ _ _ _ _ _

2. full of energy   _ _ _ _ _ _ _ _

3. tendency; inclination   _ _ _ _ _ _ _ _ _ _ _

4. stubbornly continuing   _ _ _ _ _ _ _ _ _ _

5. usual; expected   _ _ _ _ _ _ _ _ _ _

6. parentless child or animal   _ _ _ _ _ _

7. one-year-old animal   _ _ _ _ _ _ _ _

Analogies

C. DIRECTIONS: Circle the letter of the pair of words that expresses a relationship most nearly the same as the relationship of the words in CAPITAL LETTERS.

1. ORPHAN : HUMAN : :
a. dogie : cow   b. cow : calf   c. cattle : steer   d. adult : child

2. YEARLING : ONE : :
a. year : century   b. decade : ten   c. nickel : penny   d. nickel : dime

3. EAT : CONSUMPTION : :
a. hunger : food   b. dance : exhibition   c. drink : beverage   d. teach : education

4. WEAK : VIGOROUS : :
a. insistent : persistent   b. familiar : accustomed   c. slow : fast   d. healthy : exercise

Name _____   Date _____

"Sancho" by J. Frank Dobie (text page 400)
"The Closing of the Rodeo" by William Jay Smith (text page 405)

Build Spelling Skills: Using the Spelling *acc*

Spelling Strategy   A number of English words start with the letters *acc*.

• Before an *o, u, r,* or *l,* the opening letters *acc* generally have the sound of *ak*:

Examples: accomplishment   accusation   acclaim   accredit

• Before *e* or *i,* the opening letters *acc* generally have the sound of *aks*:

Examples: accelerate   accidental

A. Practice: On the lines provided, correctly complete the spelling of each word.

1. ____ ompany   6. ____ elerator   11. ____ ent

2. ____ ess   7. ____ ident   12. ____ use

3. ____ ustom   8. ____ rue   13. ____ essory

4. ____ omplish   9. ____ ord   14. ____ ountant

5. ____ eptance   10. ____ umulate   15. ____ ordion

B. Practice: On the line after each sentence, correctly spell the word in italics. If the word is already spelled correctly, write correct.

1. *According* to J. Frank Dobie's story, Sancho was an unusual young cow. _____

2. He was *akustomed* to eating hot peppers. _____

3. He *ackompanied* the others on the long cattle drive. _____

4. He could not *aksept* his new home. _____

5. At the end of Dobie's *acount*, Sancho was back in Texas. _____

Challenge: Many words associated with the American West came to English from Spanish. For example, *ranch* is from the Spanish *rancho*, "small farm." For each item below, guess the word for which the definition and Spanish origin are given. Write the word on the line provided. *Hint:* All the words can be found in the selections.

1. _____: competition in which cattle are roped; from Spanish *rodear*, "to surround"

2. _____: rope for catching horses and cattle; from Spanish *la reata*, "the rope"

3. _____: small wild horse of North America; from Spanish *mestengo*, "stray animal"

"Sancho" by J. Frank Dobie (text page 400)
"The Closing of the Rodeo" by William Jay Smith (text page 405)

Build Grammar Skills: Subjects and Predicates

The **subject** of a sentence tells who or what the sentence is about. The **predicate** tells what the subject is or does. In the following sentence, the complete subject and complete predicate are bracketed.

complete subject	complete predicate
A well with pulley wheel, rope, and bucket	furnished water for the establishment.

The **simple subject** is the main word in the complete subject, generally a noun or a pronoun. The **simple predicate** is the verb or verb phrase in the predicate.

A <u>well</u> with pulley wheel, rope, and bucket | <u>furnished</u> water for the establishment.

A. Practice: In each of these sentences, draw a vertical line separating the subject and predicate. Then draw one line under the simple subject and two lines under the simple predicate.

1. The little black-and-white calf was less than a week old.

2. Maria would give him the shucks wrapped around tamales.

3. The little chiltipiquin peppers, red when ripe, grow wild in low, shaded places.

4. The tamales gave him a tooth for corn in the ear.

5. The herd, with Sancho at the tail end of it, started the next morning.

6. Sancho sniffed southward for a whiff of the Mexican Gulf.

7. The other steers had held together.

8. The Mexican peppers on the Esperanza were red ripe now.

9. The pink phlox were sprinkling every hill and draw.

10. Old Sancho returned about six weeks ago.

B. Writing Application: Expand the subjects and predicates below into five sentences about a rodeo. Add a predicate when a subject is provided and a subject when a predicate is provided.

1. The annual rodeo _____

2. _____ competed in the events.

3. _____ roped dangerous steer.

4. _____ rode the deadly broncos.

5. The crowd of excited onlookers _____

"Sancho" by J. Frank Dobie (text page 400)
"The Closing of the Rodeo" by William Jay Smith (text page 405)

Reading Strategy: Envision a Setting

The **setting** is the time and place in which a work or event unfolds. When you **envision a setting**, you use the details to form a picture of it in your mind. To picture the scene, be sure to take note of the following details, if they are included:

- the type of place being described
- lighting and coloring
- the objects it contains
- time of day
- position (such as "left" and "in back of")
- the season and weather
- size

DIRECTIONS: Reread the opening paragraph of "Sancho" and, on the lines below, jot down details that help you envision the setting. Then, in the space below the lines, make a quick sketch or diagram of the setting you envision.

_____

_____

_____

_____

_____

"Sancho" by J. Frank Dobie (text page 400)
"The Closing of the Rodeo" by William Jay Smith (text page 405)

Literary Focus: Tone

Tone is the attitude that a writer or speaker conveys toward his or her subject, characters, or audience. For example, the tone may be formal, informal, happy, sad, angry, humorous, or matter-of-fact. To determine tone, pay attention to the author's word choice and images and to the emotional effects they have on you. You might ask yourself these questions:

- What are the emotional overtones of the words the author chooses?
- What mood or emotions does the author's imagery attempt to convey?
- What is my own emotional reaction to the writing?

DIRECTIONS: Fill in this chart to help you determine the tone of "The Closing of the Rodeo." After you are done, answer the question below the chart.

Word Choice or Image	Emotion or Mood	Your Personal Reaction

Based on what you've listed, how would you describe the poem's tone?

_____

_____

Unit 4: From Sea to Shining Sea

"A Ribbon for Baldy" by Jesse Stuart (text page 410)
"The White Umbrella" by Gish Jen (text page 414)

Build Vocabulary

Using the Word Root *-cred-*

Credibility contains the root *-cred-*, which means "to believe." *Credibility* is "the ability or power to be believed."

A. DIRECTIONS: On the line before each number, write *T* if the statement is probably true and *F* if it is probably false. Use your understanding of the root *-cred-* to help you figure out the answers.

____ 1. If someone has good *credit*, most banks believe that person will pay back his or her debts.

____ 2. A *credible* idea is hard to believe or accept.

____ 3. An *accredited* beautician school offers degrees that most others in the field accept.

____ 4. A *credulous* person is wisely suspicious of those who try to trick him or her.

____ 5. A jury is likely to accept a witness whose testimony is *incredible*.

Using the Word Bank

surveyed   envelop   bargain   discreet   credibility   constellation   revelation   anxiously

B. DIRECTIONS: Complete each sentence with the appropriate word from the Word Bank. Use each word only once.

1. Someone who refuses to gossip could be described as _____.

2. The group of stars known as Orion, the Hunter, is an example of a(n) _____.

3. A dress bought at an unusually low price might be described as a _____.

4. A person that no one believes has a problem with _____.

5. A person who worriedly wrings his or her hands is behaving _____.

6. On a foggy day, the fog can totally _____ objects, making them impossible to see.

7. When land is _____, someone carefully and completely examines the borders.

8. During a trial, the _____ of something previously unknown can change the verdict.

Recognizing Synonyms

C. DIRECTIONS: Circle the letter of the word with a meaning most nearly the same as the word in capital letters.

1. SURVEYED: a. inspected   b. conversed   c. complimented   d. demanded
2. ENVELOP: a. endear   b. enrich   c. encircle   d. mail
3. DISCREET: a. separate   b. easy   c. shy   d. tactful
4. CREDIBILITY: a. stubbornness   b. believability   c. stupidity   d. savings
5. ANXIOUSLY: a. repeatedly   b. furiously   c. nervously   d. shamefully

"A Ribbon for Baldy" by Jesse Stuart (text page 410)
"The White Umbrella" by Gish Jen (text page 414)

Build Spelling Skills: Using the Spelling *xi*

Spelling Strategy   The letters x and i combine to spell more than one sound in English.

 • The letter *x* before *i* most often has the sound of *ks*:

   Examples: ve<u>xi</u>ng   ma<u>xi</u>m   se<u>xi</u>st   anore<u>xi</u>a

 • Sometimes the *x* and *i* combine to create a *ksh* sound:

   Examples: an<u>xi</u>ous   comple<u>xi</u>on

A. Practice: On the line after each phonetic respelling, correctly spell the word.

1. BOK-sing: _____   6. TAK-sing: _____

2. kom-PLEK-si-tee: _____   7. ob-NOK-shus: _____

3. ANK-shus-lee: _____   8. TOK-sik: _____

4. NOK-shus: _____   9. MAK-si-mum: _____

5. MEK-si-kan: _____   10. FLEK-sing: _____

B. Practice: Write the correct spelling of the word in italics on the line after each sentence. If the word is spelled correctly, write *correct*.

1. The narrator's mother wanted to *macksimize* the family income. _____

2. She viewed the family's low income *anxously*. _____

3. *Mixing* the duties of job and home would not be easy. _____

4. The narrator feared being treated *obnoxshously*. _____

5. She and her sister waited in the rain because they could not afford a *taksi*. _____

Challenge: A "silent" *e* added to the end of a word will usually affect its pronunciation and meaning. On the lines provided, explain the differences in meaning, the part of speech, and the pronunciation of the following sound-alike words. The first is done as an example.

Words	Part of Speech	Meaning	Pronunciation
envelop	verb	to surround	accent on 2d syllable, short *o* in last
envelope	noun	folded packet holding a letter	accent on 1st syllable, long *o* in last
breath			
breathe			
cloth			
clothe			

Selection Support   **159**

Unit 4: From Sea to Shining Sea

"A Ribbon for Baldy" by Jesse Stuart (text page 410)

"The White Umbrella" by Gish Jen (text page 414)

Build Grammar Skills: Compound Subjects and Verbs

Sentences and clauses may have more than one subject or verb. A **compound subject** is two or more simple subjects linked by a conjunction. A **compound verb** is two or more verbs linked by a conjunction.

> **Compound Subject:**   The <u>teacher</u> **and** his <u>students</u> discussed a science project.

> **Compound Verb:**   I <u>paused</u> **and** <u>thought</u> about an idea for my project.

A. Practice: In the following sentences, draw one line under each part of a compound subject. Draw two lines under each part of a compound verb.

1. I studied and played football, both with high marks.

2. In spite of that, the boys and girls at school still made fun of me.

3. My folks and I worked hard on the farm

4. My family scrimped and saved to make ends meet.

5. I thought and thought about a good science project.

6. A cloud circled and enveloped the top of Little Baldy.

7. The mountain and the misty coils gave me an idea for my project.

8. My brother and I sawed and rolled pines to the base of the mountain.

9. With the help of Bob Lavender, I cleared and planted the mountain.

10. My family, the professor, and the science students were all amazed.

B. Writing Application: On the lines below, write five sentences about a school project in which you participated. Include the sentence part indicated in parentheses.

1. (compound subject) _____

_____

2. (compound verb) _____

_____

3. (compound verb) _____

_____

4. (compound subject) _____

_____

5. (compound subject and verb) _____

_____

"A Ribbon for Baldy" by Jesse Stuart (text page 410)
"The White Umbrella" by Gish Jen (text page 414)

Reading Strategy: Predict

To **predict** is to make reasonable guesses about what will happen before it happens. Active readers are always predicting as they read. Here are some guidelines for making predictions:

- Consider characters' traits, actions, and relationships with other characters.

- Consider the events that have already occurred.

- Consider the setting and the events likely to occur in such a setting.

- Consider the theme or moral that the writer might want to convey and the events likely to convey such a message.

- Consider any words in which the narrator **foreshadows**, or directly hints at, future events.

- Consider what future events the title may hint at.

- Take into account any outside knowledge you may have about similar situations in real life or in fictional works (books, films, plays, songs, and so on).

DIRECTIONS: Follow the guidelines as you use this chart to predict events in "A Ribbon for Baldy" and then record whether your predictions come true.

Prediction	Based On	Outcome

Unit 4: From Sea to Shining Sea

"A Ribbon for Baldy" by Jesse Stuart (text page 410)

"The White Umbrella" by Gish Jen (text page 414)

Literary Focus: Character Traits

Character traits are the qualities that make up a character's personality. Some characters have only one or two traits, but main characters—like real people—are often a mixture of several different traits, some good, some bad. Writers sometimes state character traits directly but more often reveal them through the characters' actions, appearance, speech, and the reactions of other characters. For example, this passage from "A Ribbon for Baldy" reveals that the narrator is hardworking, talented, ambitious, conceited, defensive about his poverty, and hoping to prove himself to his classmates.

> I'd made the best grade in my class in General Science. I'd made more yardage, more tackles and carried the football across the goal line more times than any player on my team. But making good grades and playing rugged football hadn't made them forget that I rode a mule to school, that I had worn my mother's shoes the first year and that I slipped away at the noon hour so no one would see me eat fat pork between slices of corn bread.

DIRECTIONS: Use the chart below to help you determine the character traits of the narrator of "The White Umbrella."

Detail	Traits Revealed

"Those Winter Sundays" by Robert Hayden (text page 424)
"Taught Me Purple" by Evelyn Tooley Hunt (text page 425)
"The City Is So Big" by Richard García (text page 427)

Build Vocabulary

Using the Word Root *-chron-*

Chronic contains the word root *-chron-*, which means "time." Something *chronic* continues over a long time, or indefinitely.

A. DIRECTIONS: Circle the letter of the choice that best completes each sentence. Use your understanding of the root *-chron-* to help you figure out the answers.

1. A *chronological* book of Civil War battles will arrange the battles ___.

    a. by state or region   b. in order of importance   c. alphabetically   d. by date

2. *Synchronized* swimmers do the same things ___.

    a. in different ways   b. at the same time   c. one after another   d. to very loud music

3. An example of an *anachronism* is a character in a historical novel using something that _____.

    a. hasn't been invented yet   b. starts a chain reaction   c. puzzles historians   d. kills a king

4. The ship's device called a *chronometer* probably features ___.

    a. seashells   b. a clock   c. bright colors   d. coins from many lands

Using the Word Bank

banked	chronic	austere	tenement	molding	quake

B. DIRECTIONS: Use the clues to fill in the puzzle with words from the Word Bank.

Across
2. to shudder or tremble
4. a rundown apartment building in a poor neighborhood
6. continuing over a long period

Down
1. showing strict self-discipline
3. burning low over a long time
5. ornamental woodwork or edging on a wall

Unit 4: From Sea to Shining Sea

"Those Winter Sundays" by Robert Hayden (text page 424)
"Taught Me Purple" by Evelyn Tooley Hunt (text page 425)
"The City Is So Big" by Richard García (text page 427)

Build Spelling Skills: Using x to Spell the Sound of y

Spelling Strategy   One way to remember the spelling of hard-to-spell words is to focus on any unusual letter repetition they contain.

- Some words have three or four *e*'s:

    Examples: re̲m̲e̲mber ce̲m̲e̲tery e̲xce̲lle̲nt de̲fe̲re̲nce

- You might remember these words more easily if you create a memory device:

    Examples: We re̲m̲e̲mber what is e̲xce̲lle̲nt.

A. Practice: Fill in the missing vowels to complete each word.

1. t __ n __ m __ nt

2. d __ t __ r __ g __ nt

3. r __ p __ ll __ nt

4. r __ f __ r __ nc __

5. __ l __ m __ nt

6. d __ p __ nd __ nt

7. s __ v __ r __

8. s __ r __ n __

9. pr __ f __ r __ nc __

10. __ ss __ nc __

11. p __ rs __ v __ r __

12. p __ rpl __ x __ d

13. __ xc __ ll __ nc __

14. ind __ p __ nd __ nt

15. v __ h __ m __ nt

B. Practice: Choose five words from the fifteen in Practice A, and create a sentence that can serve as a device for remembering how to spell the word. Write the sentence on the line provided.

Example: cemetery: In a cemetery, the dead take their e's (ease).

1. _____

2. _____

3. _____

4. _____

5. _____

Challenge: In *austere*, the sound of *aw* is spelled with *au*. The same sound has many other spellings, including *aw*, *augh*, and *ough*. On the lines below, list examples of words that illustrate theses different spellings, plus any other spellings you can think of for the *aw* sound.

au: *austere*, _____

aw: *awful*, _____

augh: *caught*, _____

ough: *bought*, _____

other spellings of *aw*:

_____

"Those Winter Sundays" by Robert Hayden (text page 424)
"Taught Me Purple" by Evelyn Tooley Hunt (text page 425)
"The City Is So Big" by Richard García (text page 427)

Build Grammar Skills: Inverted Sentences

In most English sentences, the subject comes before the verb. In an **inverted sentence**, the verb precedes the subject.

S   V

Regular: My <u>father</u> <u>rose</u> early on Sundays.

V   S

Inverted: Early on Sundays <u>rose</u> my <u>father</u>.

Poets tend to use inverted sentences more than other writers do, in part because sound is so important in poetry, and changing the word order can help create a particular rhythm, rhyme, or other sound. In addition, since inverted sentences are so rare in everyday English, they tend to stand out when they are used and so can make an idea more powerful and memorable.

A. Practice: For each sentence, put one line under the simple subject and two lines under the verb. Then, if the sentence is inverted, write *INV* on the line before it. If it uses regular subject-verb order, write *REG*.

_____ 1. So big is the city.

_____ 2. With fear quake its bridges.

_____ 3. At night I have seen the city.

_____ 4. From house to house slide the lights.

_____ 5. And trains pass brightly in the night.

_____ 6. Like a smile full of teeth shine the train windows.

_____ 7. I have seen machine-eating houses.

_____ 8. The stairways walk all by themselves.

_____ 9. On the elevator the doors open and close.

_____ 10. And people disappear inside.

B. Writing Application: On the lines below, write five sentences about a city scene. Include three inverted sentences, and label them INV. Label the other two sentences REG.

_____ 1. _____

_____ 2. _____

_____ 3. _____

_____ 4. _____

_____ 5. _____

Unit 4: From Sea to Shining Sea

"Those Winter Sundays" by Robert Hayden (text page 424)
"Taught Me Purple" by Evelyn Tooley Hunt (text page 425)
"The City Is So Big" by Richard García (text page 427)

Reading Strategy: Respond

Every reader **responds** to poetry and other literature in his or her own personal way. For example, when you read a poem, you might agree with one idea and get angry at another, or you might be pleased by the music and images in a particular stanza. You might be puzzled by something the poem says, or you might identify with a particular experience that the poem describes. Consider these lines from "Taught Me Purple" and the two student responses below it.

> My mother taught me purple
> Although she never wore it.

Student Response 1: *I admire the mother for wanting something better for the speaker than she had for herself.*

Student Response 2: *"Taught me purple" is an interesting way of using words. I'm not sure what it means, but it could have something to do with a better or more colorful life.*

DIRECTIONS: Choose one of the three poems in this grouping, and record your responses on the following chart. You might react to single lines or groups of lines.

Title of Poem:	
Lines	**Response**

"Those Winter Sundays" by Robert Hayden (text page 424)
"Taught Me Purple" by Evelyn Tooley Hunt (text page 425)
"The City Is So Big" by Richard García (text page 427)

Literary Focus: Word Choice

Word choice, or the words a writer chooses, has a powerful effect on the ideas and emotions that writing conveys. This is particularly true in poetry, where every word counts. To focus on a poem's word choice, you might ask yourself the following questions:

- What does the word mean in the context in which it is used?

- What images or associations does the word bring to mind?

- What emotional reaction do I have to the word?

- How would my reaction be different if the poet had used a different synonym? For example, if the poet chose *slender*, how would my reaction be different if the poet had chosen *skinny* instead?

DIRECTIONS: Choose one poem in this grouping, and explore its word choice by applying the preceding questions to at least four of its words or phrases. Write the results on the chart below.

Title of Poem:
Word
Line
Meaning
Images or Associations
Emotional Reaction
Different Reaction to Synonym

"Lights in the Night" by Annie Dillard (text page 443)

Build Vocabulary

Using the Root -lum-

The word *luminous* contains the root -*lum*-, which means "light." Something *luminous* produces a steady, glowing light.

A. DIRECTIONS: Circle the letter of the choice that best completes each sentence. Use your understanding of the root -*lum*- to help you figure out the answers.

1. In physics, a *lumen* is a measure of _____.

   a. sound   b. weight   c. distance   d. light

2. You *illuminate* a room when you _____.

   a. make a mess   b. speak very loudly   c. turn on the fan   d. turn on the light

3. Someone described as a *luminary* is probably _____.

   a. a celebrity   b. a joker   c. a bore   d. a shy person

Using the Word Bank

luminous	ascent	membrane	contiguous
conceivably	coincidental	elongate	

B. DIRECTIONS: Match each word in the left column with its definition in the right column. Write the letter of the definition on the line before the word it defines.

____ 1. ascent   a. a thin, soft layer

____ 2. coincidental   b. possibly

____ 3. conceivably   c. an upward climb

____ 4. contiguous   d. glowing

____ 5. elongate   e. long and narrow

____ 6. luminous   f. in contact with; touching

____ 7. membrane   g. occurring at the same time but otherwise unrelated

Recognizing Antonyms

C. DIRECTIONS: Circle the letter of the word that is most nearly the opposite of the word in capital letters.

1. ASCENT: 2. CONTIGUOUS: 3. LUMINOUS: 4. CONCEIVABLY: 5. COINCIDENTAL:
   a. refusal   a. sticky   a. famous   a. possibly   a. planned
   b. relief   b. separate   b. large   b. thoughtfully   b. cheated
   c. decent   c. puzzled   c. hectic   c. toward   c. accidental
   d. descent   d. determined   d. dark   d. never   d. worthless

"Lights in the Night" by Annie Dillard (text page 443)

Build Spelling Skills: Spelling *ei* and *ie*

Spelling Strategy   Here is the full version of the famous spelling-rule rhyme.

Use *i* before *e* (f**ie**ld, p**ie**ce, ch**ie**f, bel**ie**ve)

except after *c* (con**ce**ive, re**ce**ive)

Or when sounded like *a* as in *n**ei**ghbor* and *w**ei**gh* (v**ei**n, **ei**ght)

Exceptions: either, financier, foreign, forfeit, height, leisure, neither, protein, science, seize, sheik, stein, their, weird

A. Practice: Complete each word by writing *ie* or *ei* on the lines provided.

1. gr ___ ___ f
2. fr ___ __ nd
3. dec ___ ___ ve
4. conc ___ ___ vable
5. sl ___ ___ gh
6. c ___ ___ ling
7. r ___ gn
8. misch ___ ___ f
9. rel ___ ___ ve
10. n ___ ___ ce
11. s ___ ___ zing
12. b ___ ___ ge
13. rec ___ ___ pt
14. n ___ ___ ther
15. sc ___ ___ ntific

B. Practice: On the line after each sentence, write the correct spelling of each italicized word. If all the words are spelled correctly, write *correct*.

1. Each night I thought I saw a *wierd foriegn* shape on the wall. _____

2. Finally I *percieved* that it was a car *windsheild* reflecting the streetlight. _____

3. The car came *shreiking* through the *nieghborhood*. _____

4. I realized the things I had *beleived* could *concievably* be wrong. _____

5. I could *either* accept reason or *yield* to my vivid imagination. _____

Challenge: People often forget the silent *h* in *Pittsburgh*, Annie Dillard's home town. That's because the old term for a town or city, which still appears at the end of many place names, is sometimes spelled *-burgh* but often spelled *-burg* (*Vicksburg, Gettysburg*). On the lines provided, correctly respell the name of each city. If the spelling is already *correct*, write correct. If you are unsure of the spelling, check a dictionary or an atlas.

1. Albaquerky, N. Mex. _____
2. Cinncinnatti, Ohio _____
3. De Moine, Iowa _____
4. Hughston, Tex. _____
5. Loueyville, Ky. _____
6. Milwaukee, Wis. _____
7. Philadelphia, Pa. _____
8. Plattsburg, N.Y. _____
9. Spokan, Wash. _____
10. Touson, Ariz. _____

Selection Support **169**

"Lights in the Night" by Annie Dillard (text page 443)

Build Grammar Skills: Direct Objects

In a sentence that contains an action verb, the predicate may also contain a direct object. The **direct object** receives the action of a verb. It tells you on what or whom the subject performs the action.

> **Examples:** At night young Annie saw strange <u>shapes</u> on the wall. (Annie saw *what?* shapes)
> The eerie nighttime shadows scared <u>her</u>. (shadows scared *whom?* her)

In identifying direct objects, here are some things to keep in mind:

- Only an action verb can have a direct object.
- The direct object usually comes somewhere after the verb.
- The direct object is usually a noun or a pronoun.
- The direct object answers the question *What?* or *Whom?* after the verb.
- The direct object is never part of a prepositional phrase.

A. Practice: Underline the direct object in each sentence.

1. Sometimes the strange thing woke me.
2. The luminous, oblong shape cast strange shadows.
3. It flattened itself along the ground.
4. It had two parts, like a Chinese dragon.
5. It searched every corner of the room.
6. I did not tell my sister about it.
7. The information would only scare her.
8. One night I finally determined the identity of the intruder.
9. The windshield of a car reflected the streetlight outside.
10. Each passing car did the same thing.

B. Writing Application: On the lines below, write five sentences about a scary incident that you or someone you know has experienced. Include a direct object in each sentence. Remember that only action verbs can have direct objects; forms of *be*, such as *was* and *were*, do not have direct objects.

1. _____

2. _____

3. _____

4. _____

5. _____

Reading for Success: Strategies for Reading Critically

As a critical reader, you must take the time to analyze carefully what you read, and consider how effectively an author has put together a piece of writing.

- **Recognize the author's purpose.** Authors generally write to entertain, inform, call to action, or reflect on experiences. Notice the author's choice of words and the details he or she includes. These clues will help you determine an author's purpose. Then, judge whether the writer has achieved his or her purpose.

- **Make inferences.** It's a reader's job to fill in details the author doesn't provide. You can do so by making inferences, or drawing conclusions, based on the details that are provided, combined with your own knowledge and experience.

- **Understand the author's bias.** Look for details that might reveal a writer's opinion. Use what you know about the writer's background and knowledge.

- **Evaluate the author's message.** When you evaluate an author's message, you make a judgment about how effectively a writer has proven his or her point. First, identify the writer's message. Then, look to see whether this message has been thoroughly supported by facts and details. Also, consider whether the writer is qualified to write on that subject.

DIRECTIONS: Read the following excerpt from *Dance to the Piper* by Agnes De Mille, and use the reading strategies to increase your comprehension. In the margin, note where you recognize the author's purpose, make inferences, understand the author's bias, and evaluate the author's message. Finally, write your response to the selection on the lines provided.

from *Dance to the Piper* by Agnes De Mille

In this passage, the author explains the discipline and dedication needed to excel as a ballerina.

So she began every lesson. So I have begun every practice period since. It is part of the inviolable ritual of ballet dancing. Every ballet student that has ever trained in the classic technique in any part of the world begins just this way, never any other. They were dreary exercises and I was very bad at them but these were the exercises that built Taglioni's leg.[1] These repeated stretches and pulls gave Pavlova her magic foot and Legnani hers and Kchessinska hers.[2] This was the very secret of how to dance, the tradition handed down from teacher to pupil for three hundred years. A king had patterned the style and named the steps, the king who built Versailles.[3] Here was an ancient and enduring art whose technique stood like the rules of harmony. All other kinds of performance in our Western theater had faded or changed. What were movies to this? Or Broadway plays?

I, a complacent child, who had been flattered into believing I could do without what had gone before, now inherited the labor of centuries. I had come into my birthright. I was fourteen, and I had found my life's work. I felt superior to other adolescents as I stood beside the adults serene and strong, reassured by my vision.

[1] **Taglioni's leg:** Maria Taglioni was an Italian ballerina.
[2] **Pavlova . . . Legnani . . . Kchessinska:** famous ballerinas.
[3] **Versailles:** King Louis XIV, whose magnificent palace was in Versailles, France.

I bent to the discipline. I learned to relax with my head between my knees when I felt sick or faint. I learned how to rest my insteps by lying on my back with my feet vertically up against the wall. I learned how to bind up my toes so that they would not bleed through the satin shoes. But I never sat down. I learned the first and all-important dictate of ballet dancing—never to miss the daily practice, hell or high water, sickness or health, never to miss the barre practice; to miss meals, sleep, rehearsals even but not the practice, not for one day ever under any circumstances, except on Sundays.

I seemed, however, to have little aptitude for the business. What had all this talk about God-given talent amounted to? It was like trying to wiggle my ears. I strained and strained. Nothing perceptible happened. A terrible sense of frustration drove me to striving with masochistic[4] frenzy. Twice I fainted in class. My calves used to ache until tears stuck in my eyes. I learned every possible manipulation of the shoe to ease the aching tendons of my insteps. I used to get abominable stitches in my sides from attempting continuous jumps. But I never sat down. I learned to cool my forehead against the plaster of the walls. I licked the perspiration off from around my mouth. I breathed through my nose though my eyes bugged. But I did not sit and I did not stop.

Ballet technique is arbitrary and very difficult. It never becomes easy; it becomes possible. The effort involved in making a dancer's body is so long and relentless, in many instances so painful, the effort to maintain the technique so grueling that unless a certain satisfaction is derived from the disciplining and punishing, the pace could not be maintained. Most dancers are to an extent masochists. "What a good pain! What a profitable pain!" said Miss Fredova as she stretched her insteps in her two strong hands. "I have practiced for three hours. I am exhausted, and I feel wonderful."

[4]**masochistic:** typical of those who enjoy pain.

"Lights in the Night" by Annie Dillard (text page 443)

Literary Focus: Vignette

A **vignette** [vin-YET] is a sketch or brief narrative of a memorable scene or incident. The term *vignette*, which comes from French, was originally applied to the delicate designs used as decoration on books covers, and it still suggests a style of writing that is graceful and compact. A vignette may be a separate work or part of a longer work. You often find vignettes in biographies and in autobiographical works, like Annie Dillard's.

A. DIRECTIONS: In the space below, create a cluster diagram in which you jot down images and other details that make Dillard's vignette come alive for readers.

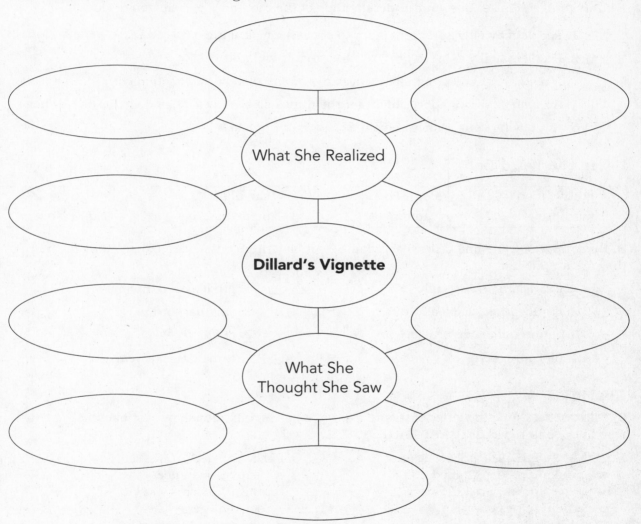

B. DIRECTIONS: How would you describe the style of Dillard's vignette? Answer on the lines below, and cite images that you listed in part A to support your evaluation.

_____

_____

_____

_____

Build Vocabulary

Using the Root *-grat-*

Gratification contains the root *-grat-*, which means "pleasing" or "satisfying." *Gratification* is "the condition of being pleased or satisfied."

A. DIRECTIONS: On the line before each statement, write *T* if the statement is probably true and *F* if it is probably false. Use your understanding of the root *-grat-* to help you decide.

____ 1. People may offer *congratulations* to show their pleasure at an event.

____ 2. People usually express *gratitude* in a thank-you note.

____ 3. A restaurant customer often leaves a *gratuity* to show satisfaction with the service.

____ 4. An *ingrate* shows appreciation for the things someone else has done for him or her.

____ 5. Not having your wishes come true is very *gratifying*.

Using the Word Bank

gratification	countenance	singular	guffawed
macabre	camouflage	predisposed	capricious

B. DIRECTIONS: On the line before each pair of words, write *S* if the words are synonyms and *A* if they are antonyms.

____ 1. capricious, reasonable

____ 2. gratification, displeasure

____ 3. countenance, expression

____ 4. macabre, eerie

____ 5. predisposed, inclined

____ 6. singular, ordinary

____ 7. guffawed, wept

____ 8. camouflage, reveal

Analogies

C. DIRECTIONS: Circle the letter of the words that express a relationship most like the relationship of the pair of words in CAPITAL LETTERS.

1. OPINION : PREDISPOSED : :
   a. decision : predetermined
   b. open-minded : prejudiced
   c. certainty : hesitated
   d. retest : pretest

2. LAUGH : GUFFAW : :
   a. chuckle : smile
   b. giggle : frown
   c. cry : sob
   d. joke : punchline

3. PLEASE : GRATIFICATION : :
   a. help : assistance
   b. anger : tease
   c. borrow : generosity
   d. entertain : boredom

4. SINGULAR : ONE
   a. group : individual
   b. special : unimportant
   c. decade : ten
   d. multiple : many

"What Stumped the Blue Jays" by Mark Twain (text page 453)
"Why Leaves Turn Color in the Fall" by Diane Ackerman (text page 458)

Build Spelling Skills: Spelling the Sound of Final *er*

Spelling Strategy The sound of *er* at the end of a word has several spellings. Learn them as you come across them in your reading, or check a dictionary if you are not sure of a spelling.

• Some words use *ar* to spell the sound of *er* at the end of a word:

Examples: begg_ar_   burgl_ar_   calend_ar_   coll_ar_   mol_ar_   regul_ar_

• Many words use *er* and *or* to spell the sound of *er* at the end of a word.

Examples: charac_ter_   maneuv_er_   upp_er_   act_or_   hon_or_   mot_or_

A. Practice: Complete each word by correctly spelling the final unstressed *er* sound. All of the words are from the two selections in this grouping.

1. flutt____   6. raft____   11. hum____   16. mort____
2. singul____   7. sug____   12. summ____   17. bak____
3. upp____   8. with____   13. shimm____   18. popl____
4. scatt____   9. wint____   14. spectacul____ 19. reconsid____
5. col____   10. flow____   15. laught____   20. maneuv____

B. Practice: On the line after each sentence, correctly respell any misspelled words in italics. If all the words in italics are spelled correctly, write *correct*.

1. He was a middle-aged *minor* who lived in a lonely *cornar* of California. _____
_____

2. He studied every *neighbar* and knew that a blue jay was the best *talker*. _____
_____

3. No *other* beast *ever* uses such good *grammer* as the blue jay. _____
_____

4. The jay's smile faded like breath on a *razor* when he saw the *singulor* hole. _____
_____

5. The other jays can *deliver* their *leathar*-headed opinions to the *sufferer*. _____
_____

Challenge: One way to remember a hard-to-spell word is to group it with other words that have the same tricky spelling. For example, to remember *camouflage* with its tricky *mou* syllable, you might remember *limousine*, which has the same spelling feature. You might try remembering that all of the following words end in *re* but are pronounced as though they end in *er*. Practice using each word in a sentence. If you're unsure of a meaning, check a dictionary.

1. ogre: _____

2. acre: _____

3. mediocre: _____

Unit 5: Extraordinary Occurrences

"What Stumped the Blue Jays" by Mark Twain (text page 453)
"Why Leaves Turn Color in the Fall" by Diane Ackerman (text page 458)

Build Grammar Skills: Indirect Objects

An **indirect object** helps a direct object complete the action of a verb by telling *to whom, for whom, to what,* or *for what* the action is performed.

> **Examples:** The jays told <u>him</u> their opinions. *(told opinions to whom? him)*
> The birds bring <u>communities</u> the gossip. *(bring gossip to what? communities)*

In identifying indirect objects, here are some points to keep in mind:

- Only an action verb can have an indirect object.

- The verb must have a direct object in order to have an indirect object.

- The indirect object usually falls between the verb and its direct object.

- The indirect object is usually a noun or a pronoun.

- The indirect object answers the question *To whom? For whom? To what?* or *For what?*

- The indirect object is never part of a prepositional phrase.

> **Example:** She plays tennis <u>with her sister</u>. (*Sister* is the object of the proposition *with,* not an indirect object.)

A. Practice: For each sentence, draw one line under the direct object and two lines under the indirect object. Some sentences may not have indirect objects. The first one has been done for you.

1. Jim Baker told <u><u>people</u></u> funny <u>tales</u> about animals.

2. In his experience, animals held conversations with one another.

3. Isolation had given Baker an understanding of this animal talk.

4. Blue jays, in particular, offered him interesting discussions.

5. Good grammar made jays the best talkers of the animal kingdom.

6. One jay brought Baker much amusement with its antics.

7. It fed a hole in the roof hundreds of acorns.

8. They offered it their diverse opinions.

9. For a long time afterward, they laughingly told visitors the story.

B. Writing Application: On the lines below, write five sentences about nature. Include an indirect object in each sentence. Remember that only action verbs can have indirect objects; forms of *be,* such as *was* and *were,* do not have indirect objects.

1. _____

2. _____

3. _____

4. _____

5. _____

"What Stumped the Blue Jays" by Mark Twain (text page 453)
"Why Leaves Turn Color in the Fall" by Diane Ackerman (text page 458)

Reading Strategy: Recognize the Author's Purpose

An **author's purpose** is his or her reason for writing a work. In most works, authors have a general purpose—usually to describe, to explain, to recount events, to persuade, and/or to entertain. In addition, the author often has a more specific purpose for including a particular detail or passage. For example, within a work in which the overall aim is to entertain or to recount events, an author may include certain details to build suspense, others to make a character more sympathetic, and still others to provoke the reader's laughter.

DIRECTIONS: Fill out the following chart to help you track Mark Twain's general and specific purposes in "What Stumped the Blue Jays." One item is done as an example.

Detail from Text	My Response	Possible Purposes
"Animals talk to each other, of course."	silly comment	to make me laugh

"What Stumped the Blue Jays" by Mark Twain (text page 453)
"Why Leaves Turn Color in the Fall" by Diane Ackerman (text page 458)

Literary Focus: Observation

An **observation** is an eyewitness account of an event or process studied over a period of time. The observer uses precise details and vivid language to re-create the event or process for readers. In her nonfictional account, Diane Ackerman carefully observes the process by which leaves turn color in the fall. In Mark Twain's fictional story, the character Jim Baker observes an odd (and humorous) example of blue jay behavior.

DIRECTIONS: On the diagram below, list the steps of the process that Diane Ackerman observes in the second and third paragraphs of "Why Leaves Turn Color in the Fall."

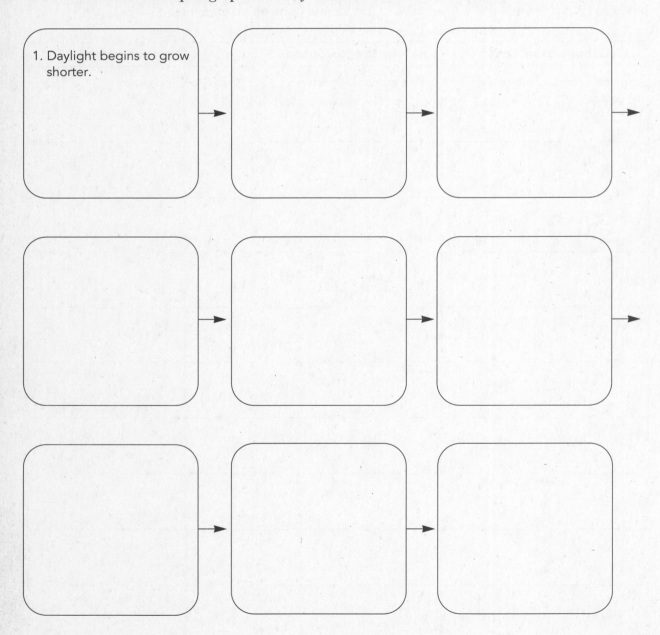

1. Daylight begins to grow shorter.

© Prentice-Hall, Inc.

"Southbound on the Freeway" by May Swenson (text page 466)
"The Story-Teller" by Mark Van Doren (text page 467)
"Los New Yorks" by Victor Hernández Cruz (text page 468)

Build Vocabulary

Using the Prefix *trans-*

The prefix *trans-* means "across" or "through." Something *transparent* is something clear enough to see through.

A. DIRECTIONS: Circle the letter of the choice that best completes each statement. Use your understanding of the prefix *trans-* to help you determine the best choice.

1. If you make a *transatlantic* call from New York City, you may be calling ____.
   a. Atlanta, Ga.   b. Los Angeles, Calif.   c. Tokyo, Japan   d. London, England

2. A *transcontinental* race that starts in San Francisco, Calif., might end in ____.
   a. Atlanta, Ga.   b. Los Angeles, Calif.   c. Tokyo, Japan   d. London, England

3. The word root *-luc-* means "light." A *translucent* fabric is one that ____.
   a. blocks light   b. lets light through   c. will not burn   d. is very thick and fuzzy

4. In a blood *transfusion,* a person ____.
   a. stops bleeding   b. bleeds internally   c. receives blood from someone else   d. breaks the law

5. A radio *transmitter* ____.
   a. sends messages   b. amplifies messages   c. encodes messages   d. changes the channels

Using the Word Bank

transparent	galore	tropical	romp

B. DIRECTIONS: Write the word from the Word Bank that best completes each sentence.

1. A _____ heat wave settled over the city.

2. Despite the heat, the children enjoyed a _____ in the park.

3. There were cars _____ on the crowded freeway.

4. The windows of the cars were _____, revealing soft shapes inside.

Recognizing Synonyms

C. DIRECTIONS: Circle the letter of the word that is closest in meaning to the word in CAPITAL LETTERS.

1. ROMP:
   a. frolic
   b. lane
   c. room
   d. division

2. TRANSPARENT:
   a. dark
   b. clear
   c. mother
   d. hidden

3. TROPICAL:
   a. northern
   b. dry
   c. humid
   d. icy

4. GALORE:
   a. joyous
   b. missing
   c. across
   d. aplenty

Unit 5: Extraordinary Occurrences

"Southbound on the Freeway" by May Swenson (text page 466)
"The Story-Teller" by Mark Van Doren (text page 467)
"Los New Yorks" by Victor Hernández Cruz (text page 468)

Build Spelling Skills: Spelling *cal* vs. *cle*

Spelling Strategy   The sound of *kul* at the end of a word is often spelled *cal* or *cle*.

- In general, use the *cal* spelling as the ending of adjectives:

   Examples: histori<u>cal</u>   medi<u>cal</u>   magi<u>cal</u>   musi<u>cal</u>   philosophi<u>cal</u>

- Use the *cle* spelling at the end of nouns and verbs:

   Examples: cy<u>cle</u>   ici<u>cle</u>   mana<u>cle</u>   mono<u>cle</u>

A. Practice: Complete each word by correctly adding *cle* or *cal* on the line provided. Check a dictionary if you're not sure of a spelling.

1. tropi _____
2. tricyc _____
3. vo _____
4. physi _____
5. un _____

6. verti _____
7. mathemati _____
8. parti _____
9. lo _____
10. recyc _____

11. ethi _____
12. topi _____
13. barna _____
14. logi _____
15. clini _____

B. Practice: On the line after each sentence, write the correct spelling of the italicized word. If the word is already spelled correctly, write *correct*.

1. What was the *tropicle* wave that settled in "Los New Yorks"? _____

2. From what *geographical* area did the wave come? _____

3. What stories did "The Story-Teller" *chronical*? _____

4. Was "Southbound on the Freeway" about a car or a *bicycal*? _____

5. Which of the three poems did you find the most *lyricle*? _____

Challenge: *Galore* is one of several words that come to English from the Celtic language family, which includes Irish and Scottish Gaelic. On the lines provided, correctly complete the words defined, which all came to English from Celtic languages.

1. L E ____ ____ ____ ____ ____ ____ ____ ____ : an elflike creature of Irish folklore

2. P L ____ ____ ____ : a checked pattern

3. G L ____ ____ : a valley

4. L O ____ ____ : a Scottish lake

5. S L ____ ____ ____ ____ : a phrase used repeatedly as a motto or to advertise a product

"Southbound on the Freeway" by May Swenson (text page 466)

"The Story-Teller" by Mark Van Doren (text page 467)

"Los New Yorks" by Victor Hernández Cruz (text page 468)

Build Grammar Skills: Predicate Adjectives

Adjectives are words that modify, or describe, nouns and pronouns. A **predicate adjective** is an adjective that comes after a linking verb and describes the subject of the sentence. In the first sample sentence below, the predicate adjective *metallic*, which comes after the linking verb *are*, describes the subject *creatures*. In the second sample sentence, the predicate adjective *strange*, which comes after the linking verb *seem*, describes the subject *They*.

The creatures of this star are <u>metallic</u>. They seem very <u>strange</u>.

In identifying predicate adjectives, here are some things to keep in mind:

- A predicate adjective always follows a linking verb, not an action verb.
- A predicate adjective always refers back to the subject of the sentence.
- A predicate adjective tells *what kind, which one, how much*, or *how many* about the subject.
- A predicate adjective is never part of a prepositional phrase.

A. Practice: For each sentence, underline the predicate adjective and circle the word it modifies. If the sentence has no predicate adjective, write *none* at the end of the sentence. The first one has been done for you.

1. To the visitor from Orbitville, the (creatures) look <u>odd</u>.

2. Their feet are round.

3. They travel on diagrams and long measuring tapes.

4. The tapes are dark with white lines.

5. Of each creature's four eyes, the two in the back are red.

6. One of the creatures has five eyes.

7. He must be special.

8. At his approach, the others become more cautious.

9. Some parts of the creatures are transparent.

10. The soft shapes inside seem shadowy.

B. Writing Application: On the lines below, write five sentences about a road or freeway. Use a predicate adjective in each sentence.

1. _____

2. _____

3. _____

4. _____

5. _____

"Southbound on the Freeway" by May Swenson (text page 466)
"The Story-Teller" by Mark Van Doren (text page 467)
"Los New Yorks" by Victor Hernández Cruz (text page 468)

Reading Strategy: Understanding the Author's Bias

Authors, like everyone else, have different ways of viewing the world. Even when they don't mean to, they present ideas through their own slant, or **bias.** For example, a poet who is a racecar fan might write a very different poem about freeways than someone who is deeply concerned about pollution from automobile exhaust. When you read a work, you need to consider what the author's bias might be and evaluate his or her ideas accordingly.

DIRECTIONS: Fill out the following chart to help you determine the authors' bias for the three poems in this grouping.

Poet	Lines	Bias

"Southbound on the Freeway" by May Swenson (text page 466)
"The Story-Teller" by Mark Van Doren (text page 467)
"Los New Yorks" by Victor Hernández Cruz (text page 468)

Literary Focus: Free Verse

Free verse is poetry that does not follow the traditional structure of poetry from centuries past. Instead of using a pattern of rhythm, free verse uses irregular rhythms created by lines of varying lengths. Instead of using a pattern of rhyme, free verse uses rhyme in irregular places, or not at all. Before the twentieth century, only a handful of English-language poets used free verse. Since 1900, however, free verse has become more and more popular. Of the three poems presented in this grouping, two of them—"Southbound on the Freeway" and "Los New Yorks"—are written in free verse.

DIRECTIONS: On the chart below, show how "Southbound on the Freeway" and "Los New Yorks" fit the definition of free verse while "The Story-Teller" does not.

Selection	Rhythm	Rhyme
"Southbound on the Freeway"	Description: Example:	Description: Example:
"The Story-Teller"	Description: Example:	Description: Example:
"Los New Yorks"	Description: Example:	Description: Example:

"The Adventure of the Speckled Band" by Sir Arthur Conan Doyle (text page 474)

Build Vocabulary

Using Forms of *convulse*

The word *convulsed* is part of the family of words related to the verb *convulse*, which means "to shake violently."

A. DIRECTIONS: Complete each sentence below with an appropriate word from the list.

Words to Use: *convulsed, convulsion, convulsive, convulsively*

1. Having injured his head in an accident, he suffered a severe _____.

2. When the earthquake hit, the ground _____ and buildings collapsed.

3. Freezing from the cold, the dog gave a _____ shake.

4. The movie audience laughed _____ at the silly monster.

Using the Word Bank

defray	manifold	morose	convulsed
imperturbably	reverie	tangible	

B. DIRECTIONS: Hidden in this puzzle are the seven words from the word bank. Their letters may read from right to left, from left to right, from top to bottom, from bottom to top, or diagonally. Find and circle the words. Then, alongside the puzzle, rewrite each word on the line next to its definition.

```
Q M E T D M U O H O E D E
B K L C F O A J A I K C X
J N I V F R H N R P P O Q
E F L E S O H E I S P N S
L S S M M S V D S F R V A
B G L C T E A V E N O U M
I M P E R T U R B A B L Y
G W T I D R J Y A R F S D
N C E C S K P H A V N E L
A N E F E X Y A R F E D C
T E B S Q D U D H F E B T
```

1. without getting excited: _____

2. having a gloomy temper: _____

3. to supply the money for: _____

4. plentiful and many-sided: _____

5. shook violently: _____

6. able to be touched: _____

7. daydream: _____

Recognizing Antonyms

C. DIRECTIONS: Circle the letter of the word that has a meaning most nearly opposite the meaning of the word in CAPITAL LETTERS.

1. IMPERTURBABLY: a. honestly   b. nervously   c. wisely   d. kindly
2. MOROSE: a. dry   b. rapid   c. lowdown   d. cheerful
3. DEFRAY: a. charge   b. drink   c. sew   d. communicate

"The Adventure of the Speckled Band" by Sir Arthur Conan Doyle (text page 474)

Build Spelling Skills: Spelling the Sound of *er*

Spelling Strategy   The sound of *er* has several spellings.

- Many words use *er* to spell the sound of *er*:

    Examples: f<u>er</u>n   mak<u>er</u>   p<u>er</u>son   Sh<u>er</u>lock

- Some words use *ur* to spell the sound of *er*:

    Examples: f<u>ur</u>nish   h<u>ur</u>t   inc<u>ur</u>   t<u>ur</u>n

- Other spellings of the *er* sound include *ar*, *ir*, *or*, and *ear*:

    Examples: begg<u>ar</u>   f<u>ir</u>   act<u>or</u>   h<u>ear</u>d

A. Practice: Complete each word by correctly spelling the missing *er* sound. All of the words are from "The Adventure of the Speckled Band."

1. s_____ prise
2. p _____ fectly
3. corrid _____
4. ret _____ ned
5. s _____ vice

6. regul _____
7. rum _____
8. maj _____
9. forw _____ d
10. inj _____ ed

11. lib _____ ty
12. horr _____
13. h _____ led
14. p _____ petrated
15. f _____ ocious

16. hagg _____ d
17. av _____ t
18. singul _____
19. s _____ viv _____
20. imp _____ t _____ bably

B. Practice: On the line after each sentence, write the correct spelling of any italicized words. If the words are already spelled correctly, write *correct.* If you're not sure of a spelling, check a dictionary.

1. The events *occurred* when Dr. Watson was still a *bacheler.* _____

2. He *obsurved* Holmes's work *firsthand* and placed it on *recurd.* _____

3. *Purhaps* the most *interesting* tale *concirned* Helen Stoner. _____

4. She *arrived early* one morning in a state of complete *terrer.* _____

5. "Kind *sur*," she *asked*, "can you throw light on the dark that *sorrounds* me?" _____

Challenge: A long *e* sound at the end of a word is often spelled with a *y.* However, it may also be spelled in many other ways, including *ie, ee, ey, i,* and even just *e.* On the lines below, add more examples of words that show the different spellings of the final long *e* sound.

final *y:*
pretty, _____

final *ie:*
reverie, _____

final *ee:*
tree, _____

final *ey:*
monkey, _____

final *i:*
confetti, _____

"The Adventure of the Speckled Band" by Sir Arthur Conan Doyle (text page 474)

Build Grammar Skills: Predicate Nouns

As you know, nouns are words that name people, places, or things. A **predicate noun** is a noun that comes after a linking verb and explains or further identifies the subject of the sentence. In the first sample sentence below, the predicate noun *detective*, which comes after the linking verb *was*, explains the subject *Sherlock Holmes*. In the second sample sentence, the predicate noun *thinker*, which also comes after the linking verb *was*, explains the subject *He*.

Sherlock Holmes was a great <u>detective</u>. He was a very logical <u>thinker</u>.

In identifying predicate nouns, here are some things to keep in mind:

- A predicate noun always follows a linking verb, not an action verb.
- A predicate noun always refers back to the subject of the sentence.
- A predicate noun is never part of a prepositional phrase.

A. Practice: Underline the predicate noun in each sentence. If the sentence has no predicate noun, write *none* at the end of the sentence.

1. Sherlock Holmes was the invention of Sir Arthur Conan Doyle.

2. A fictional character, he nevertheless became a world-famous resident of nineteeth century.

3. Watson, Holmes's friend, serves as narrator in most of the Sherlock Holmes mysteries.

4. Like Sir Arthur Conan Doyle, Watson was a medical doctor.

5. Unlike Sherlock Holmes, he was not particularly clever.

6. Early in their friendship, the two men were both bachelors.

7. They were roommates at 221B Baker Street.

8. That was a fictional house number on a real London street.

9. Later in the series, Watson became a married man.

10. His wife had been a damsel in distress in one of Holmes's adventures.

B. Writing Application: On the lines below, write five sentences about your favorite detectives in literature, in the movies, or on TV. Use a predicate noun in each sentence.

1. _____

2. _____

3. _____

4. _____

5. _____

"The Adventure of the Speckled Band" by Sir Arthur Conan Doyle (text page 474)

Reading Strategy: Identify Evidence

In a typical mystery story, the detective gathers and analyzes evidence or clues that eventually point to the solution. For most readers, one of the pleasures of reading a good mystery is trying to solve the crime along with the detective. Like the detective, you need to use your powers of observation and logical reasoning to **identify evidence** and make predictions about the solution. Sometimes you may be led astray by false clues, called **red herrings,** that mystery writers often include to make their stories more puzzling.

DIRECTIONS: Fill out the following chart to identify evidence that may help solve the mystery in "The Adventure of the Speckled Band."

Evidence	Prediction

"The Adventure of the Speckled Band" by Sir Arthur Conan Doyle (text page 474)

Literary Focus: Mystery Story

A **mystery story** is a fictional tale in which someone solves a crime or unearths the secret behind another puzzling situation. Usually the events center around a conflict in which a detective (or sometimes more than one detective) gathers evidence to solve the crime and discover the identity of the criminal (or criminals). The detective may be an experienced crime solver—private detective, police officer, insurance-company investigator, and so on—or may simply be an everyday person who cleverly manages to solve the crime by following the clues. The American short-story writer Edgar Allan Poe pioneered the mystery story in tales like "The Murders in the Rue Morgue," but it was Sir Arthur Conan Doyle and his detective Sherlock Holmes that really made the form into the popular literature it is today.

DIRECTIONS: Complete this questionnaire to show that "The Adventure of the Speckled Band" is a mystery story.

On what crime do the events center?
Who is the detective that solves the crime?
What is the identity of the culprit?
What method does the culprit use to commit the crime?
What evidence points to the solution?

"A Glow in the Dark" by Gary Paulsen (text page 504)
"Mushrooms" by Sylvia Plath (text page 508)
"Southern Mansion" by Arna Bontemps (text page 510)
"The Bat" by Theodore Roethke (text page 511)

Build Vocabulary

Using the Prefix *a-*

The prefix *a-* can mean "on" or "in." A *miss*, the opposite of a hit, is "a losing or wrong situation," and *amiss* means "in a miss," or "in a wrong way."

A. DIRECTIONS: Complete each sentence with an appropriate word formed by adding the prefix *a-* to one of the five words in italics. Use each word only once.

Words to Use: *glow, lone, sleep, wake, wash*

1. Dozing after the morning run, I fell _____ for four hours.

2. Once I was wide _____ and ready to move on, my head lamp went out.

3. The ground was _____ with puddles, and we were soon dripping wet.

4. The woods were _____ with a dim green-yellow light.

5. Except for the dogs, I was all _____ in the forest.

Using the Word Bank

discreetly	acquire	amiss

B. DIRECTIONS: Unscramble the words in the left column and write them on the lines after the scrambled words. Then match each word with its definition in the right column. Write the letter of the definition on the line before the number.

____ 1. sisma _____   a. to obtain as one's own

____ 2. deetcirlsy _____   b. wrong; not proper

____ 3. quarcei _____   c. carefully and silently

Sentence Completions

C. DIRECTIONS: Complete each sentence with the appropriate word from the Word Bank. Use each word only once.

1. Would she disturb the performance, or could she enter the room _____?

2. Have you had that dress for a long time, or did you _____ it recently?

3. Is everything all right, or is something _____?

"A Glow in the Dark" by Gary Paulsen (text page 504)
"Mushrooms" by Sylvia Plath (text page 508)
"Southern Mansion" by Arna Bontemps (text page 510)
"The Bat" by Theodore Roethke (text page 511)

Build Spelling Skills: Using *acq* and *aq* to Spell the Sound of *ak*

Spelling Strategy   The sound of *ak* has several spellings in English.

- Before a *u*, the *ak* sound is often spelled *acq* or *aq*:

    Examples: acquisition   lacquer   aqua   claque

- Use the *aq* spelling in words containing the root *-aqua-* or *-aque-*, meaning "water":

    Examples: aqua   aquamarine   aqueduct

- Always include the *c* in words containing the prefix *ac-*, meaning "toward" or "to":

    Examples: acquaint   acquisition   acquit

A. Practice: Complete each word by correctly spelling the *ak* sound on the line provided. If you are unsure of a spelling, look in a dictionary.

1. _____ uarium

2. _____ uire

3. _____ uaintance

4. l _____ uered

5. _____ uatic

6. pl _____ ue

7. _____ uisitive

8. _____ uittal

9. ra _____ uetball

B. Practice: On the line after each sentence, write the correct spelling of the italicized word. If the word is already spelled correctly, write *correct*.

1. The Smiths were *ackwainted* _____ with their neighbors.

2. In anticipation of the parade, the children were all *aqwiver* _____.

3. During the season, the track team *aquired* _____ two medals.

4. At camp we learned water-skiing and other *acquatic* _____ sports.

5. We saw many exotic fish at the *aquarium* _____.

Challenge: *Discreet* means "tactful" or "silent"; *discrete* means "separate." However, because the words have the same sound, their spellings are often confused. To remember the distinction, you might remember "The word that means 'separate' has the two *e*'s separate." On the lines below, write definitions of the pairs of words with the same sound. Then try to make up a saying that can help you remember the difference between each pair. This first one is done as an example.

1. discreet: tactful; silent   discrete: separate _____

    Saying: In the word that means "separate", the two e's are separate. _____

2. capital: _____   capitol: _____

    Saying: _____

3. principal: _____   principle: _____

    Saying: _____

"A Glow in the Dark" by Gary Paulsen (text page 504)
"Mushrooms" by Sylvia Plath (text page 508)
"Southern Mansion" by Arna Bontemps (text page 510)
"The Bat" by Theodore Roethke (text page 511)

Build Grammar Skills: Appositive Phrases

An **appositive** is a noun or pronoun placed beside another noun or pronoun to explain or identify it. An **appositive phrase** includes the appositive plus any words or phrases that modify it. In the first sample sentence below, the appositive phrase further identifies the noun *Arna Bontemps*; in the second, the appositive phrase identifies the pronoun *he*; in the third, the appositive phrase explains the noun *imagery*. Notice that appositive phrases can occur at the beginning, in the middle, or at the end of a sentence and are often set off by commas or dashes.

Today we read a poem by Arna Bontemps, <u>the famous African-American poet</u>.

<u>A talented writer</u>, he also worked as a librarian and teacher.

Imagery—<u>language with sensory appeal</u>—is an important ingredient in his poetry.

A. Practice: In the following sentences, underline each appositive phrase and circle the noun or pronoun that it further explains or defines.

1. Arna Bontemps, the noted poet, was born in Louisiana.

2. A graduate of the University of Chicago, Bontemps later was a college professor himself.

3. He was part of the Harlem Renaissance, the flowering of African-American culture in the 1920's.

4. Sylvia Plath, the popular American poet, was born in Boston in 1932.

5. For a time she was married to Ted Hughes, England's recently deceased poet laureate.

6. Plath wrote a novel—*The Bell Jar*—in addition to several poetry collections.

7. Theodore Roethke, one of Plath's influences, was also an American poet.

8. Roethke's father, a nursery owner, raised roses in his greenhouse.

9. Roethke's poems, winners of numerous awards, often contain flower images.

10. The author of more than sixty books, Gary Paulsen often writes about animals.

B. Writing Application: On each line below, write a sentence about the animal indicated. Include an appositive phrase in each sentence. Circle the appositive phrase. One example is given.

1. tarantula: The tarantula, (a large hairy spider,) lives in the desert. _____

2. polar bear: _____

3. bat: _____

4. kangaroo: _____

5. lion: _____

Unit 5: Extraordinary Occurrences

"A Glow in the Dark" by Gary Paulsen (text page 504)
"Mushrooms" by Sylvia Plath (text page 508)
"Southern Mansion" by Arna Bontemps (text page 510)
"The Bat" by Theodore Roethke (text page 511)

Reading Strategy: Make Inferences

As an active reader, it is important for you to **make inferences,** or use clues from the text to determine the writer's message or a line's meaning. For example, consider these details from "A Glow in the Dark":

> There are night ghosts. Some people say that we can understand all things if we can know them, but there came a dark night in the fall when I thought that was wrong, and so did the dogs.

From these details you might **infer,** or figure out, the following:

- The narrator is superstitious.

- The narrator was frightened by his ghostly experience.

- The narrator is pretty close to his dogs.

DIRECTIONS: Choose any of the selections in this grouping. Then, on the chart below, list clues from the selection and the inferences you draw from them.

Selection Title:	
Clues	**Inferences**

"A Glow in the Dark" by Gary Paulsen (text page 504)
"Mushrooms" by Sylvia Plath (text page 508)
"Southern Mansion" by Arna Bontemps (text page 510)
"The Bat" by Theodore Roethke (text page 511)

Literary Focus: Tone

Just as a person speaks in a certain tone of voice, so too does a writer often communicate in a certain tone. The **tone** conveys the writer's attitude toward his or her subject and audience. For example, the tone may be serious, humorous, formal, informal, happy, angry, or sad. Usually, word choice, imagery, and sentence lengths help reveal the writer's tone. For example, in these lines from "A Glow in the Dark," the choppy opening sentences and final one-sentence paragraph, the choice of the word *cold*, and the image of the heart slamming up in the narrator's throat all help to convey a frightened tone.

> It was a form. Not human. A large, standing form glowing in the dark. The light came from within it, a cold-glowing green light with yellow edges that diffused the shape, making it change and grow as I watched.
>
> I felt my heart slam up into my throat.

DIRECTIONS: On the chart below, identify the tone of the three poems in this cluster and the words, images, and/or sentence structures that point toward that tone. If you feel that the tone changes in the poem, indicate both tones and the details that point to them.

Poem	Mushrooms	Southern Mansion	The Bat
Tone(s)			
Word Choice			
Images			
Sentence Structure			

Unit 5: Extraordinary Occurrences

"A Horseman in the Sky" by Ambrose Bierce (text page 515)

Build Vocabulary

Using Words from Mythology and History

Many English words have their origins in the people, places, and objects of mythology or history. For example, *leonine* comes from Leo, the ancient Roman name for the constellation, or group of stars, shaped like a lion. Knowing the origin, you can figure out that when Bierce says "The father lifted his *leonine* head," he means that the father's head was like a lion's.

DIRECTIONS: For each story passage, figure out what the word in italics means by using the context and the information about the word's origins. Circle the letter of the most likely meaning.

1. **Passage:** One sunny afternoon in the autumn of the year 1861 a soldier lay in a clump of *laurel* by the side of a road in western Virginia. **Origin:** Ancient poets were crowned with wreathes called laurels, which were woven from the leaves of a particular tree.

   a. a type of clothing   b. a type of plant   c. a tent   d. cow manure

2. **Passage:** In *silhouette* against the sky the profile of the horse was cut with the sharpness of a cameo. **Origin:** Etienne de Silhouette, a Frenchman, created a type of picture in which a human profile or another shape was shown filled in against a lighter background.

   a. dark outline   b. sunlight   c. a type of jewelry   d. a French dance

3. **Passage:** On a *colossal* pedestal, the cliff,—motionless at the extreme edge of the capping rock and sharply outlined against the sky,—was an equestrian statue of impressive dignity. **Origin:** The Colossus of Rhodes was a giant statue of the Greek god Apollo set up in the entrance to the harbor of ancient Rhodes.

   a. very large   b. unimpressive   c. extremely odd looking   d. hidden from view

Using the Selection Vocabulary

configuration	sentinel	languor	equestrian
eminence	sublimity	mandate	impetuous

B. DIRECTIONS: On the lines provided, write the vocabulary word being defined. The letters in the shaded boxes, reading down, should spell out something that the Civil War divided.

1. arrangement; pattern    _ _ _ _ ▮ _ _ _ _ _ _ _ _

2. lack of interest or energy   _ ▮ _ _ _ _ _ _

3. a command; an order   ▮ _ _ _ _ _ _

4. a high place, thing, or ideal   _ _ ▮ _ _ _ _ _

5. nobility; majesty   _ _ _ ▮ _ _ _ _

6. moving with great force   ▮ _ _ _ _ _ _ _ _

7. on horseback   _ _ _ ▮ _ _ _ _ _ _

8. a guard   ▮ _ _ _ _ _ _

"A Horseman in the Sky" by Ambrose Bierce (text page 515)

Connecting a Story to Social Studies

"A Horseman in the Sky" is a work of **historical fiction,** writing that sets invented characters and their actions against the backdrop of real history. Even though not every detail is factual, a work of historical fiction can provide much information that is factually true and also give you a good overall sense of the times. It may even help crystallize historically important ideas or conflicts that a more accurate nonfictional account could not make as clear and memorable. The best historical fiction portrays its setting with as much accuracy as possible. It is written by someone familiar with the events portrayed, either because he or she has lived through those events or because he or she has carefully researched them.

A. DIRECTIONS: On the chart below, list the details in "A Horseman in the Sky" that you would guess are factually accurate and those that seem invented. Use the information in your textbooks and your other knowledge about the Civil War to help you decide.

Likely Fact	Likely Fiction

B. DIRECTIONS: Reread the biographical information about Ambrose Bierce on page 520 of your text. Then, on the lines provided, explain why you should or should not expect accuracy in Bierce's historical fiction about the Civil War.

_____

_____

_____

_____

"The Dinner Party" by Mona Gardner (text page 535)

Build Vocabulary

Using the Word Root *-spir-*

Spirited contains the root *-spir-*, which means "breath." The word *spirit* refers to whatever breathes life into a living creature, and *spirited* means "lively."

A. Directions: On the line before each statement, write *T* if the statement is probably true or F if it is probably false. Use your knowledge of the root *-spir-* to help you decide.

_____ 1. A *respiratory* disease has no effect on the lungs.

_____ 2. A scene that *inspires* an artist kills the artist's creativity.

_____ 3. Religious songs called *spirituals* are often enthusiastic expressions of faith.

_____ 4. Exercise is likely to make your skin *perspire*.

_____ 5. In a *conspiracy*, people work together on a secret plot or plan.

Using the Word Bank

naturalist	spirited	contracting	arresting	sobers

B. Directions: Match each word in the left column with its definition in the right column. Write the letter of the definition on the line before the word it defines.

_____ 1. arresting   a. one who observes and studies living things

_____ 2. contracting   b. enthusiastic; lively

_____ 3. naturalist   c. causes to become serious

_____ 4. sobers   d. drawing in; tightening

_____ 5. spirited   e. capturing and holding people's attention

Analogies

C. Directions: Circle the letter of the words that express a relationship most like the relationship of the pair of words in capital letters.

1. NATURALIST : SCIENTIST: :
   a. sculptor : artist
   b. plane : pilot
   c. teacher : student
   d. student : pupil
2. SOBERS : SPIRITED : :
   a. likes : loved
   b. jokes : funny
   c. arouses : lively
   d. calms : excited

3. ARRESTING : VOICE : :
   a. loud : color
   b. musical : song
   c. silent : shyness
   d. stopping : start
4. CONTRACTING : EXPANDING : :
   a. signing : agreeing
   b. dragging : pulling
   c. subtracting : adding
   d. multiplying : increasing

Name _____ Date _____

"**The Dinner Party**" by Mona Gardner (text page 535)

Build Spelling Skills: Using Single and Double Consonants

Spelling Strategy   The sound of surrounding vowels can often help you decide whether to use a single or a double consonant.

- A consonant after a long vowel sound is usually not doubled when other letters come after it.

   Examples: ro_b_ust   si_l_ent   hu_m_or

- A consonant after a short vowel sound is often doubled when other letters come after it.

   Examples: ro_bb_er   si_ll_y   hu_mm_ing

A. Practice: Complete each word by correctly inserting one or two of the consonants in parentheses.

1. (b) so _____ er
2. (g) le _____ al
3. (l) ye _____ ow
4. (p) ha _____ y
5. (m) hu _____ id

6. (n) fi _____ al
7. (t) na _____ ure
8. (m) su _____ er
9. (d) hi _____ en
10. (p) pu _____ il

B. Practice: Write the single or double letter that will correctly complete each word so that the statement accurately reflects the story.

1. The story characters are guests at a di _____ er party in India.

2. One guest says that women are not as flu _____ ery as they were in her grandmother's time.

3. Another insists that women still scream in a cri _____ is.

4. The hostess quietly su _____ ons a servant to bring in a bowl of milk.

5. The naturalist reali _____ es that the bowl is for luring a snake away.

6. He sees no snake in the li _____ eliest place, the ceiling rafters.

7. He speaks in an arresting voice that so _____ ers everyone.

8. He makes sure they remain completely still until the snake is lured from under the ta _____ le.

9. The co _____ ra had been on the hostess's foot all along.

10. Her amazing self-control proves the young girl's point in the earlier argu _____ ent about women.

Challenge: Many military ranks have unusual spellings. On the line after each sentence, write the correct spelling of the word in italics. If the word is spelled correctly, write correct.

1. Among the guests in the story was a British *kernel*. _____

2. A *serjent* is of a lower rank. _____

3. On the other hand, a *general* is of a higher rank. _____

4. The British have a strange way of pronouncing the rank of *loutenant*. _____

5. Is a person with the rank of *ensinn* found in the army or in the navy? _____

"The Dinner Party" by Mona Gardner (text page 535)

Build Grammar Skills: Clauses

A clause is a group of words with its own subject and verb. An **independent,** or **main, clause** has a subject and verb and can stand alone as a complete sentence. A **subordinate,** or **dependent, clause** has a subject and verb but cannot stand alone as a complete sentence. The sentence below contains one independent clause, *Four or five screams ring out,* and one subordinate clause, *as he jumps to the door.* In the independent clause, the subject is *screams* and the verb is *ring.* In the subordinate clause, the subject is *he* and the verb is *jumps.*

S   V   S   V
Four or five screams ring out as he jumps to the door.

A. Practice: Put one line under each independent clause and two lines under each subordinate clause. Put an *S* over the subject of each clause and the *V* over the verb.

1. When India was still a colony of Britain, a British couple threw a large dinner party.

2. As the party progressed, a lively debate began.

3. A colonel argued that women are nervous creatures.

4. A young girl argued that the two sexes have equal self-control.

5. The hostess kept her cool as a cobra threatened the group.

6. Since she had remained calm, her behavior ironically proved the young girl's point.

B. Writing Application: Expand these sentences by adding a clause to each. Write the new sentences on the lines provided.

1. A deadly cobra entered the room. _____
_____

2. It snaked around Mrs. Wynnes's foot. _____
_____

3. Mrs. Wynnes recognized the danger. _____
_____

4. She remained calm and perfectly still. _____
_____

5. A bowl of milk lured the snake to the verandah. _____
_____

Reading for Success: Strategies for Reading Fiction

Fiction, which include short stories and novels, is filled with made-up characters and events. Reading a work of fiction is similar to exploring a new world. As you read, your imagination creates a map of this world. The following strategies will help you find your way in a work of fiction.

- **Identify with the characters or the situation.** Put yourself in the characters' place or imagine yourself in their situation.

- **Predict what will happen.** Look for clues to help you predict, or make educated guesses, about how events will unfold. As your read, revise your predictions when you encounter new information.

- **Ask questions about plot, characters, and theme.** Make the reading an active experience by asking questions and trying to answer them as you read. Ask why characters behave as they do, what causes events to happen, or why the writer includes certain information.

- **Make inferences about what you read.** Writers don't always tell you everything directly. You have to make inferences in order to arrive at ideas that are only suggested by writers . You make an inference by considering the details that the writer includes or omits.

DIRECTIONS: Read the following passage from **"The Snow in Chelm"** by Isaac Bashevis Singer, and use the reading strategies to increase your comprehension. In the margin, note where you identify with the characters or the situation; predict what will happen; ask questions about plot, characters, and theme; and make inferences about what you read. Finally, write your response to the selection on the lines provided.

from **"The Snow in Chelm"** by Isaac Bashevis Singer

The following passage describes a town's efforts to collect a fleeting treasure.

Chelm was a village of fools, fools young and old. One night someone spied the moon reflected in a barrel of water. The people of Chelm imagined it had fallen in. They sealed the barrel so that the moon would not escape. When the barrel was opened in the morning and the moon wasn't there, the villagers decided that it had been stolen. They sent for the police, and when the thief couldn't be found, the fools of Chelm cried and moaned.

Of all the fools of Chelm, the most famous were its seven Elders. Because they were the village's oldest and greatest fools, they ruled in Chelm. They had white beards and high foreheads from too much thinking.

Once, on a Hanukkah night, the snow fell all evening. It covered all of Chelm like a silver tablecloth. The moon shone; the stars twinkled; the snow shimmered like pearls and diamonds.

That evening the seven Elders were sitting and pondering, wrinkling their foreheads. The village was in need of money, and they did not know where to get it. Suddenly the oldest of them all, Gronam the Great Fool, exclaimed, "The snow is silver!"

"I see pearls in the snow!" another shouted.

"And I see diamonds!" a third called out.

It became clear to the Elders of Chelm that a treasure had fallen from the sky.

But soon they began to worry. The people of Chelm liked to go walking, and they would most certainly trample the treasure. What was to be done? Silly Tudras had an idea.

"Let's send a messenger to knock on all the windows and let the people know that they must remain in their houses until all the silver, all the pearls, and all the diamonds are safely gathered up."

For a while the Elders were satisfied. They rubbed their hands in approval of the clever idea. But then Dopey Lekisch called out in consternation, "The messenger himself will trample the treasure."

The Elders realized that Lekisch was right, and again they wrinkled their high foreheads in an effort to solve the problem.

"I've got it!" exclaimed Shmerel the Ox.

"Tell us, tell us," pleaded the Elders.

"The messenger must not go on foot. He must be carried on a table so that his feet will not tread on the precious snow."

Everybody was delighted with Shmerel the Ox's solution; and the Elders, clapping their hands, admired their own wisdom.

The Elders immediately sent to the kitchen for Gimpel the errand boy and stood him on a table. Now who was going to carry the table? It was lucky that in the kitchen there were Treitle the cook, Berel the potato peeler, Yukel the salad mixer, and Yontel, who was in charge of the community goat. All four were ordered to lift up the table on which Gimpel stood. Each one took hold of a leg. On top stood Gimpel, grasping a wooden hammer with which to tap on the villagers' windows. Off they went.

At each window Gimpel knocked with the hammer and called out, "No one leaves the house tonight. A treasure has fallen from the sky, and it is forbidden to step on it."

The people of Chelm obeyed the Elders and remained in their houses all night. Meanwhile the Elders themselves sat up trying to figure out how to make the best use of the treasure once it had been gathered up.

Silly Tudras proposed that they sell it and buy a goose which lays golden eggs. Thus the community would be provided with a steady income.

Dopey Lekisch had another idea. Why not buy eyeglasses that make things look bigger for all the inhabitants of Chelm? Then the houses, the streets, the stores would all look bigger, and of course if Chelm *looked* bigger then it *would be* bigger. It would no longer be a village, but a big city.

There were other, equally clever ideas. But while the Elders were weighing their various plans, morning came and the sun rose. They looked out of the window, and, alas, they saw the snow had been trampled. The heavy boots of the table carriers had destroyed the treasure.

The Elders of Chelm clutched at their white beards and admitted to one another that they had made a mistake. Perhaps, they reasoned, four others should have carried the four men who had carried the table that held Gimpel the errand boy.

After long deliberations the Elders decided that if next Hanukkah a treasure would again fall down from the sky, that is exactly what they would do.

Although the villagers remained without a treasure, they were full of hope for the next year and praised their Elders, who they knew could always be counted on to find a way, no matter how difficult the problem.

_____

_____

_____

_____

"The Dinner Party" by Mona Gardner (text page 535)

Literary Focus: Plot

Plot refers to a story's sequence of events, with one event leading into the next. The events usually center around a **conflict,** or struggle between opposing forces. In a typical plot, the conflict is explained in an opening section called the **exposition,** which also introduces the story's chief characters and setting. After the exposition, events forming the **rising action** develop the conflict, usually by adding complications. The rising action leads to a **climax,** where the conflict reaches the point of greatest tension. After the climax, the conflict is resolved—in one way or another—in the **falling action.**

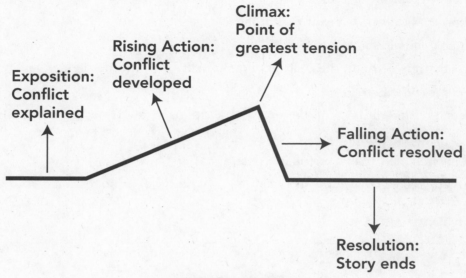

PLOT DIAGRAM

DIRECTIONS: In the second column of this chart, briefly explain the events or details that make up the four main sections of the plot in "The Dinner Party." Then, in the last column, do the same for any other story in your textbook.

Portion of Plot	"The Dinner Party"	Story Title:
Exposition		
Rising Action		
Climax		
Falling Action		

"The Tell-Tale Heart" by Edgar Allan Poe (text page 542)

Build Vocabulary

Using the Word Root *-found-*

The word root *-found-*, sometimes spelled *-fund-*, means "bottom." Something or someone *profound* comes from the bottom depths—or, in other words, is very deep.

A. DIRECTIONS: Circle the letter of the choice that best completes each sentence.

1. A teacher of great *profundity* is very ____.

   a. shallow   b. deep   c. witty   d. strict

2. A building's *foundation* is located ____.

   a. at the bottom   b. on the roof   c. on the left   d. on the right

3. America's *founders* are ____.

   a. its recent immigrants   b. its future generations   c. those who established the
   nation   d. its historians

4. A *fundamental* principle of chemistry is one that is ____.

   a. still being tested   b. undiscovered   c. basic   d. unimportant

Using the Word Bank

acute	dissimulation	profound	sagacity
crevice	gesticulations	derision	

B. DIRECTIONS: Match the words in the right column with their definitions on the left.

____ 1. deep   a. acute

____ 2. contempt; ridicule   b. sagacity

____ 3. wise understanding   c. crevice

____ 4. hand movements   d. derision

____ 5. the act of pretending   e. gesticulations

____ 6. sharpened   f. profound

____ 7. slit   g. dissimulation

Recognizing Synonyms

C. DIRECTIONS: Circle the letter of the words that is most nearly the same in meaning as the word in capital letters.

1. ACUTE:	2. CREVICE:	3. DERISION:	4. DISSIMULATION:
a. sharp	a. light	a. origin	a. reality
b. dull	b. squeak	b. idea	b. pretense
c. attractive	c. fish	c. insult	c. contrast
d. hideous	d. crack	d. prediction	d. destruction

Name _____ Date _____

"The Tell-Tale Heart" by Edgar Allan Poe (text page 542)

Build Spelling Skills: Using *sion* to Spell the Sound *zhun*

Spelling Strategy   Many English nouns end in the sound of *zhun*.

- In general, use *sion* to spell the *zhun* sound:

    Examples: allu<u>sion</u>   inci<u>sion</u>   inva<u>sion</u>   provi<u>sion</u>

- The letters *sion* may also spell the sound of *shun*, especially when the *s* is doubled:

    Examples: pa<u>ssion</u>   permi<u>ssion</u>   revul<u>sion</u>   se<u>ssion</u>

A. Practice: On the line after each sentence, write the correct spelling of the italicized word. If the word is already spelled correctly, write *correct*.

1. The main character in Poe's story has trouble separating *illution* and reality. _____

2. He commits a crime of great *revultion*. _____

3. At first, his *evajion* of the law seems successful. _____

4. Then comes the *intrudjion* of the victim's heartbeat. _____

5. The *deluzion* grows stronger and stronger. _____

6. He thinks the officers hear it too and accuses them of *derizion*. _____

7. Finally he can take it no more, and he makes a *confession*. _____

B. Practice: Complete each sentence by filling in a form of the word in parentheses.

1. (precise) Edgar Allan Poe chose his words with great _____.

2. (revise) A careful writer, he spent much time on _____.

3. (collide) Some of his descriptions are so long that there is almost a _____ of images.

4. (divide) There is no real _____ between his horror tales and his mysteries.

5. (televise) Several of his tales have been adapted for the movies and _____.

Challenge: Edgar Allan Poe may be the American author whose name is most often misspelled. It's not the *Edgar* or the *Poe* that causes trouble, but the *Allan*, which is often misspelled as *Allen* or *Alan*. On the lines provided, correctly spell the names of these famous authors. If the name is spelled correctly, write *correct*. Check your answers in a dictionary or another reference.

1. Emily Dickenson _____

2. Gwendoline Brooks _____

3. Carl Sandberg _____

4. Edward Arlington Robinson _____

5. Earnest Hemmingway _____

6. Arthur Conen Doyle _____

Name _____ Date _____

Build Grammar Skills: Adverb Clauses

An **adverb clause** is a subordinate clause that functions as an adverb, modifying a verb, an adjective, or another adverb. Adverb clauses generally tell *when, where, how, why, to what extent*, or *under what conditions*. In the sentences below, the first adverb clause tells why; the second tells when.

Poe's insane narrator kills the old man <u>because the man's eye resembles a vulture's.</u>

<u>After the narrator murders his victim,</u> he still hears the victim's heart beating.

Adverb clauses begin with **subordinating conjunctions** that help connect them to the rest of the sentence. Below is a list of common subordinating conjunctions. Note that many of them can also be used as prepositions or other parts of speech.

after	as soon as	even though	so that	when	whether
although	as though	even if	though	whenever	while
as	because	if	unless	where	
as long as	before	since	until	wherever	

A. Practice: In each of these sentences, underline the adverb clause, and circle the subordinating conjunction.

1. If Poe's stories and poetry focus on the dark side of life, it should come as no surprise.

2. Poe probably wrote of life's horrors because his own life was so horrible.

3. The son of poor actors, Poe traveled with them until his alcoholic father deserted the family.

4. When his mother died a short time later, young Poe was taken in by the Allans of Virginia.

5. Even though the Allans gave Poe a comfortable home, Mr. Allan refused to adopt him.

6. As Poe got older, he often quarreled with his stepfather, usually about money.

7. After the two broke all ties, Poe struggled for financial success as a writer.

8. Although he won fame fairly early in life, he earned very little for his efforts.

B. Writing Application: Expand these sentences about the story by adding adverb clauses that tell *when, where, how, why, to what extent*, or *under what conditions*. Write the new sentences on the lines provided.

1. The narrator sounds pretty crazy to the reader. _____

_____

2. He kills the old man. _____

_____

3. He hides the body. _____

_____

4. He imagines the old man's heartbeat. _____

_____

"The Tell-Tale Heart" by Edgar Allan Poe (text page 542)

Reading Strategy: Predict

Writers build suspense by making you wonder about future story events. As you read, you try to **predict**, or make reasonable guesses about, what will happen next and what will happen in the end. Here are some tips on what to consider when you make predictions.

- Consider characters' personalities, motives, and attitudes.

- Consider the events that have already occurred and the likely results of those events.

- Consider the setting and the events likely to occur in such a setting.

- Pay special attention to any **foreshadowing** in which the narrator makes statements that seem to hint at what is going to happen.

- Consider the themes or world view that the writer is trying to convey.

- Consider any outside knowledge you have about the author's life or the kind of writing he or she often does.

- Consider any outside knowledge you have about similar human behavior and experiences in real life or in novels, movies, and other works of fiction.

DIRECTIONS: Now that you know the clues to look for, fill in this chart to predict events in Poe's story. Also be sure to indicate whether your prediction is proved true or false.

Author's Clue	My Prediction
narrator remarks ". . . why <u>will</u> you say that I am mad?"	We'll find out that he <u>is</u> mad. Proved True _____ False _____
	Proved True _____ False _____
	Proved True _____ False _____
	Proved True _____ False _____
	Proved True _____ False _____

Name _____ Date _____

Literary Focus: Suspense in a Plot

Did you ever stay up late to finish a novel or see the end of a TV movie? Chances are, the book you were reading or movie you were watching was strong on suspense. **Suspense** is a feeling of uncertainty about future events that keeps you interested in a story's plot. Though suspense is particularly strong in mysteries, adventures, and horror tales, just about every story needs some suspense to keep readers reading. Here are some ways that writers build suspense:

- The writer adds more and more complications to the plot.

- The writer drops hints about future events and the final outcome.

- The writer delays an event that you know is coming.

- The writer makes you care about the characters and wonder what their future holds.

DIRECTIONS: On the chart below, identify points or passages in "The Tell-Tale Heart" that you found the most suspenseful—that is, points or passages where you wondered most about future events in the story. In the right column, try to explain what the writer did to get you so interested.

Suspenseful Point of Passage	Explanation of the Suspense

"An Episode of War" by Stephen Crane (text page 551)

Build Vocabulary

Using the Prefix *pre-*

Precipitate contains the prefix *pre-*, which means "before." To *precipitate* is "to cause something to happen *before* it is expected or desired."

A. DIRECTIONS: Add *pre-* to five words in the list to form new words that best complete the sentences below. Then, for the two words in the word list that you have left over, add *pre-* and use the new words in sentences on the lines provided.

determined   game   fix   historic   school   set   test

1. A _____ is a word part that you attach before the main part of the word.

2. A _____ checks what students know about a subject before the subject is taught.

3. When a dial is _____, someone else has already adjusted it to the correct position.

4. If the outcome of a contest is _____, the result was decided beforehand.

5. A dinosaur is a _____ creature.

6. (your sentence) _____

7. (your sentence) _____

Using the Word Bank

precipitate	aggregation	inscrutable	disdainfully

B. DIRECTIONS: Circle the letter of the choice that best answers each question.

1. Of the following, which would be most likely to *precipitate* a war?

a. a peace treaty   b. a cultural exchange   c. sensational journalism   d. a history book

2. What would you expect to find at an *aggregation* of soldiers?

a. an empty room   b. a diverse group   c. a memorial   d. a lack of patriotism

3. Which of the following would you be most likely to describe as *inscrutable*?

a. a puzzling ritual   b. an emotional actress   c. a popular TV show   d. an easy history test

4. Of the following people, who would you most expect to behave *disdainfully*?

a. a kindhearted neighbor   b. a shy teenager   c. a sympathetic doctor   d. an arrogant princess

Recognizing Synonyms

C. DIRECTIONS: Circle the letter of the word that is most nearly the same in meaning as the word in CAPITAL LETTERS.

1. DISDAINFULLY:
   a. wistfully
   b. meekly
   c. loudly
   d. scornfully

2. INSCRUTABLE:
   a. mysterious
   b. nervous
   c. unquestionable
   d. unkind

3. PRECIPITATE:
   a. explain
   b. question
   c. cause
   d. explode

4. AGGREGATION:
   a. collection
   b. invention
   c. friendliness
   d. loneliness

"An Episode of War" by Stephen Crane (text page 551)

Connecting Historical Fiction to Social Studies

"An Episode of War" is an example of **war literature**, which is literature about human warfare and those involved in the fighting. War literature includes works of nonfiction as well as fiction set against the backdrop of historical fact. "An Episode of War," for example, is a work of fiction set against the historical backdrop of the Civil War. Though Stephen Crane was too young to have fought in that war, he researched it carefully, interviewing many Civil War veterans for their impressions.

Most war literature falls into two categories—works that glorify war, exaggerating its heroism and downplaying its deadly violence; and works that portray war much more realistically and grimly. Overlapping with the second category is a third, **antiwar literature**, which may be realistic or may even exaggerate the negative aspects of war in order to convey a message against it.

A. DIRECTIONS: On the chart below, list the details in Crane's story that either glorify war, portray it realistically, or criticize it.

Glorify	Portray Realistically	Criticize

B. DIRECTIONS: Would you classify "An Episode of War" and war literature that glorifies war, condemns it, or simply paints it realistically? Answer on the lines provided, and use details you listed on the chart above to explain your answer.

_____

_____

_____

_____

_____

"The Day I Got Lost" by Isaac Bashevis Singer (page 559)
"Hamadi" by Naomi Shihab Nye (page 562)

Build Vocabulary

Using the Word Root *-chol-*

Melancholy contains the root *-chol-*, which comes from the Greek word for the body fluid known as bile. In times past, an excess of bile was thought to make people feel ill and unhappy. A melancholy person is one who is full of bile, or "sad and gloomy."

A. DIRECTIONS: On the line before each statement, write *T* if you think the statement is true. Write *F* if you think it is false. Use your knowledge of the root *-chol-* to help you decide.

_____ 1. A *melancholic* person is a cheerful soul.

_____ 2. The disease called *cholera* is probably very serious.

_____ 3. Food high in *cholesterol* is usually very healthy.

_____ 4. In the mental disease called *melancholia*, the patient often giggles uncontrollably.

Using the Word Bank

eternal	forsaken	pandemonium	brittle	lavish	refugees	melancholy

B. DIRECTIONS: Hidden in this puzzle are the seven words from the Word Bank. Find and circle the words. Then, alongside the puzzle, rewrite each word on the line next to its definition.

```
T M U I N O M E D N A P
S E M S E E G U F E R K
B L L K C R E J T K E V
P A A L A I M E D A O R
E N T V S E R R U S B M
W C S M I N Y D O R H A
V H L G A S N A I O A O
Q O N L A M H T T F C L
A L T R E A T G M I U N
P Y C N I L L H A Z N B
N S F E E X C B V O L I
```

1. abandoned: _____

2. unhappy: _____

3. people seeking safety: _____

4. abundant; extravagant: _____

5. total confusion: _____

6. everlasting: _____

7. easily chipped: _____

C. DIRECTIONS: Circle the letter of the word most opposite of the word in CAPITAL LETTERS.

1. PANDEMONIUM:
   a. confusion
   b. childhood
   c. welcome
   d. calm

2. ETERNAL:
   a. temporary
   b. tempting
   c. religious
   d. pale

3. BRITTLE:
   a. dry
   b. stubborn
   c. pliant
   d. shelled

4. FORSAKEN:
   a. unforgiven
   b. nurtured
   c. melancholy
   d. exaggerated

5. LAVISH:
   a. elegant
   b. colorful
   c. carefree
   d. spare

"The Day I Got Lost" by Isaac Bashevis Singer (page 559)
"Hamadi" by Naomi Shihab Nye (page 562)

Build Spelling Skills: Spelling the Unstressed *ul* Sound After *f*, *g*, and *t*

Spelling Strategy   The sound of an unstressed *ul* has several spellings when it comes at the end of a word.

- In general, use a final *le* after a double *t*, *g*, or *f* and after a single *f*.

  Examples: ke<u>ttle</u>   snu<u>ggle</u>   ba<u>ffle</u>   ri<u>fle</u>

- After a single *t* or *g*, you might use *el* or *al* as well as *le*.

  Examples: bu<u>gle</u>   ba<u>gel</u>   le<u>gal</u>   ti<u>tle</u>   lin<u>tel</u>   me<u>tal</u>

A. Practice: On the lines provided, correctly complete each word by writing *le*, *el*, or *al* to spell the final unstressed *ul* sound.

1. britt _____

2. raff _____

3. wigg _____

4. batt _____

5. pet _____

6. ting _____

7. reg _____

8. stif _____

9. waff _____

10. whist _____

11. gigg _____

12. beet _____

13. finag _____

14. ang _____ or ang _____

15. recit _____

B. Practice: On the line after each sentence, write the correct spelling of the word in italics. If the word is spelled correctly, write *correct*.

1. Isaac Bashevis Singer was one of many European Jews to *resettill* in America. _____

2. They came from big cities and *little* villages all over eastern Europe. _____

3. They helped make New York's Lower East Side a *vitle*, thriving community. _____

4. Among the new foods they introduced were the *bagle* and the knish. _____

5. The neighborhood was full of street venders with whom shoppers could *haggel*. _____

Challenge: Like *melancholy*, many other words from Greek use *ch* to spell the *k* sound. For each item below, guess the word being defined and spell it correctly on the lines provided.

1. a group of singers in a church: __ __ __ __ R

2. a chemical used to keep water in swimming pools free of germs: __ __ __ __ __ __ N E

3. a person who repairs cars: M E __ __ __ __ __ __

4. someone who designs buildings: __ __ __ __ __ T E C T

5. a king or a queen: M O N __ __ __ __

"The Day I Got Lost" by Isaac Bashevis Singer (page 559)
"Hamadi" by Naomi Shihab Nye (page 562)

Build Grammar Skills: Adjective Clause

An **adjective clause** is a subordinate clause that functions as an adjective, modifying a noun or a pronoun. In the first sentence below, the adjective clause *that European Jews spoke* modifies the noun *language*; in the second, the adjective clause *which is spoken in Israel* modifies the noun *Hebrew*.

The language <u>that European Jews spoke</u> is called Yiddish.

It is a very different language from Hebrew, <u>which is spoken in Israel</u>.

Adjective clauses usually begin with **relative pronouns** that relate them to the rest of the sentence and often serve as subjects or objects in the clauses they introduce. The five relative pronouns commonly used to open adjective clauses are listed below.

that   which   who   whom   whose

A. Practice: In each sentence, underline the adjective clause and circle the relative pronoun. Put two lines under the noun or pronoun that the clause modifies.

1. Yiddish, which comes from German, was the daily language of most European Jews.

2. The Hebrew that they used in synagogue was reserved for religious ceremony, not daily life.

3. Because of persecution, many of those who spoke Yiddish fled their homelands for America.

4. Others were killed in the Holocaust, which claimed millions of European Jewish lives.

5. Americans whose background is Jewish often sprinkle their English with Yiddish words.

6. However, those who speak and write Yiddish have steadily declined in number.

7. Isaac Bashevis Singer, who wrote in Yiddish, often translated his own works into English.

8. Had he not done so, the audience that he reached would have been very small.

B. Writing Application: Expand these sentences about "Hamadi" by adding adjective clauses. Write the new sentences on the lines provided.

1. Saleh Hamadi was a Lebanese immigrant to America. _____
_____

2. Kahlil Gibran was a famous writer born in the Middle East. _____
_____

3. Susan lived in Jerusalem until she was ten. _____
_____

4. She deeply admired Kahlil Gibran's writing. _____
_____

5. Her interest led to a friendship with Hamadi. _____
_____

"The Day I Got Lost" by Isaac Bashevis Singer (page 559)
"Hamadi" by Naomi Shihab Nye (page 562)

Reading Strategy: Identify with a Character

Often you will appreciate a story more if you identify with one or more of the characters in it. To identify with characters, think about what you may have in common with them, and compare their situations to situations in your own life. Also try to experience the characters' interests, joys, and sorrows as if they were your own.

DIRECTIONS: As you read the two stories in this grouping, try to identify with at least one character in each. You might organize your ideas on a diagram like this one.

Story Title: "The Day I Got Lost"	**Name of Character:**
Character's Reactions:	**My Reactions:**
Character's Situations:	**My Similar Situations:**
Story Title: "Hamadi"	**Name of Character:**
Character's Reactions:	**My Reactions:**
Character's Situations:	**My Similar Situations:**

"**The Day I Got Lost**" by Isaac Bashevis Singer (page 559)
"**Hamadi**" by Naomi Shihab Nye (page 562)

Literary Focus: Direct and Indirect Characters

Characterization refers to the process by which authors create memorable characters. Most authors use a combination of direct and indirect characterization. In **direct characterization**, the author includes direct statements telling you what a character is like:

Old Mrs. Bates was a nasty, miserly creature.

In **indirect characterization**, the character's personality is revealed through details about his or her appearance, speech, actions, and relationships with other characters:

With her sneering lips and beady eyes, old Mrs. Bates carefully added up her bill at the diner. "Don't you dare charge me one penny more than I owe," she barked to the young waiter.

DIRECTIONS: On the chart below, list details about the characterization of the professor in "The Day I Got Lost" or one of the characters in "Hamadi." Indicate whether each detail is direct or indirect characterization, and explain what it reveals about the character's personality and attitudes. Be sure to identify the character on the line provided.

Story Character:		
Detail	**Direct or Indirect?**	**What It States or Reveals**

"The Finish of Patsy Barnes" by Paul Laurence Dunbar (page 580)
"Tears of Autumn" by Yochiko Uchida (page 586)

Build Vocabulary

Using the Word Part *-fluence*

The word part *-fluence* is a form of the root *-flu-*, which means "flow." *Affluence*, which means "wealth," comes from the idea of money or goods flowing into someone's possession.

A. DIRECTIONS: Circle the letter of the choice that best completes each sentence. Use your understanding of the root *-flu-* to help you figure out the answers.

1. _____ is an example of a *fluid*.

   a. Water   b. A diamond   c. Iron   d. A briefcase

2. A person *fluent* in a language _____ .

   a. cannot read it   b. cannot speak it   c. knows it well   d. has just begun studying it

3. Things _____ when they are in a state of *flux*.

   a. always improve   b. never improve   c. change   d. are perfectly clear

Using the Word Bank

compulsory	meager	obdurate	diplomatic
turbulent	affluence	degrading	

B. DIRECTIONS: Complete these sentences with an appropriate word from the Word Bank. Use each word only once.

1. After the death of Patsy's father, the family finances were very _____.

2. Patsy was _____ about working at the stable, even though his mother protested.

3. Some might find sweeping the stable a _____ job, but Patsy loved it.

4. Since school was _____, a truant officer made sure that Patsy attended.

5. Not being _____, Patsy showed little tact when he insisted on riding in the race.

6. The enormously exciting race came to a _____ finish with Patsy the winner.

7. Patsy's winnings as a jockey gave his family a bit more _____.

Recognizing Synonyms

C. DIRECTIONS: Circle the letter of the words that is most nearly the same in meaning as the word in CAPITAL LETTERS.

1. DEGRADING:
   a. marking
   b. raising
   c. fascinating
   d. insulting

2. OBDURATE:
   a. stubborn
   b. cheerful
   c. temporary
   d. unpleasant

3. DIPLOMATIC:
   a. foreign
   b. elected
   c. educated
   d. tactful

"**The Finish of Patsy Barnes**" by Paul Laurence Dunbar (page 580)
"**Tears of Autumn**" by Yochiko Uchida (page 586)

Build Spelling Skills: Spelling the Long e Sound *ea*

Spelling Strategy   The sound of long e has several spellings in English.

- The letters *ea* are sometimes used to spell the sound of long *e*.

   Examples: dr<u>ea</u>m   n<u>ea</u>r   r<u>ea</u>son

- Other common spellings for the long e sound include *e, ee, ei, ie, i, ey,* and *y*.

   Examples: b<u>e</u>   bl<u>ee</u>d   rec<u>ei</u>ve   gr<u>ie</u>f   cur<u>i</u>ous   jock<u>ey</u>   cit<u>y</u>

A. Practice: Complete each word by writing the letter or letters that correctly spell the long *e* sound. All of the words appear in one of the two stories in this grouping.

1. m _____ g e r	6. ar _____ na	11. compulsor _____	16. _____ qual
2. f _____ ld	7. misd _____ d	12. mon _____	17. br _____ thed
3. dis _____ se	8. appr _____ ciate	13. degr _____ s	18. _____ gerness
4. app _____ l	9. sl _____ ve	14. _____ r _____	19. conc _____ led
5. v _____ hicle	10. qu _____ sy	15. rel _____ sed	20. _____ s _____ er

B. Practice: Circle the word that correctly completes each sentence.

1. Hana Omiya stood at the railing and watched the (sea, see) lap against the ship.

2. She had already been traveling for more than a (weak, week).

3. She had never crossed the (seas, seize) before.

4. She was scared, and her body (seamed, seemed) leaden and lifeless.

5. Her heart (beat, beet) loudly in her chest.

6. She had read Taro's letters, trying to find the (real, reel) man somewhere in the sparse prose.

7. In none of those letters did he disclose his loneliness or his (knead, need).

8. Soon she would (meat, meet) him in San Francisco.

9. He would take her to friends for (tea, tee).

10. But what would he (be, bee) like?

"The Finish of Patsy Barnes" by Paul Laurence Dunbar (page 580)
"Tears of Autumn" by Yochiko Uchida (page 586)

Build Grammar Skills: Simple and Compound Sentences

As you know, a **clause** is a group of words with its own subject and verb. A **simple sentence** consists of just one independent clause. A **compound sentence** consists of two or more independent clauses joined by a coordinating conjunction (usually *and, but, or, nor,* or *for*) or a semicolon (;).

                       S   V
Simple Sentence: Patsy grew up in Kentucky.

                                  S   V   S   V
Compound Sentence: Patsy grew up in Kentucky, but his family later moved north.

                                  S   V   S   V
Compound Sentence: Patsy grew up in Kentucky; his family later moved north.

A. Practice: On the line before each sentence, write *S* if it is a simple sentence and *C* if it is compound sentence. In each clause, underline the subject once and the verb twice.

_____ 1. Patsy's father had worked as a horse trainer in Kentucky.

_____ 2. An accident with a fiery young horse had killed Patsy's father, but Patsy still loved horses.

_____ 3. Up north, far from Kentucky, his mother struggled financially.

_____ 4. Patsy went to school grudgingly; he spent all his spare time at a nearby stable.

_____ 5. Despite his age, he exercised the horses regularly.

_____ 6. Then his mother caught pneumonia, and an incompetent doctor treated her.

_____ 7. Patsy needed money for a better doctor, or his mother might die.

_____ 8. Just around that time, a man from Kentucky brought a dangerous horse to the stable.

_____ 9. That very same horse had killed Patsy's father, but Patsy rode it anyway.

_____ 10. He won the race and used the money for the doctor's fees.

B. Writing Application: For each item, combine the two simple sentences in a single compound sentence using the conjunction or punctuation in parentheses. Write your new sentences on the lines provided.

1. (but) Hana's family had once been rich. Then her father died.

_____

2. (nor) She would not enjoy marriage to an Osaka merchant. A poor farmer would not satisfy her.

_____

3. (or) She could lead a dull life in Japan. She could go to America.

_____

4. (and) Japanese men in America often found brides back home. She sent one her photo.

_____

5. (;) She nervously traveled by ship to America. They would meet and marry in San Francisco.

_____

Name _____ Date _____

"The Finish of Patsy Barnes" by Paul Laurence Dunbar (page 580)

"Tears of Autumn" by Yochiko Uchida (page 586)

Reading Strategy: Ask Questions

When you read a story, you'll probably understand it better if you **ask questions** about the characters, events, and other details and then keep reading to see if you figure out the answers. For example, consider the opening sentence from "Tears of Autumn":

> Hana Omiya stood at the railing of the small ship that shuddered toward America in a turbulent November sea.

Here are some questions you might ask after reading this sentence:

> Who is Hana Omiya?

> Why is she going to America?

> Where in America is she going?

At times, you won't be able to answer your questions simply by reading further. Instead you will need to check outside sources. For instance, in reading "Tears of Autumn," you might have to check with your teacher, with a Japanese-American friend, or in a reference work or another nonfiction book for answers to questions about Japanese customs or the once common practice of seeking mail-order brides.

DIRECTIONS: Use this chart to record questions you ask as you read "Tears of Autumn" and your answers to those questions. In answering the questions, include reasonable guesses. Check outside sources if necessary.

Questions:	Answers:
Who is Hana Omiya?	She is a young woman who grew up in Japan and is now going to America.
Why is she going to America?	

"The Finish of Patsy Barnes" by Paul Laurence Dunbar (page 580)
"Tears of Autumn" by Yochiko Uchida (page 586)

Literary Focus: Setting

Setting is the time and place in which a work occurs. In creating a setting, the author usually provides many details about the time and place, not only to help us picture the setting but also to help us understand it better. For example, Paul Laurence Dunbar tells us several details about the fairgrounds in Dalesford and about African Americans and white Americans there so that we can understand the Barnes's situation in that community at the time "The Finish of Patsy Barnes" takes place.

DIRECTIONS: "Tears of Autumn" is set decades ago—probably in the early twentieth century—in Japan, in the Japanese-American community of California, and on a ship traveling between them. On the diagram below, list details that help you picture and understand the three settings.

```
    ( Japan )          ( ship )        ( California
       |                  |            Japanese-American
       ↓                  ↓              community )
                                             |
                                             ↓
_____   _____   _____
_____   _____   _____
_____   _____   _____
_____   _____   _____
_____   _____   _____
_____   _____   _____
_____   _____   _____
_____   _____   _____
_____   _____   _____
_____   _____   _____
_____   _____   _____
_____   _____   _____
_____   _____   _____
_____   _____   _____
```

Name _____ Date _____

"The Story-Teller" by Saki (H. H. Munro) (text page 597)
"The Medicine Bag" by Virginia Driving Hawk Sneve (text page 602)

Build Vocabulary

Using the Suffix *-less*

The suffix *-less*, which forms adjectives, means "without." Sometimes it combines with word parts to create English words: *list-* ("desire; wish") + *-less* = *listless*, "without desire." More often it combines with English nouns: *life* + *-less* = *lifeless*, "without life."

A. DIRECTIONS: Complete each sentence with an adjective formed by adding the suffix *-less* to the noun in parentheses.

1. (meaning) At first the boy thought his grandfather's customs were _____.

2. (time) Later he realized they were _____.

3. (root) Without a heritage, a person can feel _____.

4. (home) With a heritage, a person is never _____.

Using the Word Bank

bachelor	resolute	listlessly	punctuality
stately	rumpled	reluctantly	

B. DIRECTIONS: On the lines next to each definition below, write the word being defined. Then spell out the secret message by filling in the same letters on the lines with corresponding numbers.

Secret Message: __ __ __ __ __ __ __ __ __ __ __ __ __ __ __ __ __ __ __ __ __ __ __
                     1 2 3 4   5 6 1 2   7   8 9 10 4   8 11 4 12 4 13 4 12 4   7

__ __ __ __ __ __ __ __ __ __ __ __ __ __ __ __ __
15 7 16 15 1 17   7 2 16   8 13 1 15 7 16 18 9 12 19 20

1. firm of purpose: __ __ __ __ __ __ __ __
                     12 4 20 1 19 5 8 4

2. in an unenergetic manner: __ __ __ __ __ __ __ __ __ __
                               19 9 20 8 19 4 20 20 19 17

3. the quality of being on time: __ __ __ __ __ __ __ __ __ __ __
                                   6 5 2 3 8 5 7 19 9 8 17

4. an unmarried man: __ __ __ __ __ __ __ __
                      15 7 3 11 4 19 1 12

5. unwillingly: __ __ __ __ __ __ __ __ __ __ __
                12 4 19 5 3 8 7 2 8 19 17

6. messy; creased: __ __ __ __ __ __ __
                    12 5 10 6 19 4 16

7. elegant: __ __ __ __ __ __ __
            20 8 7 8 4 19 17

"**The Story-Teller**" by Saki (H. H. Munro) (text page 597)
"**The Medicine Bag**" by Virginia Driving Hawk Sneve (text page 602)

Build Spelling Skills: Using *or* to Spell the Unstressed Final *ur* Sound

Spelling Strategy   The sound of an unstressed *ur* at the end of a word has several spellings.

- In general, use *or*, *er*, or sometimes *ar* in nouns formed from verbs:

  Examples: direct [arrow] direct<u>or</u>   broil [arrow] broil<u>er</u>   beg [arrow] beg<u>gar</u>

- Use *er* to spell the final unstressed *ur* sound in comparative adjectives:

  Examples: cold<u>er</u>   nic<u>er</u>   pretti<u>er</u>   bett<u>er</u>   farth<u>er</u>   furth<u>er</u>

- In most other cases, use *or*, *er*, or, occasionally, *ar* for the final unstressed *ur* sound:

  Examples: horr<u>or</u>   mot<u>or</u>   pri<u>or</u>   wav<u>er</u>   form<u>er</u>   forev<u>er</u>   mol<u>ar</u>

  Exceptions: aug<u>ur</u>, glam<u>our</u>, murm<u>ur</u>, sat<u>yr</u>

A. Practice: Complete each word by correctly spelling the final unstressed *ur* sound. All of the words appear in the selections in this grouping.

1. corn __
2. bachel __
3. moth __
4. charact__
5. murm __

6. flick __
7. fav __
8. behavi __
9. hon __
10. answ __

11. clev __
12. col __
13. supp__
14. neighb __
15. doct __

16. leath __
17. warri __
18. coll __
19. soldi __
20. should __

B. Practice: Complete each sentence by turning the verb in parentheses into a noun.

1. (visit) A _____ to the train compartment would have been shocked by the noise.

2. (rescue) The man longed for a _____ to remove him from the noisy scene.

3. (conduct) He wished the _____ would come along and change his seat.

4. (listen) Not one of the children was a good _____ .

5. (tell) The aunt was a very poor _____ of stories.

6. (act) Only a good _____ can tell a really good story.

Challenge: Complete each sentence by writing the comparative form of the adjective in parentheses.

1. (small) The carriage held a small girl, a _____ girl, and a small boy.

2. (far) The _____ seat was occupied by someone the children did not know.

3. (good) "Why is the grass in that field _____?" asked Cyril.

4. (big) "That's the stupidest story I've ever heard," said the _____ of the small girls.

Name _____ Date _____

"The Story-Teller" by Saki (H. H. Munro) (text page 597)
"The Medicine Bag" by Virginia Driving Hawk Sneve (text page 602)

Build Grammar Skills: Complex Sentence

A **complex sentence** is a sentence that contains one independent clause and one or more subordinate clauses. In each of the two complex sentences below, the independent clause is in dark print; the subordinate clause is in italics.

             S   V   S   V
When I was young, **I always bragged to friends about my Sioux grandpa.**

            S   S   V   V
Our friends, *who always had lived in the city,* **knew about Indians only from movies and TV.**

A. Practice: In each complex sentence below, put one line under the independent clause and two lines under the subordinate clause or clauses.

1. The Asian nation of Burma, which is now called Myanmar, was once ruled by Britain.

2. Many people of British background lived in Burma when it was part of the British Empire.

3. Hector Hugh Munro grew up in Burma, where his father worked as a police officer.

4. After his mother died, he was sent back to Britain, where he was raised by two aunts.

5. These aunts, who were very strict, made a lifelong impression on the young boy.

6. Because he was often ill, Hector did not become a policeman as his father had been.

7. Instead he adopted a writing career that soon won him fame.

8. His stories, which he wrote under the pen name of Saki, were known for their humor and irony.

9. Many featured the mischievous young boy Cyril, who often misbehaved.

10. Saki's brilliant career ended in 1916 in World War I, when an enemy sniped killed him.

B. Writing Application: For each item, combine the two sentences into a complex sentence that uses the relative pronoun or subordinating conjunction in parentheses. Write your new sentence on the lines provided.

1. (who) My Sioux Grandpa came to the city. He lived on a reservation.

_____

2. (because) He was old and weak. I was embarrassed by his appearance.

_____

3. (when) My city friends met him. He dressed in his Sioux finery.

_____

4. (that) He told them many stories. The stories impressed them.

_____

5. (after) My grandfather died. I kept up his Sioux traditions.

_____

"The Story-Teller" by Saki (H. H. Munro) (text page 597)
"The Medicine Bag" by Virginia Driving Hawk Sneve (text page 602)

Reading Strategy: Make Inferences

When you read, you must **make inferences,** or reach reasonable conclusions based on evidence that the writer supplies. The evidence may include the events that take place, the things characters do and say, the changes that characters undergo, and the contrasts between characters. Consider these details from "The Medicine Bag":

We never showed our friends Grandpa's picture. Not that we were ashamed of him, but because we knew that the glamorous tales we told didn't go with the real thing. Our friends would have laughed at the picture because Grandpa wasn't tall and stately like TV Indians.

From these details you might infer, or figure out, the following:

- The narrator is overly concerned with what his peers think.

- Despite what he says, the narrator really is a bit ashamed of his grandfather's appearance.

Directions: Choose one of the two selections in this grouping. Then, on the chart below, list details and the inferences you draw from them.

Selection Title:	
Details	**Inferences**

"The Story-Teller" by Saki (H. H. Munro) (text page 597)
"The Medicine Bag" by Virginia Driving Hawk Sneve (text page 602)

Literary Focus: Theme

A story's **theme** is a general insight about life that the story conveys to readers. Usually, you can sum up a theme in a sentence or two: "Friendship is more valuable than riches," for example, or "Life is short; make the most of it while you can." Sometimes a theme is directly stated in a story, but more often it is **implied,** or suggested, and you must figure it out yourself from the story's details. Among the details that can point to a story's theme are the title, the conflict and its outcome, the characters' remarks or actions, and the contrasts between the characters.

DIRECTIONS: Choose either story, and fill out this chart explaining how the details help point to the theme of the story. If you feel that one type of detail does not point to the theme, leave that part of the chart blank. At the top of the chart, state the theme in one or two sentences on the lines provided.

Theme: _____

_____

Title:	How It Points to Theme:
Conflict & Outcome:	How They Point to Theme:
Characters' Remarks or Actions:	How They Point to Theme:
Contrasts Between Characters:	How They Point to Theme:

"Animal Craftsmen" by Bruce Brooks (text page 625)

Build Vocabulary

Using Forms of *habitable*

Habitable, which means "fit to live in," is one of several English words from the Latin verb *habitare*, "to live." Here are four other English words in the same family:

   habitat, "the environment in which a plant or animal lives"   *inhabited*, "lived"

   inhabitants, "those who live in a particular area"   *uninhabited*, "not lived in"

A. DIRECTIONS: Complete each sentence with one of the four words defined above—*habitat, inhabited, inhabitants,* or *uninhabited.* Use each word only once.

1. The narrator wondered who _____ the small nest in the barn.

2. After a time, he realized that the nest was the _____ of a group of wasps.

3. He did not think that the _____ of the nest had built their home themselves.

4. When he returned in winter, the wasps were gone, and the nest was _____.

Using the Word Bank

subtle	infusion	habitable	dispelled
attributing	empathize	adroitness	replicated

B. DIRECTIONS: Match each word in the left column with its definition in the right column. Write the letter of the definition on the line before the word it defines.

____ 1. adroitness   a. injecting one thing into another

____ 2. attributing   b. duplicated; copying

____ 3. dispelled   c. delicate; not obvious

____ 4. empathize   d. drove off; got rid of

____ 5. habitable   e. to share the thoughts and feelings of another

____ 6. infusion   f. the ability to move easily and skillfully

____ 7. subtle   g. able to be lived in

____ 8. replicated   h. applying

Recognizing Antonyms

C. DIRECTIONS: Circle the letter of the word that has a meaning most nearly opposite the meaning of the word in capital letters.

1. DISPELLED:
   a. removed
   b. pronounced
   c. attracted
   d. gossiped

2. SUBTLE:
   a. graceful
   b. costly
   c. tactful
   d. conspicuous

3. ADROITNESS:
   a. clumsiness
   b. maturity
   c. education
   d. dryness

4. HABITABLE:
   a. uncertain
   b. incapable
   c. unusual
   d. unlivable

"**Animal Craftsmen**" by Bruce Brooks (text page 625)

Build Spelling Skills: Spelling the Silent *b*

Spelling Strategy   The letter b is silent, or unsounded, in certain words.

- A silent *b* often occurs just after an *m* at the end of a word or syllable:

    Examples: cli<u>mb</u>   co<u>mb</u>   doorja<u>mb</u>   plu<u>mb</u>er

- A silent *b* sometimes occurs just before a *t*:

    Examples: de<u>b</u>t   dou<u>b</u>t   su<u>b</u>tle

A. Practice: For each item, write the word for which the pronunciation is given in parentheses.

Example: (DETur): <u>debtor</u>

1. (NUM): _____

2. (LIM): _____

3. (TOOM): _____

4. (DUM): _____

5. (KRUM): _____

6. (DOUTful): _____

7. (NUMskul): _____

8. (PLUMing): _____

9. (DUMbel): _____

10. (SUTultee): _____

11. (BAHMshel): _____

12. (inDETid): _____

B. Practice: On the line after each sentence, write the correct spelling of the italicized word. If the word is already spelled correctly, write *correct*.

1. As a youngster, Bruce Brooks *climed* up the outside ladder of an old barn. _____

2. Inside there wasn't a horse, a cow, or a *lamb*, but there was a wasps' nest. _____

3. The design of the nest was very *suttle*. _____

4. It looked a bit like a bee's *honeycome*. _____

5. Brooks *douted* that the wasps themselves had built the nest. _____

Challenge: If you add a suffix that begins with a vowel to a word that ends in a single vowel plus a single consonant (other than *w, x,* or *y*), double the consonant if the stress is on the final syllable: *dispel + -ed = dispelled; forget + -ing = forgetting; propel + -er = propeller.* For each item, write the word formed by adding the suffix.

1. dispel + -ing = _____

2. admit + -ance = _____

3. commit + -ee = _____

4. propel + -ed = _____

5. occur + -ence = _____

6. regret + -able = _____

7. remit + -al = _____

8. begin + -er = _____

9. repel + -ent = _____

"Animal Craftsmen" by Bruce Brooks (text page 625)

Build Grammar Skills: Subjective Case Pronouns

Many pronouns change form depending on their grammatical role in a sentence. For example, when the pronoun referring to a female is the subject of a sentence, we use *she* (*She saw Jon*); when it is an object, we use *her* (*Jon saw her*). This change in form based on grammatical use is called the **case** of a pronoun. The **subjective case** should be used when the pronoun is the subject of a verb:

> **Subject:** He explored the barn.

Be careful to use the subjective case in compound subjects:

> The wasps and he (not him) explored the barn.

In proper English, the subjective case should also be used when the pronoun replaces a predicate noun after a linking verb:

> The last creatures in the area were the wasps and he (not him).

The following pronouns are the chief pronouns in the subjective case.

> I   you   he   she   it   we   they

A. Practice: Underline the pronouns in parentheses that correctly complete the sentences.

1. Our relative and (we, us) spent time together throughout the year.

2. My family and (I, me) periodically visited the relative in the country.

3. Nearby were a farmer and his wife, and the farmer and (she, her) owned an old barn.

4. To my knowledge, the only visitor to their barn was (I, me).

5. With each visit, the wasps and (I, me) grew less wary of one another.

6. The following winter, however, the nest and (they, them) were gone.

7. The farmer may have built the nest, or perhaps (he, him) and his wife built it together.

8. (He, Him) and his wife were amused by my mistake.

9. Neither the farmer nor (she, her) had built the nest.

10. The surprised one was (I, me).

B. Writing Application: On the lines below, write five sentences about an experience in which you and your friends or relatives learned something about nature. Use the pronouns in parentheses—for item 4, you can use *she* or *he*. Include at least one pronoun after a linking verb.

1. (we) _____

2. (it)_____

3. (I) _____

4. (she *or* he) _____

5. (they)_____

Reading for Success: Strategies for Reading Nonfiction

You're bombarded with facts and ideas at all times and from every direction. When you scan a cereal box, read a textbook, or cruise the internet, you make decisions about what, who, and how much to believe. These strategies will help you read the nonfiction you encounter every day.

- **Set a purpose for reading.** Before you begin, set a goal for reading a work of nonfiction. Your goal may be to find facts, to analyze a writer's theory, to understand an opinion, or simply to be entertained. Keep your purpose in mind as you read.

- **Identify the author's main points.** Ask yourself what the author wants you to learn or think as a result of reading his or her nonfiction work. These main points are the most important ideas in the piece.

- **Understand the author's purpose.** Authors of nonfiction have a reason, or a purpose, for writing. Their details and information support their purpose. They also adopt a tone, or attitude, toward their topic and their reader. Consider the details and tone to determine an author's purpose.

DIRECTIONS: Read the following passage from "Grace Hopper: Amazing Grace" by Mary Northrup, and use the reading strategies to increase your comprehension. In the margin, note where you satisfy your purpose for reading, understand the author's purpose, identify the author's main points, and identify the evidence for the author's main points. Finally, write your response to the selection on the lines provided.

from **"Grace Hopper: Amazing Grace"** by Mary Northrup

The following passage explores the life of a pioneer in computers.

"There's a bug in the system!" A programmer says this when something goes wrong with a computer. It does not mean an ant or a beetle is crawling around inside. However, the very first computer bug was a real one. A moth flew into the Mark II, an early computer, and caused a short circuit. Grace Hopper and her co-workers pulled it out with a tweezer. They taped their "computer bug" into the log book. Afterward they told their boss they were "debugging" the computer.

Grace Hopper did much more than invent colorful phrases. She programmed some of the first computers. She contributed to the development of Common Business-Oriented Language (COBOL), a computer language. Early on she realized that computers were essential. Through teaching and in speeches, she told people how important computers could be. She served in the Navy and the Naval Reserve for more than forty years. There, she reached the rank of rear admiral. For several years, she had the rare honor of being the oldest naval officer on active duty.

This remarkable woman was born in New York City on December 9, 1906. Grace Brewster Murray was the oldest child of Walter Fletcher Murray and Mary Campbell Van Horne Murray. She had one brother, Roger, and one sister, Mary.

Hopper's grandfather was a civil engineer for New York. From him, she learned to love maps. When he measured for new streets, she tagged along and held the surveyor's pole.

Hopper had a happy childhood growing up in New York City. She went to private schools, where she was good at mathematics. She especially liked geometry. The family spent summers in New Hampshire.

Hopper was fascinated with how machines run. One day her mother found all the alarm clocks in their summer home in pieces.

What had happened was that I'd taken the first one apart and I couldn't get it together so I opened the next one. I ended up with all seven of them apart. After that I was restricted to one clock. It's that kind of curiosity: How do things work?

When Hopper was a teenager, many people did not approve of education for women. Yet Hopper's father was different. He wanted his daughters to go to college. So Hopper went off to Vassar, an all-female college. After graduating in 1928, she earned her master's degree in 1930 from Yale University. That same year she married Vincent Foster Hopper. She returned to Vassar as a math professor, teaching there from 1931 to 1944. She also went on to earn a Ph.D. in mathematics from Yale in 1934.

During World War II (1939–1945), many young women were eager to join the Navy, including Hopper. Females were not allowed to serve aboard any ship. Yet women could enlist in the Women Accepted for Volunteer Emergency Service (WAVES). After training, Grace became Lieutenant Hopper.

She was assigned to the Bureau of Ordnance Computation Project. Part of her job was to calculate firing distances for weapons. She worked at Harvard University. Here, the Navy ran a computer, the Mark I. Grace had never seen a computer before. She recalled, "I've always loved a good gadget. When I met Mark I, it was the biggest, fanciest gadget I'd ever seen. I had to find out how it worked."

Mark I was huge: fifty-one feet long. Its computing power, though, was slow. It could do three additions each second. (Today a supercomputer can do one trillion additions per second.) Still, for the time, it was amazing. Hopper quickly learned how Mark I worked. She wrote some of its early programs and the user's manual.

Computers were not used yet in many places. Yet Hopper believed that they would be good at work other than the military. The business uses of computers began to attract her. Her technical skills were in demand. So she wrote some programs for companies. She developed a knack for marketing, too. Soon, she knew, companies would have to rely on fast, accurate computing machines.

_____

_____

_____

_____

_____

_____

"Animal Craftsmen" by Bruce Brooks (text page 625)

Literary Focus: Reflective Essay

An **essay** is a short nonfiction piece on writing that focuses on a particular subject. In a **reflective essay,** the writer presents his or her thoughts about a topic of personal interest. Often the writer re-creates and evaluates personal experiences to make a point about his or her life or about life in general. In "Animal Craftsmen," Bruce Brooks recalls how his childhood experience of finding a wasps' nest led to his lifelong appreciation of nature's wonders.

DIRECTIONS: In the space below, complete the flow chart showing the steps that led to Brooks's conclusion about nature's wonders. Include both Brooks's experiences and his ideas and opinions about them.

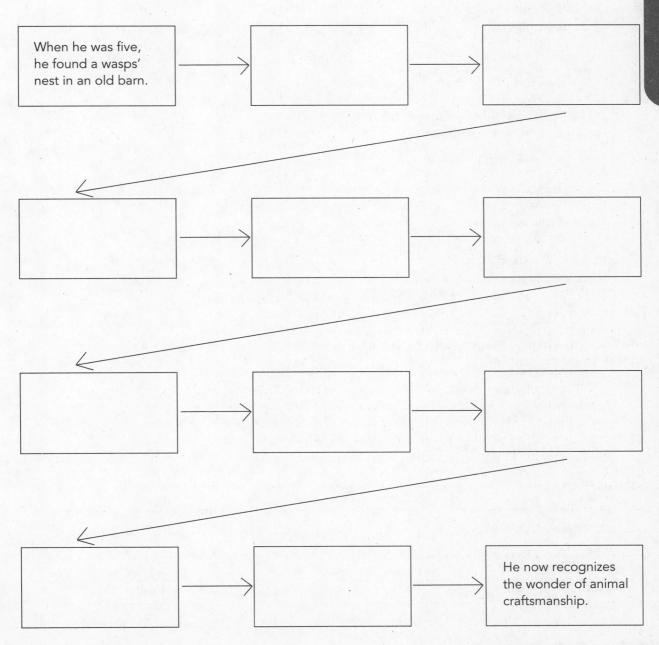

from **One Writer's Beginnings** by Eudora Welty (text page 634)

"Baseball" by Lionel G. García (text page 636)

Build Vocabulary

Using the Root *-vis-*

Visible contains the root *-vis-*, which means "to see." *Visible* means "able to be seen."

A. DIRECTIONS: Circle the letter of the choice that best completes each sentence. Use your understanding of the root *-vis-* to help you figure out the answers.

1. When you *revise* a paper, you ___.
   a. see it for the first time
   b. look at it again
   c. read it aloud
   d. grade it

2. *Invisible* ink ___.
   a. is red
   b. is black
   c. fills an old-fashioned fountain pen
   d. fades and disappears

3. A *visor* is something that protects the ___.
   a. eyes
   b. ears
   c. nose
   d. throat

Using the Word Bank

visible	reigning	respectively	constellations
eclipses	devices	evaded	

B. DIRECTIONS: On the line before each pair of words, write *S* if the two words are synonyms or *A* if they are antonyms.

___ 1. constellations, stars   ___ 4. evaded, faced   ___ 6. reigning, ruling

___ 2. devices, techniques   ___ 5. eclipses, blockages   ___ 7. visible, hidden

___ 3. respectively, haphazardly

Analogies

C. DIRECTIONS: Circle the letter of the words that express a relationship most nearly the same as the relationship in capital letters.

1. ECLIPSES : DARK ::
   a. craters : moon
   b. sunlight : shadow
   c. rainfall : wet
   d. star : sky

2. STARS : CONSTELLATIONS ::
   a. bones : skeletons
   b. flowers : roses
   c. triangles : squares
   d. beans : vegetables

3. VISIBLE : EYE ::
   a. fragrant : smell
   b. invisible : unseen
   c. audible : ear
   d. reliable : person

from **One Writer's Beginnings** by Eudora Welty (text page 634)
"Baseball" by Lionel G. García (text page 636)

Build Spelling Skills: Spelling *ei* and *ie*

Spelling Strategy   The rhyme about when to use *i* before *e* is a famous spelling rule.

- Use *i* before *e* except after *c*

   Examples: gr<u>ie</u>f   sh<u>ie</u>ld   c<u>ei</u>ling   perc<u>ei</u>ve

- Or when sounded like *a* as in *neighbor* and *weigh:*

   Examples: b<u>ei</u>ge   r<u>ei</u>gn   sl<u>ei</u>gh   surv<u>ei</u>llance

- Like most rules there are some exceptions:

   Exceptions: <u>ei</u>ther, financ<u>ie</u>r, for<u>ei</u>gn, forf<u>ei</u>t, h<u>ei</u>ght, h<u>ei</u>r, l<u>ei</u>sure, n<u>ei</u>ther, prot<u>ei</u>n, sc<u>ie</u>nce, s<u>ei</u>ze, sh<u>ei</u>k, sover<u>ei</u>gn, st<u>ei</u>n, th<u>ei</u>r, w<u>ei</u>rd

A. Practice: Complete each word by writing *ie* or *ei* on the lines provided.

1. y____ ____ ld

2. r____ ____ gning

3. rec ____ ____ pt

4. ____ ____ ther

5. ____ ____ ghteen

6. w ____ ____ ght

7. ach ____ ____ ve

8. conc ____ ____ t

9. bel ____ ____ ve

10. n ____ ____ gh

11. for ____ ____ gner

12. n ____ ____ ce

13. dec ____ ____ ve

14. v ____ ____ n

15. sc ____ ____ ntist

B. Practice: On the line after each sentence, write the correct spelling of each italicized word. If all the words are spelled correctly, write *correct.*

1. In our *nieghborhood* my *freinds* and I played baseball often. _____

2. Most of the players had *thier* positions in the *outfield.* _____

3. Usually *either* Juan or Cota *reigned* on the pitcher's mound. _____

4. Matías sometimes pitched, but he *cheifly recieved* the ball as catcher. _____

5. I recall when he *shreiked* out the score: *eight* to one. _____

Challenge: *Device,* which ends in an *s* sound, is a noun; *devise,* which ends in a *z* sound, is a verb. Because these related words have similar sounds, their spellings are easy to confuse. On the lines below, identify the part of speech and meaning of each pair of words. Also distinguish their pronunciations. **Example:**   device: (final s sound) n. a thing   devise: (final z sound) v. to

1. advice: _____

   advise: _____

2. loose: _____

   lose: _____

from **One Writer's Beginnings** by Eudora Welty (text page 634)
"Baseball" by Lionel G. García (text page 636)

Build Grammar Skills: Objective Case Pronouns

As you know, pronouns change **case,** or form, based on their grammatical use. The **objective case** should be used when the pronoun is the object of a verb or a preposition:

Direct Object: The image of the moon deeply impressed <u>me</u>.

Indirect Object: Dad showed <u>me</u> the telescope.

Object of a Preposition: The telescope brought the moon's image to <u>me</u>.

Be careful to use the objective case in compound objects:

The telescope stood between Dad and <u>me</u> (not <u>I</u>).

In proper English, the objective case should *not* be used when the pronoun replaces a predicate noun after a linking verb:

The people at the telescope were Dad and <u>I</u> (not <u>me</u>).

The following pronouns are the chief pronouns in the objective case.

me   you   him   her   it   us   them

A. Practice: Underline the pronouns in parentheses that correctly complete the sentences.

1. A strange game of baseball attracted my friends and (I, me).

2. Juanita played with her brother and (we, us).

3. The pitchers were Matìas and (she, her).

4. Matìas told the others and (she, her) the location of first base.

5. Father Zavala watched the other students and (he, him).

6. Juanita pitched to her brothers and (they, them).

7. The next three players were Juan, Cota, and (I, me).

8. The pitcher stood between first base and (I, me).

9. Sometimes my uncle Adolfo also viewed Matìas and (we, us).

10. Adolfo told the others and (he, him) the correct baseball positions.

B. Writing Application: On the lines below, write five sentences about a sporting event in which you were a player or spectator. Use the pronouns in parentheses.

1. (us)_____

2. (it)_____

3. (me) _____

4. (him *or* her)_____

5. (them) _____

from **One Writer's Beginnings** by Eudora Welty (text page 634)
"Baseball" by Lionel G. García (text page 636)

Reading Strategy: Understand the Author's Purpose

Authors have reasons for writing. Often they have one or more of the following purposes in mind:

- to describe   • to teach or explain   • to recount or narrate   • to persuade   • to entertain

To **understand the author's purpose,** ask yourself, "Why is he or she telling me this?" For example, if you ask that question about the opening line of the selection by Eudora Welty— "Learning stumps you with its moments"—you might conclude that the author's possible purpose at that point is to teach the reader something.

DIRECTIONS: Fill in the chart below to help you determine the author's purpose in the selection from *One Writer's Beginnings.* An example is done for you.

Text from Selection	How It Affects Me	Possible Purpose(s)
"Learning stumps you with its moments."	It makes me stop and think.	to teach

Unit 7: Nonfiction

from **One Writer's Beginnings** by Eudora Welty (text page 634)
"Baseball" by Lionel G. García (text page 636)

Literary Focus: Autobiography

An **autobiography** is person's account of his or her own life. Usually the writer uses first-person pronouns, *I* and *me*, to write about personal experiences and impressions that the writer considers significant in his or her life. The autobiography may cover the writer's whole life (up until the point at which it was written) or it may focus on only a portion of that life. The two selections in this grouping, for example, focus on portions of each author's childhood.

DIRECTIONS: Choose one of the two selections in this grouping and, on the chart below, list some of the personal memories that the writer provides. In the second column, indicate why you think those memories are important to the writer.

Selection Title:	
Memory	**Significance**

"The United States v. Susan B. Anthony" by Margaret Truman (text page 643)

Build Vocabulary

Using the Prefix *retro-*

Retrospect contains the prefix *retro-*, which means "backward" or "behind." *Retrospect* is a looking back at events in the past.

A. DIRECTIONS: Complete each sentence below with the best word from the list in italics. Use each word only once.

retroactive   retrofit   retrogress   retrospective

1. After the new parts are perfected, we will have to _____ the equipment.

2. If a _____ law passed on May 1, people who broke it before May 1 can be prosecuted.

3. The _____ film festival showed many Hollywood classics of the past.

4. It's bad enough we made no progress, but we certainly don't want to _____.

Using the Selection Vocabulary

unremitting	oratory	inadvertently	intimidated
retrospect	consternation	futile	

B. DIRECTIONS: Write the word from the box above on the lines after its definition below. The shaded boxes, reading down, will spell out a famous name in the women's suffrage movement.

1. a backward glance   _ _ _ _ _ ▮ _ _ _ _

2. having no effect   _ _ ▮ _ _ _ _

3. great upset that leaves one helpless   _ _ _ _ _ _ _ _ _ ▮ _ _ _

4. without intention; by accident   _ _ _ _ _ _ _ _ _ ▮ _ _ _

5. made cowardly by fear   _ _ _ _ _ _ _ ▮ _ _ _

6. public speaking   _ _ _ _ ▮ _ _

7. unending; persistent   _ _ _ _ _ _ _ _ ▮ _

Recognizing Synonyms

C. DIRECTIONS: Circle the letter of the word that has a meaning most like the meaning of the word in capital letters.

1. FUTILE:
   a. angry
   b. useless
   c. puzzling
   d. ancient

2. RETROSPECT:
   a. clarity
   b. hindsight
   c. vision
   d. foresight

3. INADVERTENTLY:
   a. word
   b. word
   c. unclearly
   d. unintentionally

4. INTIMIDATED:
   a. frightened
   b. empowered
   c. word
   d. word

"The United States v. Susan B. Anthony" by Margaret Truman (text page 643)

Connecting a Biographical Essay to Social Studies

A **biography** is a nonfiction account of one person's life written by another person. The person whose life is being recorded is called the **subject** of the biography; the writer is called the **biographer.** The biographer may have been personally acquainted with the subject or may have researched the subject's life. Though a biased, one-sided biography can make for good reading, the best biographies from a historical point of view are those that portray their subjects accurately and fairly. If the subject is a historical figure of some importance or a witness to important historical events, a well-written biography can also provide valuable information about past events and about life in earlier times.

DIRECTIONS: On the chart below, list details from the selection that supply information about Susan B. Anthony, the historical events of which she was a part, and the time in which she lived. To get you started, three details are listed as examples.

The Person	The Events	The Times
Susan B. Anthony was a stern and single-minded woman.	In1872, in Rochester, N.Y., she and four other women tried to register to vote.	In 1872, barbershops were used as centers for voter registration.

"Hokusai: The Old Man Mad About Drawing" by Stephen Longstreet (text page 654)
"Not to Go With the Others" by John Hersey (text page 656)

Build Vocabulary

Unit 7: Nonfiction

Using the Prefix *en-*

The prefix *en-*, which means "in; into; onto" or "cause to be," is usually used to form verbs. A *gulf* is a large gap or body of water; the verb *engulf* is "to cause to be in a gulf; to overflow and enclose; to swallow up or overwhelm."

A. DIRECTIONS: Complete these sentences with a verb formed by adding the prefix *en-* to the word in parentheses.

1. (close) Be sure to _____ you check in the envelope before you mail it.

2. (joy) Try to relax and _____ yourself at the party.

3. (circle) In the dance, we all join hands and _____ the maypole.

4. (trap) Cheese is often used as bait when you _____ a mouse.

5. (dear) She used flattery in an effort to _____ herself to others.

Using the Word Bank

apprenticed	commissioned	engulfing	mania	feigned
ensued	prostate	dispatched	pretense	immersed

B. DIRECTIONS: Hidden in this puzzle are the ten words from the Word Bank. Their letters may read from right to left, from left to right, from top to bottom, from bottom to top, or diagonally. Find and circle the words. Then, alongside the puzzle, rewrite each word on the line next to its definition.

```
L V D E H C T A P S I D R
C K M Q E X D J I I S E Y
D E N O I S S I M M O C J
V F N E T A H S R O P I B
P R E T E N S E H J I T G
R H M I A S P W P L O N D
O L N E B K J A F C I E E
S D A D E N G I E F F R S
T C E D J I E H L W O P R
A N U U E Y X U D A E P E
T W Q F S S G J A I N A M
E X L B C N N V P R E N M
F G U W E D E E A K H V I
```

1. contracted to learn a trade:_____

2. plunged into: _____

3. overflowing and swallowing up:_____

4. uncontrollable enthusiasm: _____

5. a false showing:_____

6. imitated; took on the role of: _____

7. ordered to make something:_____

8. sent to death:_____

9. lying flat or prone: _____

10. came afterward: _____

"Hokusai: The Old Man Mad About Drawing" by Stephen Longstreet (text page 654)
"Not to Go With the Others" by John Hersey (text page 656)

Build Spelling Skills: Words With Silent *g*

Spelling Strategy   The letter *g* is silent, or unsounded, in certain words.

- A silent *g* often occurs just before an *n* when the two letters are part of the same syllable:

Examples: gnaw   reign   resigned

- A silent *g* often occurs just before a silent *h* in the middle or at the end of a word or syllable:

Examples: light   neighbor   through

A. Practice: For each item, unscramble the letters in parentheses to spell the word being defined.

Example: to quit a job (ingers):   resign _____

1. a tiny insect (tang): _____

2. not day (ihtng): _____

3. to pretend (finge): _____

4. pattern (ginsed): _____

5. battled (otghuf): _____

6. the sound a horse makes (ghein): _____

7. past tense of teach (ghttua): _____

8. leg part above the knee (hhgit): _____

9. an elflike creature (neomg): _____

10. to arrange in a line (linga): _____

B. Practice: On the line after each sentence, write the correct spelling of each italicized word. If all the words are already spelled correctly, write *correct*.

1. A *highly* gifted artist, Hokusai lived when the shogun *reined* in Japan. _____

2. *Althouh* he *desined* greeting prints, he is best known for landscapes. _____

3. In a series *thought* to be his finest, *lightning* plays around Mount Fuji. _____

4. He *feined* maple leaves by having a rooster walk *strait* across a surface. _____

5. He lived past *eigty* and *throughout* his life *sined* his name differently. _____

Challenge: The word *dispatched* has the smaller word *patched* within it, although the two words are not related in meaning. What other small words can you find in *dispatched*? Find four more words within *dispatched*, and write them on the lines below.

_____   _____   _____   _____

"Hokusai: The Old Man Mad About Drawing" by Stephen Longstreet (text page 654)
"Not to Go With the Others" by John Hersey (text page 656)

Build Grammar Skills: Using *Who* and *Whom*

The pronouns *who* and *whom* are often confused. *Who,* the subjective case, should be used as the subject of a sentence or clause or in place of a predicate noun after a linking verb. *Whom,* the objective case, should be used as the object of a verb or preposition. In the first example below, *who* is the subject of the sentence; in the second, *whom* is the object of the preposition *from.*

Subjective: Who escaped death by hiding in a storehouse box?

Objective: From whom was he trying to escape?

Who and *whom* are often confused because they are used in questions and subordinate clauses, two places where a direct object usually comes before the verb and so can be confused with the subject. Remember that the subject performs the action of the verb; the direct object receives the action.

Question: Whom did he avoid? *(He did avoid whom?)*

Subordinate Clause: The people whom he feared belonged to the Gestapo. *(he feared whom)*

Also remember that when the pronoun replaces a predicate noun after a linking verb, you should use *who,* not *whom.*

Who (not Whom) was Frantizek Zaremski? *(Frantizek Zaremski was who?)*

The prisoner who he was then became the heroic figure of today. *(he was who then)*

A. Practice: Underline the pronoun in parentheses that correctly completes each sentence.

1. (Who, Whom) created *Thirty-six Views of Fuji?*

2. The person (who, whom) it was sometimes signed his name Sori and Shunro.

3. He was really Hokusai, a talented artist (who, whom) lived in eighteenth-century Japan.

4. An older artist (who, whom) Hokusai admired was named Shunsho.

5. Shunsho was the artist (who, whom) Hokusai studied under.

6. For (who, whom) did Hokusai paint?

7. One person for (who, whom) he created art was the shogun of Japan.

8. (Who, Whom) was the shogun?

B. Writing Application: On the lines below, write three questions about a famous artist. Use the pronouns indicated in parentheses.

1. (who) _____

2. (whom) _____

3. (who) _____

"Hokusai: The Old Man Mad About Drawing" by Stephen Longstreet (text page 654)
"Not to Go With the Others" by John Hersey (text page 656)

Reading Strategy: Identify the Author's Main Points

You'll get more from your nonfiction reading if you try to **identify the author's main points,** or most important ideas, in a selection. To do so, ask yourself what the author wants you to discover or think as you read. In a well-written short selection, you can often piece together the main point of the selection as a whole by identifying the main points of individual paragraphs. The main point of the selection may also be mentioned in an introductory opening paragraph and restated in a concluding final paragraph.

DIRECTIONS: On the diagram below, identify the authors main points in "Hokusai: The Old Man Mad About Drawing." The first one is done as an example.

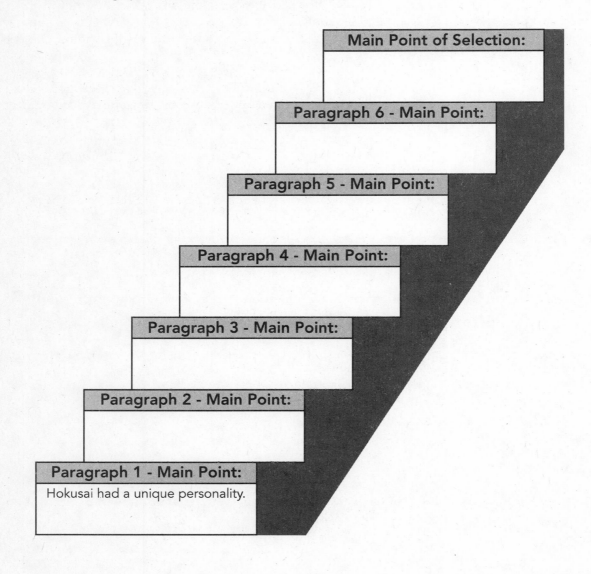

Main Point of Selection:

Paragraph 6 - Main Point:

Paragraph 5 - Main Point:

Paragraph 4 - Main Point:

Paragraph 3 - Main Point:

Paragraph 2 - Main Point:

Paragraph 1 - Main Point:
Hokusai had a unique personality.

"Hokusai: The Old Man Mad About Drawing" by Stephen Longstreet (text page 654)

"Not to Go With the Others" by John Hersey (text page 656)

Literary Focus: Biography

A **biography** is a written account of a person's life. Most biographies tell the stories of famous or admirable people. Although a biography is nonfiction, a good biography has the same elements as good narrative (storytelling) fiction:

- **plot,** or series of events
- **conflict,** a struggle around which plot events center
- **setting,** or time and place
- **characters,** the people in the narrative
- **dialogue,** the conversation of the characters
- **theme,** or message about life

For example, the plot of "Hokusai: The Old Man Mad About Drawing" is a series of events tracing Hokusai's achievements, all focusing on his conflict or struggle to achieve greatness and maintain creativity. The setting is eighteenth- and nineteenth-century Japan, especially in the area around Edo (now Tokyo). Characters include Hokusai, Shunsho, and the shogun. Although there is no real dialogue, the selection quotes Hokusai himself ("From the age of six I had a mania . . . "). Two likely themes are that artists are sometimes eccentric and that creativity must and can be renewed over the years.

DIRECTIONS: On the chart below, list the narrative elements in "Not to Go With the Others."

Plot (Events)
Conflict
Setting
Characters
Dialogue (Examples)
Theme

"Debbie" by James Herriot (text page 670)
"Forest Fire" by Anaïs Nin (text page 675)
from **Netiquette** by Virginia Shea (text page 678)

Build Vocabulary

Using the Root *-vac-*

Evacuees contains the root *-vac-*, which means "empty." *Evacuees* are people who are removed from a place, leaving that place empty.

A. DIRECTIONS: On the line before each statement, write *T* if the statement is probably true and *F* if it is probably false. Use your understanding of the root *-vac-* to help you figure out the answers.

____ 1. A *vacant* lot usually has a large building on it.

____ 2. A fire alarm may cause people to *vacate* the premises.

____ 3. To get rid of a *vacancy* on the staff, you would need to fire a lot of people.

____ 4. A *vacuous* expression indicates great intelligence and concentration.

____ 5. During a hurricane, people on the coast may be asked to *evacuate*.

Using the Word Bank

privations	evacuees	pungent	tenacious
dissolution	ravaging	implemented	encompasses

B. DIRECTIONS: Unscramble the words in the left column and write them on the lines that follow the scrambled words. Then match each word with its definition in the right column. Write the letter of the definition on the line before the number.

____ 1. diilnoosstu _____ a. having a sharp, stinging smell

____ 2. aceemnopsss _____ b. strongly damaging; destroying

____ 3. aceeesuv _____ c. provided the tools or means to achieve something

____ 4. deeeilmmnpt _____ d. contains; includes

____ 5. aiinoprstv _____ e. holding on firmly

____ 6. egnnptu _____ f. falling apart; crumbling

____ 7. aagginrv _____ g. lack of basic needs

____ 8. aceinostu _____ h. people who leave a place to escape danger

Sentence Completions

C. DIRECTIONS: Circle the letter of the word that best completes each sentence.

1. Internet access ___ both Web sites and e-mail.
   a. encompasses   b. privations   c. evacuees   d. ravages

2. Some days the 'Net moves so slowly that only a(n) ___ person would bother using it.
   a. pungent   b. encompassing   c. tenacious   d. ravaging

"Debbie" by James Herriot (text page 670)
"Forest Fire" by Anaïs Nin (text page 675)
from **Netiquette** by Virginia Shea (text page 678)

Build Spelling Skills: Using *g* to Spell the Sound of *j*

Spelling Strategy The letter *g* is sometimes used to spell the sound of *j*.

• A *g* often has a *j* sound when it comes right before an *e*, an *i*, or a *y*:

Examples: gem   danger   aging   giant   gyp   biology

• When a *g* comes right after a *d*, the two letters together also have a *j* sound:

Examples: badge   edgy   judgment   lodging   ridge

A. Practice: For each numbered item, write the word for which the pronunciation is given in parentheses. All of the words appear in the selections in this grouping.

Example: (BUJ):   budge _____

1. (EDJ): _____

2. (MESij): _____

3. (RAvujing): _____

4. (TRAJik): _____

5. (ENjin): _____

6. (DAMij): _____

7. (JIBurish): _____

8. (HYOOJ): _____

9. (JESchur): _____

10. (PUNjint): _____

11. (JENdur): _____

12. (PASSij): _____

B. Practice: On the line after each sentence, write the correct spellings of the words in italics. If all the words are already spelled correctly, write *correct*.

1. Every now and then Debbie came into the *lounje*, shy and *apolojetic.*_____

_____

2. Mrs. Ainsworth was the *jenerous* kind of client veterinary *surjeons* dream of._____

_____

3. I *managed* to touch Debbie and *jently* stroked her cheek with one finger. _____

_____

4. After visiting the Ainsworths, she darted through a *large* hole in the *hedje.*_____

_____

5. The aroma of turkey and *sage* and onion stuffing set my gastric juices *surjing.*_____

_____

Challenge: How is the word *dissolution* related to the word *solution?* Keeping in mind that the prefix *dis-* means "the opposite of," explain the relationship of the two words on the lines below. Feel free to use a dictionary to help you.

_____

_____

_____

"**Debbie**" by James Herriot (text page 670)
"**Forest Fire**" by Anaïs Nin (text page 675)
from **Netiquette** by Virginia Shea (text page 678)

Build Grammar Skills: Pronoun-Antecedent Agreement

A **pronoun** is a word that takes the place of a noun in a sentence, serving as a subject, as an object, or in another role typically served by a noun. The specific word to which the pronoun refers is called its **antecedent;** it is usually a noun but can also be another pronoun. A pronoun must agree with its antecedent in gender (masculine, feminine, or neither) and number (singular or plural—that is, one or more than one). In the sample sentence below, the feminine singular pronoun *her* agrees in gender and number with its antecedent, *Debbie*, and the gender-neutral plural pronoun *they* agrees in number with its antecedent, *dogs*.

Sometimes Debbie sat near the dogs, but they ignored her.

A. Practice: Complete each sentence by underlining the correct pronoun from the choices given in parentheses. Circle the antecedent of the pronoun.

1. Since Mrs. Ainsworth was a pet owner, (she, they) often called the vet.

2. The vet cared for Mrs. Ainsworth's three Basset hounds when (he, they) fell ill.

3. One day, when (he, it) came to treat one of the hounds, the vet saw a stray cat.

4. Mrs. Ainsworth welcomed the stray to (her, their) home.

5. Debbie, the stray, sat near the fire and really enjoyed (him, it).

6. The flames of the forest fire had a deadly look to (it, them).

7. Evacuees left (your, their) cabin and arrived at the rescue station.

8. We parked the car on the field below (me, us).

9. When people use e-mail, (you, they) should try to be polite to others.

B. Writing Application: Rewrite this paragraph on the lines provided, replacing the repetitious nouns in italics with pronouns. Be sure that the pronouns you use agree with their antecedents.

One Christmas Mrs. Ainsworth phoned because *Mrs. Ainsworth* was worried about Debbie, a stray cat. Debbie was suffering from a malignant tumor but *Debbie* struggled to the Ainsworth house to drop off *Debbie's* young kitten before *Debbie* died. Mrs. Ainsworth had three dogs, but *the dogs* seemed to welcome *the dogs'* playful new companion. When James Herriot visited a year later, *Herriot* was not surprised when Mrs. Ainsworth told *Herriot* that the kitten was *Mrs. Ainsworth's* best Christmas present ever.

_____

_____

_____

_____

"Debbie" by James Herriot (text page 670)

"Forest Fire" by Anaïs Nin (text page 675)

from **Netiquette** by Virginia Shea (text page 678)

Reading Strategy: Set a Purpose for Reading

When you read nonfiction, you will focus your reading better if you **set a purpose** for what you read. Follow these steps:

1. Identify the subject by

- considering the title

- skimming the selection

- reading the opening paragraph or any special introductory material

2. Consider what you already know about the subject.

3. Determine what you want to know about the subject, and use that to set your purpose.

4. Once you've set your purpose, continue reading the selection with that purpose in mind.

DIRECTIONS: Fill out the following KWL diagram for one of the selections. Indicate what you already **K**now about the subject, what you **W**ant to know, and what you **L**earn from your reading. The middle column should help you set your purpose.

K	W	L

"Debbie" by James Herriot (text page 670)

"Forest Fire" by Anaïs Nin (text page 675)

from **Netiquette** by Virginia Shea (text page 678)

Literary Focus: Essay

An **essay** is a short nonfiction work that focuses on a particular topic.

- A **narrative essay** tells a true story about real people. Like a fictional story, it presents a plot, or series of events, in which the reader usually learns about the characters through their actions and words and sometimes even their thoughts.

- A **descriptive essay** describes a real-life event, scene, or object by providing vivid images that show how things look, sound, smell, taste, or feel. Most descriptive essays also include the writer's emotional responses to the event, scene, or object being described.

- An **expository essay** presents factual information, clarifies ideas, or explains a process. Often it includes numbered or lettered steps, definitions, and diagrams or charts that make the explanation clearer.

DIRECTIONS: Choose one selection from this grouping and, on the chart below, show how that selection displays the properties of one of the three essay types defined above.

Essay Type:	
Essay Title:	
Properties:	

© Prentice-Hall, Inc.

Name _____ Date _____

Build Vocabulary

Using the Prefix *anti-*

Antithesis contains the prefix *anti-*, which means "opposite" or "opposed to." A *thesis* is a statement that is logically supported; an *antithesis* is a statement that contradicts the thesis.

A. DIRECTIONS: Complete each sentence with a word formed by adding the prefix *anti-* to one of these five words: *hero, poverty, social, theft, war.* Use each word only once.

1. A burglar alarm is an _____ device.

2. A main character who does not display admirable qualities is often called an

   _____.

3. In the late 1960's, "hawks" supported the Vietnam War, while "doves" were _____.

4. Job training and food stamps are two kinds of _____ programs.

5. A very shy or unfriendly person may be described as _____.

Using the Word Bank

diverts usurps august pervading antithesis paradoxes dilemma devoid

B. DIRECTIONS: Match each Word Bank word on the left with its definition on the right.

____ 1. usurps   a. spreading throughout

____ 2. dilemma   b. draws attention from

____ 3. pervading   c. completely without

____ 4. paradoxes   d. a contrasting argument

____ 5. august   e. highly regarded

____ 6. diverts   f. contradictory statements

____ 7. antithesis   g. a serious problem

____ 8. devoid   h. takes over

Recognizing Synonyms

C. DIRECTIONS: Circle the letter of the word that is closest in meaning to the word in capital letters.

1. AUGUST:
   a. warm
   b. argumentative
   c. restful
   d. honored

2. DILEMMA:
   a. openness
   b. sourness
   c. problem
   d. conversation

3. DEVOID:
   a. filled
   b. lacking
   c. meeting
   d. faithful

4. DIVERT:
   a. distract
   b. join
   c. sadden
   d. rest

Unit 7: Nonfiction

"The Trouble with Television" by Robert MacNeil (text page 686)
"The American Dream" by Martin Luther King, Jr. (text page 690)

Build Spelling Skills: Spelling the Sound of *oy*

Spelling Strategy   The sound of *oy* has more than one spelling.

- In general, use *oy* to spell the *oy* sound at the end of a word, or when a word already ending in *oy* adds a suffix or becomes a plural:

  Examples: ann<u>oy</u> ann<u>oy</u>ed b<u>oy</u> b<u>oy</u>hood j<u>oy</u> j<u>oy</u>s

- Otherwise, at the beginning or in the middle of a word, generally use *oi*:

  Examples: av<u>oi</u>d b<u>oi</u>ler c<u>oi</u>l n<u>oi</u>se <u>oi</u>l v<u>oi</u>d

  Exception: <u>oy</u>ster

A. Practice: Complete each word by writing *oi* or *oy* on the lines provided.

1. sp ___ ___ l
2. destr ___ ___
3. dev ___ ___ d
4. f ___ ___ led
5. enj ___ ___ ed
6. ___ ___ ntment
7. p ___ ___
8. h ___ ___ st
9. l ___ ___ n
10. empl ___ ___ ment
11. p ___ ___ se
12. ___ ___ ly
13. ___ ___ nk
14. v ___ ___ ces
15. dec ___ ___ s
16. ann ___ ___ ance
17. conv ___ ___
18. m ___ ___ sture
19. b ___ ___ ling
20. ___ ___ sters

B. Practice: Cross out each misspelled italicized word, and write it correctly above the line. If an italicized word is spelled correctly, write *correct*.

1. To Robin MacNeil, television is a slow *poyson destroying* our society.

2. Broadcasters *avoyd* anything that might *emploi* thought or concentration.

3. Instead they *toyl* to create shows that are totally *devoyd* of meaning.

4. MacNeil is *annoid* by the amount of time *boys* and girls spend watching TV.

5. MacNeil asks readers to *join* his crusade against this dangerous *toy*.

Challenge: The word *august* has the same spelling (except for the capital *A*) as the month *August*, even though the two words are pronounced differently. What other pairs of words with the same spellings but different meanings are described on the lines below?

Example: Capitalized and with the stress on the first syllable, it comes after July: <u>August</u>
Not capitalized and with the stress on the second syllable, it means "honored": <u>august</u>

1. Capitalized and pronounced with a long *o*, it is the language of Poland: _____

   Not capitalized and pronounced with a short *o*, it shines and protects furniture:

   _____

2. With a stressed *oo* sound in the second syllable, it means "tiny": _____

   With an unstressed *i* sound in the second syllable, it is 60 seconds: _____

"The Trouble with Television" by Robert MacNeil (text page 686)
"The American Dream" by Martin Luther King, Jr. (text page 690)

Build Grammar Skills: Pronoun Agreement with Indefinite Pronouns

Indefinite pronouns stand for unidentified or unclearly identified people or things. Nevertheless, they do give an indication of number (singular or plural—that is, one or more than one). Other pronouns that refer to them must therefore agree with them in number. In the sentences below, for example, the singular pronoun *he or she* refers to the singular indefinite pronoun *Nobody*. The plural pronoun *they* refers to the plural indefinite pronoun *few*.

Singular: Nobody concentrates when he or she watches television.

Plural: TV draws people of all ages, but few concentrate when they watch.

While most indefinite pronouns are either singular or plural, a few can be either, depending on the people or things to which they refer. In the following sentences, the indefinite pronoun *most* refers first to one chunk of television and then to more than one TV program.

Singular: Most of television aims mainly to fulfill its role as a profitable means of advertising.

Plural: Most of the TV programs want only to increase their ratings to attract advertisers.

Below are the common indefinite pronouns. (Many of them can also be used as adjectives.)

Always Singular	another, anybody, anyone, anything, anywhere, each, either, everybody, everyone, everything, much, neither, nobody, no one, nothing, nowhere, one, other, somebody, someone, something, somewhere
Always Plural	both, few, many, others, several
Singular or Plural	all, any, enough, more, most, none, some, such

A. Practice: In the following sentences, underline the correct pronouns from the choices given in parentheses. Then circle the indefinite pronouns to which the underlined pronouns refer.

1. In America today, many spend (his or her, their) time watching television.

2. Almost everyone has (his or her, their) favorite shows.

3. Most of the shows present (its, their) events in a swift, kaleidoscopic series.

4. Several gain (its, their) audiences' attention with violence or other shocking acts.

5. None of the nightly network news is presented in depth to (its, their) audience.

6. Anyone who watches TV is not using (his or her, their) full concentration.

B. Writing Application: Complete these sentences with ideas from Martin Luther King's essay. In each of your complete sentences, use a pronoun to refer back to the indefinite pronoun.

1. Everyone in the nation _____

2. Many of our founding principles _____

3. Most of America in the 1960's _____

4. Much of the American dream _____

Unit 7: Nonfiction

"The Trouble with Television" by Robert MacNeil (text page 686)
"The American Dream" by Martin Luther King, Jr. (text page 690)

Reading Strategy: Persuasive Techniques

Persuasion is writing that tries to convince its audience to think or act in a certain way. To be convincing, writers often employ some of these **persuasive techniques**:

- **supporting evidence:** Writers support their main points with facts, statistics, and quotations. This is the most reasonable technique, though persuasive writers often pick and choose their supporting evidence and omit details that do not support their positions.

- **emotional language:** Writers use images with strong emotional appeal and pay attention to the emotional associations of the words they choose. For example, to sell a diet product, a writer might choose the words *slim* and *slender*, which have positive associations. To criticize the same product, a writer might use *skinny* and *anorexic*, which have negative associations.

- **popular references:** Writers refer to popular movies, books, songs, TV shows, sporting events, etc., with the hope that the popularity of these things will spill over and make the writers' views more popular and convincing.

- **repetition:** Writers repeat key ideas and beliefs hoping that they will sink in.

- **slogans:** Writers use catchy statements or chants to stir an audience or sell a product or idea.

DIRECTIONS: Use the chart below to list examples of persuasive techniques that the writer uses in one of the two persuasive essays in this grouping.

Title of Selection:	
Techniques	**Examples**
supporting evidence	
emotional language	
popular references	
repetition	
slogans	

Name _____ Date _____

"The Trouble with Television" by Robert MacNeil (text page 686)
"The American Dream" by Martin Luther King, Jr. (text page 690)

Literary Focus: Persuasive Essay

An **essay** is a short piece of nonfiction writing on a particular subject. A **persuasive essay** is an essay in which the writer tries to convince readers to act or think in a certain way. A good persuasive essay takes a position and supports it with strong arguments or reasons to convince readers that the position is correct. For example, in "The Trouble with Television," Robin MacNeil states a central position of his essay at the start of the third paragraph: "The trouble with television is that it discourages concentration." He then offers a logical argument to support his position before restating it at the end of the third paragraph: "In short, a lot of television usurps one of the most precious of all human gifts, the ability to focus your attention yourself, rather than just passively surrender it."

DIRECTIONS: On the chart below, list the main positions that each writer takes in the two persuasive essays in this grouping. Then, for each position, identify the supporting argument.

Author	Position	Supporting Argument
MacNeil	The trouble with television is that it it discourages concentration.	

The Diary of Anne Frank, **Act I** by Frances Goodrich and Albert Hackett
(text page 713)

Build Vocabulary

Using the Prefixes *un-* and *in-*

The prefixes *un-* and *in-* both mean "not." An *unabashed* person is someone who is not abashed, or not ashamed. An *insufferable* condition is one that is not able to be suffered, or not endured.

A. DIRECTIONS: Complete each sentence with a word formed by adding *in-* or *un-* to these words from the play: *ashamed, dignified, exposed, furnished, tolerable*. Use each word only once.

1. Was Anne's room _____, or did it have a bed and a dresser?

2. The staircase was hidden behind the wall, _____ to the view of the factory workers.

3. At one point Anne called Peter the most horrible, _____ boy she had ever met.

4. Anne looked very _____ in Peter's clothing.

5. Though Peter was embarrassed, his mother felt he should be _____ to have a girl-friend.

Using the Word Bank

conspicuous	mercurial	leisure	unabashed
insufferable	meticulous	fatalist	ostentatiously

B. DIRECTIONS: Match each word in the left column with its definition in the right column. Write the letter of the definition on the line before the word it defines.

____ 1. conspicuous   a. changeable

____ 2. fatalist   b. noticeable

____ 3. insufferable   c. unbearable; horrible

____ 4. leisure   d. not ashamed

____ 5. mercurial   e. one who believes events are predetermined

____ 6. meticulous   f. in a showy manner

____ 7. ostentatiously   g. free time

____ 8. unabashed   h. very careful about details

Recognizing Antonyms

C. DIRECTIONS: Circle the letter of the word that is most nearly the opposite of the word in capital letters.

1. METICULOUS:
   a. silent
   b. sloppy
   c. sneaky
   d. elastic

2. CONSPICUOUS:
   a. dry
   b. decisive
   c. hidden
   d. creative

3. UNABASHED:
   a. stubborn
   b. enthusiastic
   c. dented
   d. embarrassed

4. LEISURE:
   a. stroll
   b. dress
   c. work
   d. recreation

***The Diary of Anne Frank*, Act I** by Frances Goodrich and Albert Hackett
(text page 713)

Build Spelling Skills: Spelling *ie* or *ei*

Spelling Strategy A famous rhyme tells when to use *ie* and *ei*—although there are exceptions.

- Put *i* before *e* except after *c*
  Or when sounded like *a* as in *neighbor* and *weigh*

  Examples: chi<u>e</u>f   fi<u>e</u>ld   dec<u>ei</u>ve rec<u>ei</u>pt   n<u>ei</u>gh   v<u>ei</u>l

- Here are some exceptions to the rhyme:

  <u>ei</u>ther   financ<u>ie</u>r   for<u>ei</u>gn   forf<u>ei</u>t   h<u>ei</u>ght   h<u>ei</u>r   l<u>ei</u>sure   n<u>ei</u>ther
  prot<u>ei</u>n   s<u>ei</u>ze   sh<u>ei</u>k   sover<u>ei</u>gn   st<u>ei</u>n   th<u>ei</u>r   w<u>ei</u>rd

- The rule also does not apply when the *e* and *i* are not in the same syllable.

  Examples: de•ity   sci•ence   see•ing

A. Practice: On the line after each sentence, write the correct spelling of each italicized word. If all the words are spelled correctly, write *correct*.

1. All *eight* people crowded into three small rooms above the factory *cieling*. _____

2. "We'll have plenty of *liesure*," Mr. Frank joked to *relieve their* tension. _____

3. Dussel, a man in his *fifties, carried* a *breifcase*. _____

4. "I don't like *being dignified!*" Anne told her *freind* Peter. _____

5. *Niether* the Nazis nor the war stopped Anne from *believing* in human goodness.
   _____

B. Complete the sentences below with words that are exceptions to the *ie/ei* rhyme. Do not use a word more than once.

1. To Mr. and Mrs. Frank, who had fled Germany, Dutch was a _____ language.

2. _____ Miep or Mr. Kraler brought food to the people in hiding.

3. As food became scarce, it was hard for Anne to get enough _____ in her diet.

4. In the daytime, she and the others had to keep _____ voices down to a whisper.

5. They lived in fear that the Nazis would _____ them and send them to the death camps.

Challenge: The word *mercurial* comes from Mercury, the Roman messenger god known for his swiftness. On the line after each god listed below, write and define an English word that you think comes from the name of that god. Check your answers in a dictionary.

Example: Mercury, messenger god: <u>mercurial—having swiftly changing moods</u>

1. Ceres, goddess of grain: _____

2. Mars, god of war: _____

3. Titan, one of several giant gods: _____

Unit 8: Drama

The Diary of Anne Frank, **Act I** by Frances Goodrich and Albert Hackett
(text page 713)

Build Grammar Skills: Subject and Verb Agreement

A verb must agree in number with its subject, which may be singular (one) or plural (more than one). Verbs in the present tense usually add *s* or *es* to agree with a singular subject. For example, in the first two sentences below, the verb *rise* adds an *s* to agree with the singular subject *curtain*, and the verb *cross* adds *es* to agree with the singular subject *Mr. Frank*.

                          s   v   s   v

Singular: The <u>curtain</u> <u>rises</u> on an empty scene. Then <u>Mr. Frank</u> <u>crosses</u> the room.

                          s   v   s   v

Plural: Occasionally faint <u>sounds</u> <u>float</u> up from below. <u>Children</u> <u>play</u> in the street.

Remember that the subject of a sentence or clause is never part of a prepositional phrase. In the first sentence below, the subject is *one*, not *employees*, and so takes the singular verb *hides*. In the second sentence, the subject is *Employees*, not *Mr. Frank*, and so takes the plural verb *hide*.

                        s   v

Singular: <u>One</u> of Mr. Frank's employees <u>hides</u> him and his family.

                        s   v

Plural: <u>Employees</u> of Mr. Frank <u>hide</u> him and his family.

A. Practice: Underline the correct form of the verb in parentheses, and circle the subject with which it agrees.

1. The scene (remains, remain) the same throughout the play.

2. The three rooms of the factory's top floor (forms, form) the scene.

3. The door at the foot of the stairs (swings, swing) open.

4. Mr. Frank, a gentle, cultured European, (comes, come) up the steps.

5. He (stand, stands) in the room, looking slowly around.

6. An object among the furnishings (catches, catch) his eye.

7. Footsteps on the stair (signals, signal) the entrance of Miep.

8. Her attitude toward the events (shows, show) great compassion.

9. The notes in the book (proves, prove) to be Anne's diary.

10. The voice of the young girl (echoes, echo) across the years.

B. Writing Application: On the lines below, write three sentences about *The Diary of Anne Frank*. Use the verbs in parentheses in the present tense, and make sure the subjects and verbs agree.

1. (hide)_____

2. (angers) _____

3. (grow) _____

***The Diary of Anne Frank*, Act I** by Frances Goodrich and Albert Hackett
(text page 713)

Reading Strategy: Be Aware of Historical Context

Whenever you read a work of literature that takes place in the past, you will better understand and appreciate it if you are **aware of the historical context**. For example, knowing the events of World War II and the Holocaust will help you to understand the reasons for the Frank family's situation.

DIRECTIONS: In the left column of the following chart, enter details of the dialogue or action that portray the characters' situation. In the right column, write what you know or can determine about the historical context.

Characters' dialogue or action	Historical context
Anne: As my family is Jewish, we emigrated to Holland when Hitler came to Power.	Hitler, Germany's leader, made life hard for the Jews.

Unit 8: Drama

The Diary of Anne Frank, Act I by Frances Goodrich and Albert Hackett
(text page 713)

Literary Focus: Staging

Staging is the act of putting on a play. It includes all the elements that bring a drama to life such as scenery, props (movable objects), costumes, lighting, sound effects, directing, and acting. Playwrights generally provide information about staging as part of the play. This information, called **stage directions**, usually appears in special print and may be set off in brackets or parentheses. In the following example, the stage directions appear in italic print and brackets. Notice that the directions give information about the scene; about Anne's actions, appearance, personality, movements, and costume; and about Mr. Frank's actions.

[*ANNE comes running up the stairs. She is thirteen, quick in her movements, interested in everything, mercurial in her emotions. She wears a cape, long wool socks and carries a schoolbag.*]

MR. FRANK. [*Introducing them*] My wife, Edith. Mr. and Mrs. Van Daan . . . their son, Peter . . . my daughters, Margot and Anne.

DIRECTIONS: On the chart below, list details that provide information about the staging of Act I.

Scene: _____   _____   _____
Scenery & Props: _____   _____   _____
Lighting: _____   _____   _____
Sound: _____   _____   _____
Costumes: _____   _____   _____
Characters: _____   _____   _____

***The Diary of Anne Frank*, Act II** by Frances Goodrich and Albert Hackett
(text page 749)

Build Vocabulary

Using Forms of *effect*

The word *ineffectually* means "in a way that does not produce the desired result." Here are some other words in the same family:

> *effect*: "result"
>
> *effective*: "having the desired result"
>
> *effectively*: "in a way that produced the desired result; actually"
>
> *ineffective*: "not having the desired result"

A. Directions: Complete each sentence with one of the words defined above—*effect, effective, effectively,* or *ineffective.* Do not use the same word twice.

1. The Nazis thought fear was an _____ way of getting people to do their bidding.

2. However, in the case of Miep and Mr. Kraler, Nazi methods proved

   _____.

3. Nazi methods had little _____ on Miep and Mr. Kraler, who tried to save the Franks.

Using the Word Bank

inarticulate   apprehension   intuition   sarcastic   indignant   stealthily   ineffectually

B. Hidden in this puzzle are the seven words from the Word Bank. Their letters may read from right to left, from left to right, from top to bottom, from bottom to top, or diagonally. Find and circle the words. Then, alongside the puzzle, rewrite each word on the line next to its definition.

```
B E T A L U C I T R A N I
K C N O I T I U T N I Q Y
X D A E O M T N S L V L P
F W N I G R S O D E I J C
T H G L C O A J P H B K M
L O I I A E C D T U W T H
I N D I G Y R L F A I E P
Q S N S E V A H J E S R F
O C I T K E S H C E O R S
A Y U W T Y X D A U E W E
N O I S N E H E R P P A Y
I N E F F E C T U A L L Y
```

1. mocking in a critical way: _____

2. the ability to sense without reason: _____

3. tongue-tied: _____

4. in a sneaky way: _____

5. fear of what will happen: _____

6. without having any result: _____

7. angry at some injustice: _____

Selection Support **257**

Unit 8: Drama

The Diary of Anne Frank, Act II by Frances Goodrich and Albert Hackett
(text page 749)

Build Spelling Skills: Using *tu* to Spell the Sound of *choo*

Spelling Strategy The *choo* sound can be spelled in more than one way.

- In the middle of a word, the *choo* sound is usually spelled *tu*:

   Examples: ac<u>tu</u>al   for<u>tu</u>nate   na<u>tu</u>re   si<u>tu</u>ated

- At the beginning or end of a word, the *choo* sound is usually spelled *choo* or *chew*:

   Examples: a<u>choo</u>   <u>choo</u>se   <u>chew</u>   <u>chew</u>y

A. Practice: Complete each word by correctly spelling the *choo* sound.

1. ineffec ____ ally
2. ri ____ al
3. ac ____ ally
4. ____ sing
5. adven ____ re

6. punc ____ al
7. na ____ ral
8. ____ ed
9. for ____ ne
10. ma ____ re

11. punc ____ ation
12. infa ____ ated
13. ____ ing
14. unfor ____ nate
15. rup ____ re

B. Practice: On the line after each sentence, correctly spell the word in italics. If the word is already spelled correctly, write *correct*.

1. Anne Frank had the *misforchoon* of being a Jewish girl in 1940's Holland.

   _____

2. When the Nazis overran Holland, the Jews there were in a deadly *sichooation*.

   _____

3. Those who were *capchoored* were sent to concentration camps and usually killed.

   _____

4. The Nazi efforts to wipe out human decency proved *ineffechooual*.

   _____

5. Although Anne *evenchooally* was killed, she still believed in human goodness.

   _____

Challenge: The word *indignant* contains five smaller words: *in, dig, a, an,* and *ant*. Find at least three smaller words in each word listed below. Write the smaller words on the lines provided.

1. inarticulate: _____

2. apprehension: _____

3. sarcastic: _____

***The Diary of Anne Frank*, Act II** by Frances Goodrich and Albert Hackett
(text page 749)

Build Grammar Skills: Verb Agreement with Indefinite Pronouns

Indefinite pronouns stand for unidentified people or things. However, they do give an indication of whether they are singular or plural, and when they are subjects, their verbs must agree with them in number. In the sentences below, for example, the singular indefinite pronoun *everybody* requires the singular verb *knows*. The plural indefinite pronoun *many* requires the plural verb *visit*.

Singular: Virtually everybody in Amsterdam knows the story of Anne Frank.

Plural: Many now visit the building where she and her family hid.

A few indefinite pronouns can be either singular or plural, depending on the people or things to which they refer. In the following sentences, the indefinite pronoun *most* refers first to one single thing, the building, and then to more than one tourist.

Singular: Most of the building displays items from Anne's stay there.

Plural: Most of the tourists find the visit moving and sad.

Below is a chart of common indefinite pronouns.

Always Singular	another, anybody, anyone, anything, anywhere, each, either, everybody, everyone, everything, much neither, nobody, no one, nothing, nowhere, one, other, somebody, someone, something, somewhere
Always Plural	both, few, many, others, several
Singular or Plural	all, any, enough, more, most, none, some, such

A. Practice: Underline the correct verb from the choices in parentheses. Also circle the subject with which the verb agrees.

1. Everyone in the hiding place (shares, share) three small rooms.

2. Each of the hidden guests (recognizes, recognize) the danger of being captured.

3. Most of the day (passes, pass) slowly.

4. During the day, no one in the rooms (talks, talk) above a whisper.

5. Anyone needing the toilet (waits, wait) until nightfall.

B. Writing Application: On the lines below, write five sentences about *The Diary of Anne Frank.* Use present tense verbs with the subjects in parentheses.

1. (everyone) _____

2. (some) _____

3. (all) _____

4. (several) _____

Unit 8: Drama

The Diary of Anne Frank, Act II by Frances Goodrich and Albert Hackett
(text page 749)

Reading Strategy: Envision

Plays are meant to be performed. When you read them, instead of seeing them, you need to **envision**, or picture, what the performance would be like. The **stage directions**, which usually appear in italics, parentheses, and/or brackets, can help you envision the performance. Follow these guidelines:

- Use the stage directions near the beginning of each scene to help you envision the setting.

- Pay attention to the character labels to know who is speaking and to the accompanying stage directions to actors, which will help you picture how the characters speak and move.

- If the stage directions include any physical descriptions of characters, take those into account in picturing the characters.

- Take note of stage directions that indicate sound effects—the buzzing of a door bell, for example, or a loud crashing sound.

DIRECTIONS: On the chart below, list the details that help you picture the start of Act II, Scene 1, in *The Diary of Anne Frank.*

Setting	Directions to Actors	Characters' Appearance	Sound Effects

***The Diary of Anne Frank*, Act II** by Frances Goodrich and Albert Hackett
(text page 749)

Literary Focus: Characterization and Theme in Drama

Characterization is the method by which writers reveal characters' personalities. In a play, the usual means of characterization include a character's speech and actions as well as the remarks of other characters about him or her. In addition, in the stage directions, the playwright may make direct statements about a character's personality.

The growth or changes that take place in characters in the course of a drama may point to one or more of the work's **themes**. A theme is a general message about life that a work of literature communicates. Often, the characters' behavior and the outcome of events help points to a particular theme, or message, about human experience in general.

DIRECTIONS: On the chart below, list details of characterization in Act II of *The Diary of Anne Frank*, what they reveal about the character, and the themes to which you think they may point. An example is done to get you started.

Character's Words/Actions	What They Reveal	Possible Theme
Mr. Van Daan leaves Margot out when dividing the cake.	He is hungry and growing more selfish and less humane.	People forced to live under harsh conditions often grow selfish and inhumane.

Unit 8: Drama

from *A Walk in the Woods* by Lee Blessing (text page 773)

Build Vocabulary

Using Compound Words

A **compound word** is one that is formed from two smaller words. For example, *warmonger* is a compound of *war* + *monger*, an old word meaning "dealer or trader." Understanding the parts helps you understand the meaning of the compound: A *warmonger* is someone who deals in war.

A. DIRECTIONS: Complete each sentence with a compound word formed by combining these smaller words: *blue, safe, war, guards, eye, heads, prints, drops.* Use each smaller word only once.

1. The _____ simply map out a plan for a treaty.

2. There are built-in _____ to protect both sides from danger.

3. The tips of the missiles do not have multiple _____, according to Honeyman.

4. After using the _____, Botvinnik's vision was momentarily blurred.

Using the Selection Vocabulary

obsolete	technology	arsenals	comprehensive
reductions	verifications	warmongers	

B. DIRECTIONS: Write the word from the box above on the lines after its definition below. The shaded boxes, reading down, will spell out a famous twentieth-century conflict.

1. checks on truth or accuracy

2. science applied for practical use

3. out of date

4. acts that cut down on amount or number

5. those who promote warfare

6. storehouses for weapons

7. complete; all encompassing

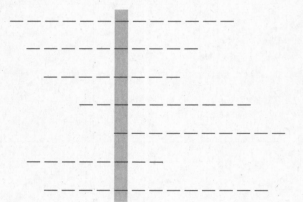

Recognizing Synonyms

C. DIRECTIONS: Circle the letter of the word that has a meaning most like the meaning of the word in capital letters.

1. OBSOLETE:
   a. unused
   b. worthwhile
   c. outmoded
   d. unpleasant

2. REDUCTIONS:
   a. fattenings
   b. lessenings
   c. entrances
   d. trails

3. VERIFICATIONS:
   a. lies
   b. poems
   c. sentences
   d. checks

4. COMPREHENSIVE:
   a. total
   b. creative
   c. oral
   d. thoughtless

from *A Walk in the Woods* by Lee Blessing (text page 773)

Connecting Drama to Social Studies

A **satire** is a work that blends criticism with humor in order to change something in society. It may take the form of a play, a movie, a novel, a story, or even a more visual medium, such as a political cartoon. Most satires criticize or poke fun at an aspect of human behavior or at a broader social, economic, or political issue. *A Walk in the Woods* is a satire that criticizes the Cold War.

A. DIRECTIONS: On the chart below, identify specific criticisms and humorous details in the passage from *A Walk in the Woods*.

Criticisms	Humorous Details

B. DIRECTIONS: In the space below, try creating a political cartoon that might have run in a newspaper in the Cold War era. In your cartoon, blend humor and criticism to convey the same basic message that you think the passage from *A Walk in the Woods* conveys.

Unit 8: Drama

from *A Midsummer Night's Dream* by William Shakespeare (text page 784)
from *Much Ado About Nothing* by William Shakespeare (text page 790)
from *The Life and Death of King Richard III* by William Shakespeare (text page 792)

Build Vocabulary

Using the Suffix *-ous*

The suffix *-ous*, which means "full of," is generally used to turn nouns into adjectives. For example, when you add the suffix to the noun *office*, meaning "an important position, job, or duty," you get *officious*, "full of the importance of one's position, job, or duty; devoted or overly devoted to service or duty."

A. DIRECTIONS: Complete each sentence with an appropriate adjective formed from the noun in parentheses. You may have to drop or change some letters before adding the suffix *-ous*.

1. (caution) When she began reciting Shakespeare's lines, the new actress was _____.

2. (nerve) As she spoke the lines, she became more and more _____.

3. (humor) She did not expect the audience to find the speech so _____.

4. (ridicule) The audience thought the actress's heavy Brooklyn accent was _____.

5. (courtesy) In Shakespeare's day, audiences were not very _____ either.

Using the Word Bank

| apprehension | confederacy | officious | discourse | censured | adversaries |

B. DIRECTIONS: On the line before each pair of words, write *S* if the words are synonyms and *A* if they are antonyms.

____ 1. apprehension, confusion   ____ 4. confederacy, plot

____ 2. discourse, reasoning   ____ 5. officious, obliging

____ 3. adversaries, friends   ____ 6. censured, praised

Sentence Completions

C. DIRECTIONS: Circle the letter of the choice that best completes each sentence.

1. Hermia's _____ of her surroundings comes from her ears as well as her eyes.
   a. adversaries   b. apprehension   c. confederacy   d. discourse

2. Helena considers Hermia to be part of the _____ that is plotting to deceive her.
   a. censured   b. apprehension   c. confederacy   d. officious

3. Benedick seeks a woman of sound _____, not an illogical creature.
   a. adversaries   b. officious   c. confederacy   d. discourse

4. King Richard recalls when Edward fought his _____ in battle.
   a. adversaries   b. officious   c. censured   d. discourse

from *A Midsummer Night's Dream* by William Shakespeare (text page 784)
from *Much Ado About Nothing* by William Shakespeare (text page 790)
from *The Life and Death of King Richard III* by William Shakespeare (text page 792)

Build Spelling Skills: Using *cious* to Spell the Sound of *shus*

Spelling Strategy   Many adjectives end in the *shus* sound, which has several spellings.

- In most cases, the *shus* sound is spelled *cious*:

    Examples: atro<u>cious</u>   fero<u>cious</u>   judi<u>cious</u>

- If the adjective is formed from a noun ending in *tion*, the *shus* sound is often spelled *tious*:

    Examples: cau<u>tion</u>   cau<u>tious</u>   infec<u>tion</u>   infec<u>tious</u>

- Other spellings include *seous, scious,* and, when a *k* sound is included, *xious*.

    Examples: nau<u>seous</u>   con<u>scious</u>   an<u>xious</u> (*k* sound before the *shus*)

A. Practice: On the line after each phonetic respelling, write the correct spelling of the word.

1. (preshus): _____

2. (ofishus): _____

3. (delishus): _____

4. (nootrishus): _____

5. (malishus): _____

6. (nawshus): _____

7. (sooperstishus): _____

8. (konshus): _____

9. (obnokshus): _____

10. (vishus): _____

B. Practice: Complete each sentence with an adjective formed from the word in parentheses. Write the adjective on the line provided.

1. (flirtation) Several characters in *A Midsummer Night's Dream* seem very _____.

2. (grace) Hermia tries to be _____ in her conversations.

3. (suspicion) Helena is _____ of the others' trickery.

4. (ambition) Richard III is very _____.

5. (anxiety) He is _____ to replace Edward as king.

Challenge: The *s* in *censured* has an *sh* sound: *senshurd*. Can you think of other words in which an *s* followed by a *u* has the sound of *sh*? List as many as you can on the lines below.

_____   _____   _____

_____   _____   _____

_____   _____   _____

from *A Midsummer Night's Dream* by William Shakespeare (text page 784)
from *Much Ado About Nothing* by William Shakespeare (text page 790)
from *The Life and Death of King Richard III* by William Shakespeare (text page 792)

Build Grammar Skills: Subject and Verb Agreement in Inverted Sentences

In a typical English sentence, the subject comes before the verb, but in an **inverted sentence**, the subject follows the verb. Many inverted sentences today begin with the words *there* and *here*. In Shakespeare's day, inverted sentences of all kinds were more common. Whatever the words and their order, the verb in an inverted sentence must still agree with its subject in number. In the following sentences, the verb *comes* agrees with the singular subject *sound*, and the verb *are* agrees with the plural subject *brows*.

Regular: The <u>sound</u> of Lysander's voice <u>comes</u> to my ear.

Inverted: To my ear <u>comes</u> the <u>sound</u> of Lysander's voice.

Regular: Our <u>brows</u> <u>are</u> now bound with victorious wreaths.

Inverted: Now <u>are</u> our <u>brows</u> bound with victorious wreaths.

A. Practice: Underline the correct verb from the choices in parentheses, and circle its subject. On the line before the sentence, write *R* if the sentence uses regular subject-verb order and *I* if it is an inverted sentence.

_____ 1. There (is, are) many English writers of great brilliance.

_____ 2. At the top of the list (sits, sit) William Shakespeare.

_____ 3. For a writer of the past, Shakespeare (expresses, express) remarkably modern ideas.

_____ 4. Brilliant (is, are) his understanding of human beings and their problems.

_____ 5. In the lines of his writing there (lies, lie) many sharp insights into the human heart.

_____ 6. Delightful, too, (is, are) the poetry of his lines.

_____ 7. There (is, are) a memorable speech at the opening of his play about Richard III.

_____ 8. Here Shakespeare powerfully (conveys, convey) Richard's attitudes and feelings.

_____ 9. With these lines (comes, come) a memorable depiction of Richard's character.

_____ 10. Nowhere (is, are) there other playwrights of such brilliance today.

B. Writing Application: On the lines below, write five sentences about Shakespeare and his plays. Use inverted order and present tense verbs in all of your sentences.

1. _____

2. _____

3. _____

4. _____

5. _____

from *A Midsummer Night's Dream* by William Shakespeare (text page 784)
from *Much Ado About Nothing* by William Shakespeare (text page 790)
from *The Life and Death of King Richard III* by William Shakespeare (text page 792)

Reading Strategy: Summarizing

The powerful poetry of Shakespeare's plays, written centuries ago, uses language that you may not always understand completely. Nevertheless, you should be able to grasp the main action of the scenes and the key ideas that characters express. Summarizing can help you focus on these main points. When you **summarize**, you state in your own words the main ideas and details of a piece of writing.

DIRECTIONS: Fill out the following chart to help you summarize the scene from *A Midsummer Night's Dream*. An example is done to get you started.

Passage	Summary
lines 1–7	Hermia asks Lysander why he has left her.

Unit 8: Drama

from *A Midsummer Night's Dream* by William Shakespeare (text page 784)
from *Much Ado About Nothing* by William Shakespeare (text page 790)
from *The Life and Death of King Richard III* by William Shakespeare (text page 792)

Literary Focus: Scenes and Soliloquies

Most plays are divided into **acts**, which are further divided into **scenes**. A scene usually consists of the dramatic interaction between two or more characters. The characters speak directly to each other in **dialogue**, or conversation between characters, and the play's events unfold as the characters interact. Sometimes, however, Shakespeare includes a **soliloquy** in which only one character appears on stage and reveals his or her thoughts in a **monologue**, or speech by one character. The character delivering the soliloquy may simply speak his or her thoughts aloud, as if talking to himself or herself. The speeches by Benedick and Richard III are both soliloquies.

DIRECTIONS: Use the chart below to record the thoughts and attitudes expressed in either Richard's or Benedick's soliloquy.

Character's Name:		
Remark	**Line Number(s)**	**What It Reveals**

"The Secret Heart" by Robert P. Tristram Coffin (text page 809)

Build Vocabulary

Using the Word Root -semble-

A. DIRECTIONS: The word root -semble- means "to seem" or "appear." Choose the word below that matches each definition. Write the word in the blanks at the right, one letter per blank.

resemble   resemblance   semblance   resembling

1. a look that seems like another   _ _ _ _ _ _ _ _ _ _ _

2. appearing like something else   _ _ _ _ _ _ _ _ _ _

3. to seem or appear like something else   _ _ _ _ _ _ _ _

4. a seeming likeness   _ _ _ _ _ _ _ _ _

Now write an original sentence using each word above with the root -semble-.

5. _____

6. _____

7. _____

8. _____

Using the Word Bank

kindled	semblance

B. DIRECTIONS: Write the Word Bank word that best completes each sentence.

1. The boy cleaned his messy room in an effort to give it some _____ of neatness.

2. The novel _____ the reader's interest in other books by the same author.

Recognizing Antonyms

C. DIRECTIONS: Circle the letter of the word that is most *opposite* in meaning to the word in CAPITAL LETTERS.

1. KINDLED
   a. lit
   b. burned
   c. deadened
   d. drew

2. SEMBLANCE
   a. difference
   b. likeness
   c. resemblance
   d. look

Unit 9: Poetry

"The Secret Heart" by Robert P. Tristram Coffin (text page 809)

Build Spelling Skills: The *uhl* Sound Spelled *le*

Spelling Strategy The Word Bank word *kindled* is a form of the word *kindle*, which ends with the *uhl* sound spelled *le*. In most English words that end with the *uhl* sound, the sound is spelled *le*.

Examples: apple   trouble   rattle

A. Practice: Complete each sentence with a word that ends with the *uhl* sound spelled *le*. The first letter of the word is given as a clue. Write the entire word.

1. When some people smile, a d_____ forms on each cheek.

2. A t_____ is a reptile that travels with a hard shell on its back.

3. If your electricity goes out, you might light a c_____ in order to see.

4. When throwing out a pile of old magazines, tie them up in a b_____.

5. When your aunt marries, her husband becomes your u_____.

6. Most babies drink from a b_____ before learning how to use a cup.

B. Practice: In each sentence, find a word ending with the *uhl* sound that is spelled wrong. Cross out the word and write it correctly above the line.

1. In "The Secret Heart," the father is presented as a shining exampel of what a good and loving parent should be.

2. Every night, the father performs the simpel task of checking on his son by lighting a match in the dark.

3. The match glows for just a littel bit and then burns out in the dark room.

4. No doubt the boy never finds it hard to settel back to sleep after seeing his father's secret heart.

Challenge: Although the Word Bank word *kindled* begins with the letters *kind*, it is not related in meaning to the word *kind*. Other words in English also begin with the letters *kind*. Use a dictionary to help you explain the meanings of these words.

1. kindergarten _____

2. kindhearted _____

3. kindred _____

4. kindling _____

"The Secret Heart" by Robert P. Tristram Coffin (text page 809)

Build Grammar Skills: Comparison of Modifiers

There are two kinds of modifiers:

- An **adjective** modifies (describes) a noun or pronoun.

- An **adverb** modifies a verb, adjective, or other adverb.

Modifiers may appear in different forms:

- The **positive** form is used when no comparison is being made.

- The **comparative** form is used when two things are being compared.

- The **superlative** form is used when three or more things are being compared.

Positive	Comparative	Superlative
slow	slower	slowest
costly	costlier	costliest
slowly	more slowly	most slowly

A. Practice: Underline each modifier. Above the modifier, write C if its form is comparative and S if it is superlative. Then circle the word that is modified. The first one is done for you.

1. The father visited his son at the quietest (hour) of the night.

2. The father entered the room more quietly than a mouse.

3. His heart-shaped hands were the happiest sight the son ever saw.

4. The father gazed at his son most tenderly at this late hour.

5. The boy slept more soundly after his father left the room.

6. An older child might not have appreciated the experience as much.

B. Writing Application: Imagine that the boy or his father kept a diary in which they described their inner thoughts and feelings about each another. Write sentences that the character might have written. Use each adjective or adverb below in the form that is indicated.

1. kind (superlative) _____

2. loving (comparative) _____

3. precious (comparative) _____

4. fine (superlative) _____

5. sweet (comparative) _____

6. gently (superlative) _____

Unit 9: Poetry

Reading for Success: Strategies for Reading Poetry

Poetry is unlike other types of literature. Poets use language imaginatively to create images, tell stories, explore feelings and experiences, and suggest meanings. They choose and combine words carefully to enable you to see your world in a new and fresh way. To appreciate and enjoy poetry fully, use the following reading strategies:

- **Read lines according to punctuation.** Don't automatically stop at the end of every line. Pause as you always would, briefly for commas and semi-colons, and longer for end marks like periods and question marks.

- **Identify the speaker.** The speaker in poetry is the voice that the poet creates to communicate his or her message. Sometimes the speaker is identified; sometimes the speaker is a nameless voice; and sometimes the speaker is the poet.

- **Use your senses.** Poetry is full of images that appeal to your senses of sight, hearing, taste, smell and touch. You must use your senses to experience the world that the poem introduces you to.

- **Paraphrase the lines.** Restate a line or passage in your own words to be sure you understand it.

DIRECTIONS: Read the following poem by Sandra Cisneros, and use the reading strategies to increase your comprehension. In the margin, note where you read lines according to punctuation, identify the speaker, use your senses, and paraphrase the lines.

"Twister Hits Houston" by Sandra Cisneros

Papa was on the front porch.
Mama was in the kitchen.
Mama was trying
to screw a lightbulb into a fixture.
Papa was watching the rain.
Mama, it's a cyclone for sure,
he shouted to his wife in the kitchen.
Papa who was sitting on his front porch
when the storm hit
said the twister ripped
the big black oak to splinter,
tossed a green sedan into his garden,
and banged the back door
like a mad cat wanting in.
Mama who was in the kitchen
said Papa saw everything,
the big oak ripped to kindling,
the green sedan land out back,
the back door slam and slam.
I missed it.
Mama was in the kitchen Papa explained.
Papa was sitting on the front porch.
That light bulb is still sitting
where I left it. Don't matter now.
Got no electricity anyway.

"The Secret Heart" by Robert P. Tristram Coffin (text page 809)

Literary Focus: Symbols

A **symbol** is an object, person, or idea that stands for something beyond itself. For example, a dove is literally a kind of bird. But a dove is also a universal symbol for peace. A sunrise is a sunrise, but in a story or poem, it might also be the symbol for a new beginning. Writers use symbols as a way of making a point or reinforcing a theme.

In "The Secret Heart," several elements may be considered symbols for ideas greater than themselves. For example, the father in the poem could be considered a symbol representing the ideas of love and protection.

DIRECTIONS: In the chart below, read each element listed under "Symbol." Then explain the larger idea that the element might represent. One example is provided.

Symbol	Larger Idea It Represents
the father	love, protection, security
the boy	
the lighted match	
the heart-shaped hands	
the room's darkness	

Unit 9: Poetry

"The Wreck of the Hesperus" by Henry Wadsworth Longfellow (text page 817)
"The Centaur" by May Swenson (text page 820)

Build Vocabulary

Using the Suffix -ful

A. DIRECTIONS: In each sentence, replace the italicized phrase with one of the following words ending in -ful, meaning "full of" or "having the qualities of":

hopeful   mournful   restful   joyful

1. The family's vacation by the beach was relaxing and *(having the qualities of rest)* _____.

2. The city was *(full of hope)* _____ about the Olympics coming there.

3. The lottery winner was clearly happy and *(full of joy)* _____.

4. The mood at the funeral was sad and *(having the qualities of mourning)* _____.

Using the Word Bank

scornful	gale	breakers	cinched	canter	negligent

B. DIRECTIONS: Write the Word Bank word that best completes each sentence.

1. The diver _____ the equipment firmly around his waist.

2. The _____ guard was asleep when the thieves slipped past him.

3. The _____ enemies sneered at each other as they passed.

4. The jockey tried to _____ the horse at a slow, steady pace.

5. The unexpected _____ blew the roofs off several houses.

6. Swimmers came ashore when they saw the tall _____ rolling toward them.

Analogies

C. DIRECTIONS: For each related pair of words in CAPITAL LETTERS, choose the pair that best expresses a *similar* relationship. Circle the letter of your choice.

1. GALE : WIND ::
   a. rain : drop
   b. wind : blow
   c. blizzard : snow
   d. tornado : volcano

2. NEGLIGENT : RESPONSIBLE ::
   a. top : high
   b. late : tardy
   c. messy : mess
   d. bad : good

3. SCORNFUL : HATRED ::
   a. beautiful : beauty
   b. hope : hopeful
   c. cheerful : sad
   d. successful : lovely

4. CINCHED : FASTENED ::
   a. tied : untied
   b. ran : raced
   c. looked : hid
   d. clapped : laughed

5. BREAKERS : OCEAN ::
   a. dunes : desert
   b. mountain : hill
   c. rainforest : rain
   d. water : wet

6. CANTER : SLOW ::
   a. horse : rider
   b. gallop : fast
   c. oats : food
   d. car : key

"The Wreck of the Hesperus" by Henry Wadsworth Longfellow (text page 817)
"The Centaur" by May Swenson (text page 820)

Build Spelling Skills: Add the Suffix *-ful* Without Doubling the Final *l*

Spelling Strategy The Word Bank word *scornful* is formed by adding the suffix *-ful* to the word *scorn*.

• When the suffix *-ful* is added to a word, never double the final *l*.

WRONG: scorn + ful = scornfull

RIGHT: scorn + ful = scornful

A. Practice: Add the suffix *-ful* to each of the words below. Write the new word.

1. wonder _____   6. soul _____

2. power _____   7. hand _____

3. help _____   8. mouth _____

4. basket _____   9. dread _____

5. rest _____   10. grace _____

B. Practice: Complete each sentence by adding the suffix *-ful* to the word in parentheses. Write the new word.

1. In "The Wreck of the Hesperus," the narrator describes the (fright) _____ voyage of the schooner.

2. The skipper was a (boast) _____ man.

3. As the storm increased, his daughter grew more and more (fear) _____.

4. During the (fate) _____ voyage, the girl's father became a frozen corpse.

5. Eventually the girl also died a (woe) _____ death, lashed close to a drifting mast.

6. In "The Centaur," the narrator describes her (event) _____ summer afternoons.

7. Each day, the (cheer) _____ girl would cut a tree branch and pretend it was a riding horse.

8. As part of her (play) _____ routine, the girl imagined that she herself was a racing horse.

9. The girl was not (care) _____ about keeping herself clean or tidy.

Challenge: By changing just one letter in the Word Bank word *gale*, you get the word *gate*. How many other words can you make by changing just one letter in *gale*? Can you find at least eight? Write them on the lines provided.

_____ _____ _____ _____

_____ _____ _____ _____

Unit 9: Poetry

"The Wreck of the Hesperus" by Henry Wadsworth Longfellow (text page 817)
"The Centaur" by May Swenson (text page 820)

Build Grammar Skills: Comparisons With *more* and *most*

Some adjectives and adverbs, when used in comparisons, have the word *more* or *most* added to them.

- When comparing two things, add the word *more*.

- When comparing three or more things, add the word *most*.

Comparative: Which of the two poems do you find *more inspiring*?
(compares two poems)

Superlative: It is the most *inspiring* poem I ever read.
(compares all the poems ever read by the speaker)

A. Practice: Read each sentence. If a comparative or superlative form of an adjective is used incorrectly, cross out the wrong word and write it correctly.

1. "The Wreck of the Hesperus" is one of Longfellow's more famous poems of all.

2. The skipper was most confident than his little daughter was.

3. As the voyage continued, the storm grew most violent than before.

4. Seeing her father's frozen corpse was perhaps the girl's more horrifying experience.

5. "The Centaur" is a most cheerful poem than "The Wreck of the Hesperus" is.

6. The girl had the more fun of all when riding her make-believe horse.

7. By the end of her ride, she was most filthy than she had been earlier.

8. Riding her horse was the more exciting thing the girl could do.

B. Writing Application: Imagine you were a passenger on the Hesperus or a playmate of the girl in "The Centaur." Write sentences that describe your experiences. Use the phrases below in your sentences.

1. more dangerous _____

2. most tiring _____

3. more quickly _____

4. most courageous _____

5. more satisfying _____

6. most unforgettable _____

"The Wreck of the Hesperus" by Henry Wadsworth Longfellow (text page 817)
"The Centaur" by May Swenson (text page 820)

Reading Strategy: Read Lines According to Punctuation

When you read poetry, you should **read according to the punctuation** rather than stopping automatically at the end of each line. Punctuation refers to marks such as periods, commas, colons, semicolons, dashes, question marks, and exclamation marks. Each type of punctuation serves as a signal that tells you how to read. For example, a dash tells you to pause briefly; a comma also tells you to pause. The semicolon in the sentence you just read also told you to pause! And the exclamation mark at the end of the previous sentence told you to read with special emphasis.

DIRECTIONS: For each poem, record examples of punctuation that help you understand how the poem should be read. One example is provided.

Name of Poem	Example of Punctuation	What It Tells You About Reading
"The Wreck of the Hesperus"	comma after the word *Hesperus* in line 1	Pause briefly before reading second line.
"The Wreck of the Hesperus"		
"The Wreck of the Hesperus"		
"The Centaur"		
"The Centaur"		
"The Centaur"		

"The Wreck of the Hesperus" by Henry Wadsworth Longfellow (text page 817)
"The Centaur" by May Swenson (text page 820)

Literary Focus: Narrative Poetry

A **narrative poem** is a poem that tells a story. Like a short story, a narrative poem has a plot, setting, characters, dialogue, and a theme. The plot consists of these elements:

- exposition—the introduction to the story

- rising action—the events that tell how characters try to solve a problem they face

- climax—the highest dramatic moment in the story

- falling action—events that follow the climax

- resolution—the story's outcome, or result

Unlike a short story, a narrative poem has rhythm and rhyme. In addition, the poem is broken into stanzas instead of paragraphs.

DIRECTIONS: Complete the following outline with details from either "The Wreck of the Hesperus" or "The Centaur."

I. Plot
   A. Exposition: _____

   _____

   B. Rising action: _____

   _____

   C. Climax: _____

   _____

   D. Falling action: _____

   _____

   E. Resolution: _____

II. Setting: _____

   _____

III. Characters: _____

   _____

IV. Dialogue: _____

   _____

V. Theme: _____

   _____

"Harlem Night Song" by Langston Hughes (text page 828)
"Blow, Blow, Thou Winter Wind" by William Shakespeare (text page 829)
"love is a place" by E. E. Cummings (text page 830)
"The Freedom of the Moon" by Robert Frost (text page 831)

Build Vocabulary

Using the Word Root *-lus-*

A. DIRECTIONS: Each word below on the left contains the root *-lus-*, meaning "to light." Match each word with its definition. Write the letter of the definition on the line next to the word it defines.

____ 1. lustrous   a. an example that makes something clear

____ 2. illustrator   b. brilliantly outstanding

____ 3. illustration   c. reflecting light evenly without sparkle

____ 4. illustrious   d. one who gives an example

Using the Word Bank

roam	keen	feigning	breadth	luster

B. DIRECTIONS: Write the Word Bank word that best matches each clue.

1. It's what a gemstone might have. _____

2. It's what an actor is doing on stage. _____

3. It's what a person who is lost might do. _____

4. It's something a builder might measure. _____

5. It might describe the edge of a knife. _____

Recognizing Synonyms

C. DIRECTIONS: Circle the word or phrase that is most *similar* in meaning to the word in CAPITAL LETTERS.

1. KEEN
   a. dull
   b. crooked
   c. sharp
   d. selfish

2. ROAM
   a. stop
   b. spill
   c. clean
   d. wander

3. FEIGNING
   a. fainting
   b. pretending
   c. penalizing
   d. helping

4. BREADTH
   a. width
   b. length
   c. depth
   d. height

5. LUSTER
   a. scratch
   b. darkness
   c. shine
   d. smell

Unit 9: Poetry

"Harlem Night Song" by Langston Hughes (text page 828)
"Blow, Blow, Thou Winter Wind" by William Shakespeare (text page 829)
"love is a place" by E. E. Cummings (text page 830)
"The Freedom of the Moon" by Robert Frost (text page 831)

Build Spelling Skills: *i* Before *e* Except After *c* . . .

Spelling Strategy In the Word Bank word *feigning*, the letters *e* and *i* appear together. Note that the *e* comes before the *i*.

- A well-known rule states: "Use *i* before *e* except after *c* or when sounded like *ay* as in *neighbor* and *weigh*." In the word *feigning*, *e* comes before *i* because the word has the *ay* sound, as in *neighbor* and *weigh*.

     Examples: f<u>ie</u>ld   fr<u>ie</u>nd   rec<u>ei</u>ve   c<u>ei</u>ling   n<u>ei</u>gh   w<u>ei</u>ght

     Exceptions: The words *seize, either, leisure, weird, height,* and *protein* are exceptions to the above rule. In all those words, *e* comes before *i*, even though the letters do not follow *c* and are not sounded as *ay*.

A. Practice: Choose the correctly spelled word to complete each sentence. Write the word on the line. If you are unsure of an answer, consult a dictionary.

1. The (neighbors, nieghbors) _____ threw a block party.

2. Everyone was very (friendly, freindly) _____ to the newcomers.

3. The radio can both send and (recieve, receive) _____ signals.

4. What is the (wieght, weight) _____ of the package you wish to send?

5. (Neither, Niether) _____ of the twins was in school today.

6. I measured my (hieght, height) _____ with a yardstick.

7. Did you save the (receipt, reciept) _____ for the item you wish to return?

8. My (niece, neice) _____ and nephew will be visiting me next week.

B. Practice: In each sentence, find a word with the letters *e* and *i* together. If the word is misspelled, cross it out and write it correctly.

1. In "Harlem Night Song," the speaker invites the reader to roam through the nieghborhood.

2. The speaker's repetition of "I love you" indicates that he considers the reader to be a good freind.

3. In "Blow, Blow, Thou Winter Wind," the speaker describes most friendships as fiegning.

4. The speaker seems to beleive that most people are insincere and ungrateful.

5. In "love is a place," the speaker percieves the world as a positive and powerful place of love.

6. He does not seem to view the world as feircely as does the speaker in Shakespeare's poem.

7. In "The Freedom of the Moon," the speaker seems to enjoy his liesure moments gazing at the moon.

"Harlem Night Song" by Langston Hughes (text page 828)
"Blow, Blow, Thou Winter Wind" by William Shakespeare (text page 829)
"love is a place" by E. E. Cummings (text page 830)
"The Freedom of the Moon" by Robert Frost (text page 831)

Build Grammar Skills: Irregular Comparisons of Modifiers

Although many modifiers make their comparative and superlative forms by adding -er and -est, some modifiers do not. These modifiers have **irregular forms of comparisons**.

Positive	Comparative	Superlative
bad	worse	worst
good	better	best
well	better	best
little	less	least
many, much	more	most

A. Practice: Underline the modifier in each sentence. Above the modifier, write C if it is comparative and S if it is superlative.

1. Langston Hughes is better known than the average poet.

2. Some of his most famous poems are about life in Harlem.

3. "Blow, Blow, Thou Winter Wind" seems to portray man in the worst way.

4. The speaker describes friendship as less sincere than it appears.

5. "love is a place" is more positive in its attitude than Shakespeare's poem is.

6. E. E. Cummings is considered one of the best poets of his generation.

7. "The Freedom of the Moon" is one of Robert Frost's least known poems.

8. In terms of its quality, however, you could find no better work!

B. Writing Application: Imagine you were asked to comment on the four poems you read. Write your comments, using each of the irregular modifiers below.

1. best _____

2. worse _____

3. less _____

4. most _____

5. least _____

6. better _____

Unit 9: Poetry

"Harlem Night Song" by Langston Hughes (text page 828)
"Blow, Blow, Thou Winter Wind" by William Shakespeare (text page 829)
"love is a place" by E. E. Cummings (text page 830)
"The Freedom of the Moon" by Robert Frost (text page 831)

Reading Strategy: Identify the Speaker

The **speaker** in a poem is the imaginary character or voice assumed by the poet. Sometimes the speaker may represent the poet. Other times the speaker may be someone entirely different from the poet. In either case, you can learn much about the speaker by paying close attention to the poem's details. The things that speakers say, and the ways they express themselves, tell you a lot about their personality and attitudes.

For example, in "Harlem Night Song," the speaker repeats the phrase "I love you." This detail helps you to infer, or guess, that the speaker has a warm and generous heart and enjoys his companion's company.

DIRECTIONS: Use the following chart to help you analyze the speakers in the four poems. In the left column, record details from each poem that are clues to the speaker's personality. In the right column, explain what inferences you can make about the speaker, based on the details. One example is provided.

Name of Poem	Clue	Inference About the Speaker
"Harlem Night Song"	The speaker repeats the phrase, "I love you."	The speaker has a warm and generous heart.
"Harlem Night Song"		
"Blow, Blow, Thou Winter Wind"		
"love is a place"		
"The Freedom of the Moon"		

"Harlem Night Song" by Langston Hughes (text page 828)
"Blow, Blow, Thou Winter Wind" by William Shakespeare (text page 829)
"love is a place" by E. E. Cummings (text page 830)
"The Freedom of the Moon" by Robert Frost (text page 831)

Literary Focus: Lyric Poetry

Lyric poetry expresses the poet's thoughts and feelings in lively and musical language. It creates a mood through vivid images, descriptive words, and the musical quality of its lines. In a lyric poem, you can almost "see" and "hear" the images that the poet presents. For example, in "Harlem Night Song," it is almost possible to "hear" the band that is playing down the street. As you read a lyric poem, concentrate on the images created by the words, and try to experience those images as if you were "inside" the poem.

DIRECTIONS: For each of the four poems, use the chart below to record the most vivid images you find. One example is provided.

Poem	Image
"Harlem Night Song"	A band is playing down the street.
"Harlem Night Song"	
"Blow, Blow, Thou Winter Wind"	
"love is a place"	
"The Freedom of the Moon"	

Unit 9: Poetry

"January" by John Updike (text page 836)
Two Haiku by Bashō and Moritake (text page 837)
"Identity" by Julio Noboa Polanco (text page 838)
"400-Meter Free Style" by Maxine Kumin (text page 839)

Build Vocabulary

Using Forms of *fertile*

The word *fertile* is an adjective that means "rich" or "productive." The word *fertile* has several related words that are other parts of speech. For example, the word *fertilize* is a verb, and the word *fertilizer* is a noun.

A. DIRECTIONS: Use one of the following words to complete each sentence below.

fertilizer   fertility   fertilize   fertile

1. Someone with a _____ imagination has a lot of ideas.

2. A _____ contains minerals and other nutrients that help plants grow.

3. Doctors use _____ drugs to help some women become pregnant.

4. Farmers often use manure to _____ their soil.

Using the Word Bank

harnessed	abyss	shunned	fertile
catapults	cunningly	extravagance	nurtures

B. DIRECTIONS: Write the Word Bank word that best matches each clue.

1. It's how a clever fox behaves. _____

2. It's what classmates did to a student they didn't like. _____

3. It's what a loving gardener does to her flowers. _____

4. It's how the horse was kept near the fence. _____

5. It describes a field that grows lots of crops. _____

6. It's something you don't want to fall into. _____

7. It's a waste of money. _____

8. It's how a pole-vaulter gets over the bar. _____

Recognizing Antonyms

C. DIRECTIONS: Circle the letter of the word that is most *opposite* in meaning to the word in CAPITAL LETTERS.

1. CUNNINGLY: a. cleverly b. quickly c. slowly d. stupidly

2. SHUNNED: a. attended b. ignored c. shouted d. injured

"January" by John Updike (text page 836)
Two Haiku by Bashō and Moritake (text page 837)
"Identity" by Julio Noboa Polanco (text page 838)
"400-Meter Free Style" by Maxine Kumin (text page 839)

Build Spelling Skills: The Short *i* Sound Spelled *y*

Spelling Strategy   The Word Bank word *abyss* contains the short *i* sound spelled *y*.

- In most words in English, the short *i* sound is spelled *i*. However, in some words the short *i* sound is spelled *y*.

   Examples: rhythm   system   myth

A. Practice: Fill in the missing letter in each word. Write the entire word. Then write its meaning. Finally, use the word in a sentence. Use a dictionary for help, if necessary.

1. m___stery   Meaning: _____

   Sentence: _____

2. s___non___m   Meaning: _____

   Sentence: _____

3. ab___smal   Meaning: _____

   Sentence: _____

4. t___pical   Meaning: _____

   Sentence: _____

5. l___nx   Meaning: _____

   Sentence: _____

B. Practice: In each sentence, find a word with the short *i* sound that is spelled wrong. Cross out the word and write it correctly.

1. The lines in "January" have a steady rhithm that doesn't change throughout the entire poem.

2. The first of the Two Haiku offers a lirical description of the sounds and sights of the night.

3. The speaker in "Identity" sees a tall, ugly weed as a simbol for true freedom.

4. The shape of the lines in "400-Meter Free Style" helps readers envision the phisical movements of the swimmer.

Challenge: The Word Bank word *catapults* comes from the Greek word *katapeltes*, meaning "to throw down." Write the Word Bank word that matches each clue below. Use a dictionary for help, if necessary.

1. Which word comes from the Greek words *a* and *byssos* meaning "without bottom"?
   _____

2. Which word comes from the Latin word *ferre*, meaning "bear"? _____

3. Which word comes from the Old French word *harneis*, meaning "armor"? _____

"January" by John Updike (text page 836)
Two Haiku by Bashō and Moritake (text page 837)
"Identity" by Julio Noboa Polanco (text page 838)
"400-Meter Free Style" by Maxine Kumin (text page 839)

Build Grammar Skills: Coordinate Adjectives

Coordinate adjectives are adjectives that modify the same noun separately and equally.

> **Example:** A *tall, handsome* stranger rode into town.

- To test whether two adjectives are coordinate, switch the order of the adjectives. If the new order still makes sense, the adjectives are coordinate.

> **Example:** A *handsome, tall* stranger rode into town.

- Use a comma to separate coordinate adjectives.

A. Practice: Read each sentence. If it contains coordinate adjectives, underline each adjective. Insert a comma between the adjectives.

1. In "January," there are fat snowy footsteps that track the floor.

2. The river is a cold icy place that remains still beneath the trees.

3. In Two Haiku, a bright thunderous bolt of lightning appears in the sky.

4. A beautiful fragile butterfly flutters onto a tree branch.

5. In "Identity," the speaker does not wish to be an admired watered flower.

6. The speaker envies the freedom of a wild musty weed.

7. In "400-Meter Free Style," a coordinated strong swimmer moves steadily.

8. The long difficult challenge is completed after more than four hours.

B. Writing Application: For each noun below, supply two coordinate adjectives. Then write a complete sentence using your adjectives and the noun they modify.

1. sky _____

_____

2. storm _____

_____

3. weed _____

_____

4. flower _____

_____

5. athlete _____

_____

"January" by John Updike (text page 836)
Two Haiku by Bashō and Moritake (text page 837)
"Identity" by Julio Noboa Polanco (text page 838)
"400-Meter Free Style" by Maxine Kumin (text page 839)

Reading Strategy: Paraphrase Lines

When you **paraphrase lines**, you restate in your own words what someone else has written. One purpose of paraphrasing lines is to see how well you really understand what you have read. With a poem, you might attempt to restate the meaning of each line or stanza in your own words. If you succeed, it shows that you understand the poem well. When you paraphrase, try not to use too much of the writer's original phrasing. At the same time, be careful not to change the meaning of the original passage; just express it in a different way.

For example, in "January" the poet writes: "The river is/A frozen place/Held still beneath/The trees of lace." You might paraphrase the lines like this: The river has turned to ice and remains motionless under the icy trees.

DIRECTIONS: Select your favorite lines from each of the four poems. For each passage or stanza, paraphrase the main idea in your own words. One example is provided.

Name of Poem	Original Text	Paraphrase
"January"	The river is/A frozen place/Held still beneath/The trees of lace.	The river has turned to ice and remains motionless under the icy trees.
"January"		
Two Haiku		
"Identity"		
"400-Meter Free Style"		

Name _____ Date _____

"January" by John Updike (text page 836)
Two Haiku by Bashō and Moritake (text page 837)
"Identity" by Julio Noboa Polanco (text page 838)
"400-Meter Free Style" by Maxine Kumin (text page 839)

Literary Focus: Poetic Form

Poetic form is the structure of a poem, or how it is shaped. Poems, like houses, may comes in different shapes and sizes.
- In a **lyric poem**, the lines are usually grouped into stanzas. "January," for example, is a lyric poem divided into four stanzas. Each stanza contains four lines.
- In Japanese **haiku**, the poem consists of three lines. The first and third lines have five syllables each. The second line has seven syllables. Count the syllables in each line of Two Haiku as an example.
- In **free verse**, the poem has no set structure. Its line breaks and stanzas are created however the poet wishes. "Identity" is an example of free verse.
- In **concrete poetry**, the poem takes on a special shape to represent an idea or image within the poem. "400-Meter Free Style" is an example of concrete poetry.

DIRECTIONS: Write your answers to the following questions.

1. If you were to rewrite "January" as a concrete poem, what shape do you think would best express the main idea of the poem? Why?

   _____

   _____

2. If you were to rewrite "January" as a haiku, how might you rewrite the phrase "The river is a frozen place" as a five- or seven-syllable line?

   _____

   _____

3. If you were to rewrite Two Haiku as two concrete poems, what shape would you choose for each poem? Why?

   _____

   _____

4. If you were to rewrite "Identity" as a haiku, how might you rewrite the phrase "I'd rather be a tall, ugly weed" as a five- or seven-syllable line?

   _____

   _____

5. If you were to rewrite "400-Meter Free Style" as a lyric poem, how many stanzas would you include? What would be the main idea in each stanza?

   _____

   _____

6. Do you think "400-Meter Free Style" works better as a concrete poem than it would as a haiku? Why?

   _____

   _____

"Wahbegan" by Jim Northrup (text page 845)

Build Vocabulary

Jim Northrup's poem is a powerful tribute to the American soldiers who fought in and survived the Vietnam War. The words of the speaker help you understand the pain and difficulties that stayed with survivors and their families long after the fighting had ended. How do the words in the box help to convey the suffering that Vietnam survivors underwent? What other words might you use to describe the pain and suffering of war?

A. DIRECTIONS: Replace the italicized word or phrase in each sentence with the appropriate word from the box. Then write the new sentence on the line.

tortured	flashbacks	casualty	comfort	memorial

1. Families were notified immediately about each *person killed, wounded, or captured* in the war.

   _____

   _____

2. The town decided to create a statue as a *thing whose purpose is to help people remember* to all war veterans.

   _____

   _____

3. Many soldiers who came back from the war continued to live lives that were *filled with great pain.*

   _____

   _____

4. War veterans back home had to cope with *memories of the past* that haunted their dreams.

   _____

   _____

5. There was little anyone could do or say to give *aid and encouragement* to the former soldiers.

   _____

   _____

B. DIRECTIONS: Write two words that you would use to describe war veterans or their experiences. Then write a sentence using both words.

Word: _____ Word: _____

Sentence:_____

_____

Unit 9: Poetry

"Wahbegan" by Jim Northrup (text page 845)

Connect a Poem to Social Studies

In "Wahbegan," the poet offers insight into the life of a war veteran. He describes how the survivor's experiences continue to haunt him long after the fighting has ended. In addition, he details the suffering that the survivor's family undergoes both before and after the eventual death of the veteran.

Although "Wahbegan" describes a soldier from the Vietnam War, its powerful images could easily apply to any soldier in any war. Participants in war suffer many of the same traumas, regardless of the time or place of the battle. War, the poet seems to suggest, creates a universal suffering.

DIRECTIONS: Use the details in the poem to answer the following questions.

1. What can cause the memories of war to be triggered in a veteran's mind?

_____

_____

2. Why aren't many veterans able to live in complete peacefulness after the war has ended?

_____

_____

3. What do cities or nations often do as a memorial or tribute to fallen war veterans?

_____

_____

4. How do families suffer after the eventual death of a war survivor?

_____

_____

5. What kind of comfort often is offered to families after the loss of a soldier?

_____

_____

6. What kind of memorial does the speaker in "Wahbegan" wish to see established? Why?

_____

_____

7. Based on the poem, in what ways would you say war is harmful to any generation?

_____

_____

"Silver" by Walter de la Mare (text page 856)
"Forgotten Language" by Shel Silverstein (text page 857)
"Drum Song" by Wendy Rose (text page 858)
"If I can stop one Heart from breaking" by Emily Dickinson (text page 859)

Build Vocabulary

Using Word Pairs

Sometimes words appear in pairs because they are opposites. For example, the word *warm-blooded* describes an animal whose body heat stays the same, regardless of the climate it is in. The word *coldblooded* describes an animal whose body temperature matches the climate.

A. DIRECTIONS: Write the meanings of the word pairs below. You may use a dictionary for help.

1. a. *Typical* means _____ b. *Atypical* means _____

2. a. *Unilateral* means _____ b. *Nonpartisan* means _____

3. a. *Partisan* means _____ b. *Bilateral* means _____

4. a. *Sacred* means _____ b. *Profane* means _____

Now write a sentence that uses each pair of words together.

5. _____

6. _____

7. _____

8. _____

Using the Word Bank

vertical	burrow	gourds

B. DIRECTIONS: Write the Word Bank word that best completes each sentence.

1. The rabbit crawled down its _____ and disappeared from sight.

2. A flagpole is a _____ structure often made out of steel.

3. I photographed the pumpkin _____ that we had carved into jack-o'-lanterns.

C. DIRECTIONS: For each related pair of words in CAPITAL LETTERS, choose the lettered pair that best expresses a similar relationship. Circle the letter of your choice.

1. VERTICAL : HORIZONTAL ::
   a. big : fat
   b. wide : narrow
   c. awake : busy
   d. horizon : sky

2. RABBIT : BURROW ::
   a. head : tail
   b. home : shelter
   c. ocean : whale
   d. bird : nest

"Silver" by Walter de la Mare (text page 856)
"Forgotten Language" by Shel Silverstein (text page 857)
"Drum Song" by Wendy Rose (text page 858)
"If I can stop one Heart from breaking" by Emily Dickinson (text page 859)

Build Spelling Skills: The Long *o* Sound Spelled *ow*

Spelling Strategy   The Word Bank word *burrow* contains the long *o* sound spelled *ow*. There are many other words in which the long *o* sound is spelled *ow*.

Examples: low, grow, sorrow, tomorrow

A. Practice: Complete each sentence with a word having the long *o* sound spelled *ow*. The first letter of the word is provided as a clue. Write the entire word.

1. A hurricane is the result of winds that b_____ with great force.

2. A c_____ is a bird that is black all over.

3. The waters of the Mississippi River f_____ through several states.

4. Water freezes into ice when the temperature drops b_____ 32°F.

5. If I run out of money, may I b_____ a little from you?

6. A colorful r_____ may appear in the sky after a rainstorm.

7. The pitcher is ready to t_____ the baseball to the catcher.

8. If it's too hot for you in here, just open a w_____.

9. You can see your s_____ when the sun shines above you.

10. The cows and the sheep grazed in the m_____.

B. Practice: In each sentence, find a word with the long *o* sound that is spelled wrong. Cross out the word and write it correctly.

1. In "Silver," the speaker describes the shadoey coat of feathers on a dove.

2. The speaker clearly admires how the moon gloes on the earth below.

3. In "Forgotten Language," the speaker is somewhat sorroful that his childhood has passed.

4. He seems to want to knoe how the years went by so quickly.

5. In "Drum Song," the speaker describes the very slo movement of the turtle.

6. She also describes how the snowhare moves from bush to burroe.

7. In "If I can stop one Heart from breaking," the speaker hopes she can ease the sorro of another person.

8. Though she mentions helping a robin, she'd probably be just as happy to help a cro.

"Silver" by Walter de la Mare (text page 856)
"Forgotten Language" by Shel Silverstein (text page 857)
"Drum Song" by Wendy Rose (text page 858)
"If I can stop one Heart from breaking" by Emily Dickinson (text page 859)

Build Grammar Skills: Correct Use of Adjectives and Adverbs

People are sometimes confused about the correct use of adjectives and adverbs.

- An **adjective** modifies (describes) a noun or pronoun.

> **Examples:** The *train* was <u>slow</u>.   *I* feel <u>bad</u> about your accident.
> You did a <u>good</u> job.

- An **adverb** modifies a verb, adjective, or other adverb.

> **Examples:** The train *moved* <u>slowly</u>.   *I behaved* <u>badly</u>.
> You *sang* the song <u>well</u>.

A. Practice: Choose the correct word in parentheses to complete each sentence. Write the word.

1. In "Silver," the moon shines (silent, silently) _____ over the trees.

2. The poet details the effects of the moonlight very (good, well) _____ .

3. The speaker in "Forgotten Language" feels (bad, badly) _____ about forgetting the language.

4. He once knew the language quite (good, well) _____ .

5. In "Drum Song," the turtle's legs move (steady, steadily) _____ along the rocks.

6. The poet does a (good, well) _____ job of creating images for the reader to picture.

7. In "If I can stop one Heart from breaking," the speaker may feel (bad, badly) _____ if she is unable to comfort anyone.

8. Her (sole, solely) _____ desire is to help someone in need.

B. Writing Application: Complete the sentences that have been started below. In each sentence, use the word that appears in parentheses.

1. (brightly) The moon _____

_____

2. (sad) The speaker of the forgotten language _____

_____

3. (well) The woodpecker _____

_____

4. (good) A person who comforts others _____

_____

Unit 9: Poetry

"Silver" by Walter de la Mare (text page 856)
"Forgotten Language" by Shel Silverstein (text page 857)
"Drum Song" by Wendy Rose (text page 858)
"If I can stop one Heart from breaking" by Emily Dickinson (text page 859)

Reading Strategy: Make Inferences

When you **make inferences** in a poem, you make guesses and reach conclusions based on details. You supply information that the poet did not state directly in the poem. In order to make reliable inferences, you must pay close attention to details such as sound devices, pictures and images the poem creates, and thoughts or feelings it expresses. Then, compare these details, and think about the meaning they suggest.

For example, notice how the speaker in "Drum Song" begins each stanza with the word *Listen*. This detail can help you infer, or guess, that the speaker is very much aware of nature and its sounds.

DIRECTIONS: Use the following chart to record inferences that you make based on details in each poem. One example is provided.

Poem	Detail	Inference
"Drum Song"	Each stanza starts with the word *Listen*.	The speaker is very much aware of nature and its sounds.
"Silver"		
"Forgotten Language"		
"Drum Song"		
"If I can stop one Heart from breaking"		

"Silver" by Walter de la Mare (text page 856)
"Forgotten Language" by Shel Silverstein (text page 857)
"Drum Song" by Wendy Rose (text page 858)
"If I can stop one Heart from breaking" by Emily Dickinson (text page 859)

Literary Focus: Sound Devices

Poets often use **sound devices** to create musical effects in poetry. Three of the most popular techniques are *rhyme*, *repetition*, and *alliteration*.

- **Rhyme** is created when identical sounds are heard at the ends of different lines. In "Silver," rhymes include *moon* and *shoon*, as well as *sees* and *trees*.

- **Repetition** is created when the same words or phrases are repeated several times, often at the beginnings of lines or stanzas. In "Forgotten Language," the line "How did it go?" is repeated at the end of the poem.

- **Alliteration** is created when the same sound is repeated at the beginning of several words. In "Drum Song," the phrase "feet of four claws" repeats the *f* sound.

DIRECTIONS: As you read the four poems, record examples of rhyme, repetition, and alliteration. One example is provided.

Poem	Rhyme	Repetition	Alliteration
"Silver"	moon/shoon; sees/trees		
"Silver"			
"Forgotten Language"			
"Drum Song"			
"If I can stop one Heart . . .			

Build Vocabulary

Using the Word Root -cede-

The word root -cede- means "to go or move." For example, the word *precede* means "to go before." Sometimes the word root -cede- is spelled -ceed, as in *proceed*, which means "to go forward."

A. Directions: Complete each sentence below with one of the following words having the word root -cede-:

       proceed   exceed   recede   succeed   intercede   concede   precede   secede

1. Although many new businesses open each year, very few of them _____.

2. During the Civil War, many states chose to _____ from the Union.

3. As a responsible driver, you should never _____ the speed limit.

4. A negotiator was hired to _____ on behalf of the prisoner.

5. If there is no rain, we will _____ as planned with our picnic tomorrow.

6. A colorful half-time show will _____ the second half of the football game.

7. As many people get older, their hairline tends to _____.

8. Many people are too proud to _____ that they are wrong.

Using the Word Bank

glistens	borne	low	hover	recede	luminance

B. Directions: Match each word on the left with its meaning on the right. Write the letter of the meaning on the line next to the word it defines.

____ 1. glistens	a. move back
____ 2. borne	b. make the sound a cow makes
____ 3. low	c. brightness, brilliance
____ 4. hover	d. shines, sparkles
____ 5. recede	e. flutter in the air
____ 6. luminance	f. carried

C. Directions: For each related pair of words in CAPITAL LETTERS, choose the lettered pair that best expresses a *similar* relationship. Circle the letter of your choice.

1. COW : LOW ::
   a. sheep : farm
   b. pig : duck
   c. horse : neigh
   d. farmer : feed

2. HOVER : AIR ::
   a. float : water
   b. run : hide
   c. fly : airplane
   d. helicopter : land

3. LUMINANCE : DARKNESS ::
   a. sun : star
   b. earth : grass
   c. light : bulb
   d. ease : difficulty

"New World" by N. Scott Momaday (text page 864)
"One Time" by William Stafford (text page 866)
"Lyric 17" by José Garcia Villa (text page 867)
"For My Sister Molly Who in the Fifties" by Alice Walker (text page 868)

Build Spelling Skills: The *seed* Sound Spelled *cede*

Spelling Strategy The Word Bank word *recede* contains the seed sound spelled *cede*.

• In most words having the *seed* sound, the sound is spelled *cede*.

Examples: recede   secede   concede

• Three words that have the *seed* sound spelled *ceed* are *exceed*, *proceed*, and *succeed*.

A. Practice: Complete the spelling of each word with either *ceed* or *cede*. Write the entire word. Then write the word's meaning.

1. se__ __ __ __   _____

   Meaning: _____

2. ex__ __ __ __   _____

   Meaning: _____

3. pre__ __ __ __   _____

   Meaning: _____

4. pro__ __ __ __   _____

   Meaning: _____

5. suc__ __ __ __   _____

   Meaning: _____

B. Practice: In each sentence, find the word with the *seed* sound spelled incorrectly. Cross out the word and write it correctly.

1. In "New World," the speaker procedes to describe all the beauty of nature that he beholds.

2. He describes how meadows receed through planes of heat and pure distance.

3. In "One Time," the speaker relates how he once interceeded on his friend's behalf.

4. The speaker succeded in bringing home Tina, a blind girl, in the dark.

5. In "Lyric 17," the speaker conceeds that a poem must be both magical and musical.

Challenge: The Word Bank word *glistens* contains the smaller word *listen*, though the two words are not related in meaning. How many other smaller words can you find within the word *glistens*? Write the words on the lines provided.

_____ _____ _____ _____

Name _____ Date _____

"**New World**" by N. Scott Momaday (text page 864)
"**One Time**" by William Stafford (text page 866)
"**Lyric 17**" by José Garcia Villa (text page 867)
"**For My Sister Molly Who in the Fifties**" by Alice Walker (text page 868)

Build Grammar Skills: Pronouns in Comparisons With *than* or *as*

When a pronoun appears after the word *than* or *as* in a **comparison**, sometimes the verb that follows the pronoun is implied rather than stated.

> **Example:** We traveled faster than they.

> **Implied:** We traveled faster than they traveled.

It is important to recognize the verb that is implied in a comparison, so that you use the correct form of the pronoun.

> **Wrong:** I type faster than him.

> **Right:** I type faster than he. (Implied: I type faster than he types.)

A. Practice: Read each sentence. If it contains an incorrect pronoun, cross out the pronoun and write the correct pronoun above it.

1. N. Scott Momaday writes beautiful poetry; few write as well as him.

2. No one in class was more affected by his poem "New World" than me.

3. When the boy walked Tina home, no other youngsters were as happy as them.

4. Ironically, children who have their sight might not be as perceptive as her.

5. Other classes did not analyze Villa's "Lyric 17" as deeply as us.

6. Few poets have described a poem as vividly as him.

7. No one enjoyed Alice Walker's poem more than me.

8. I'll bet no one in her family admired Walker's sister more than her.

B. Writing Application: Complete the sentences that have been started below. In each sentence, include a pronoun that follows the word *than* or *as*.

1. Momaday's visions of a new world _____

_____

2. Tina's companion _____

_____

3. The qualities of a poem _____

_____

4. Sister Molly's creativeness _____

_____

"New World" by N. Scott Momaday (text page 864)
"One Time" by William Stafford (text page 866)
"Lyric 17" by José Garcia Villa (text page 867)
"For My Sister Molly Who in the Fifties" by Alice Walker (text page 868)

Reading Strategy: Use Your Senses

Poems are often filled with vivid images, or word pictures. To experience the image as fully as possible, you must **use your senses**. What things does the speaker describe that you can see? Feel? Hear? Taste? Smell? By using your senses, the poem will become transformed from mere words on a page to a living experience that you participate in.

For example, in "New World" the speaker describes how "the earth glitters with leaves." Close your eyes and picture that description. Can you see the glittering leaves? What colors are they? What do they remind you of? By answering questions such as these, you are using your senses well.

DIRECTIONS: In the chart, record images from the four poems that you experience by using your senses. One example is provided.

Poem	Image	Sense Involved	My Experience
"New World"	"the earth glitters with leaves"	sight	I see red and gold leaves glittering like gold
"New World"			
"One Time"			
"Lyric 17"			
"For My Sister Molly . . ."			

Unit 9: Poetry

Name _____ Date _____

"New World" by N. Scott Momaday (text page 864)
"One Time" by William Stafford (text page 866)
"Lyric 17" by José Garcia Villa (text page 867)
"For My Sister Molly Who in the Fifties" by Alice Walker (text page 868)

Literary Focus: Imagery

Imagery is language that appeals to your senses. Poets use imagery to help you visualize and experience their writing in an intense, lively fashion. Often an image is a visual description of color, shape, or movement. However, it may also appeal to your sense of hearing, taste, touch, or smell.

For example, the poet writes that "Pollen is borne on winds that low . . ." The poet could have written "winds that blow." But the word *low* enables you to hear exactly *how* the winds are blowing.

DIRECTIONS: In each of the four poems, find imagery that appeals to one or more of your senses. Record each word or phrase on the chart where it belongs. One example is provided.

Poem	Sight	Sound	Smell	Taste	Touch
"New World"		"winds that low"			
"New World"					
"One Time"					
"Lyric 17"					
"For My Sister . . ."					

"The Dark Hills" by Edwin Arlington Robinson (text page 876)
"Solar" by Philip Larkin (text page 877)
"Incident in a Rose Garden" by Donald Justice (text page 878)

Build Vocabulary

Using Commonly Confused Words

Some pairs of words look and sound similar, which is why many people tend to confuse their usages. Such commonly confused word pairs include *continuously/continually, beside/besides,* and *imply/infer.*

A. DIRECTIONS: Complete each sentence with one of the two words in parentheses. Write the correct word on the line. If you are unsure of the meaning of a word, look in a dictionary.

1. The phone rang (continually, continuously) _____ for ten minutes.

2. I am (continually, continuously) _____ bothered by junk mail.

3. Place your suitcase (beside, besides) _____ the wall.

4. Who else will be at the party (beside, besides) _____ the twins?

5. May I (imply, infer) _____ from your smile that you're happy?

6. I hope my criticisms don't seem to (imply, infer) _____ that I hate your entire outfit.

Using the Word Bank

| hovers   legions   unrecompensed   continuously   scythe   beckoned   gestures |

B. DIRECTIONS: Write the Word Bank word that matches each definition.

1. not rewarded

2. uninterrupted

3. suspends, lingers

4. large number

5. grass cutter

6. motions

7. called

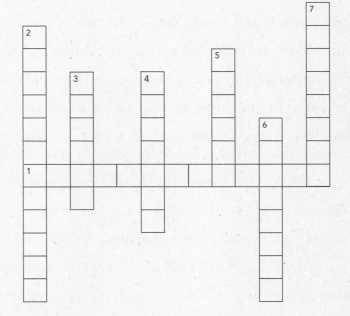

Unit 9: Poetry

"The Dark Hills" by Edwin Arlington Robinson (text page 876)
"Solar" by Philip Larkin (text page 877)
"Incident in a Rose Garden" by Donald Justice (text page 878)

Build Spelling Skills: The *uh* Sound Spelled *o*

Spelling Strategy The Word Bank word *hovers* contains the *uh* sound spelled *o*.

- In most words, the *uh* sound is spelled *u*: up   cut   gush
- In some words, the *uh* sound is spelled *o*: of   done   brother

A. Practice: Complete each sentence with a word having the *uh* sound spelled *o*. The first letter of the word is provided as a clue. Write the entire word.

1. The woman who gave birth to you is your m_____.

2. A son of your parents is your b_____.

3. Many people get married after they fall in l_____.

4. I memorized the first part of the Declaration o_____ Independence.

5. Be sure to wear your g_____ if you plan to play in the snow.

6. The d_____ is a bird that symbolizes peace.

7. If you don't like my gift, you can exchange it for a_____ one.

8. We cannot see many stars that hover far a_____ the universe.

B. Practice: In each sentence, find the word with the *uh* sound spelled incorrectly. Cross out the word and write it correctly.

1. In "The Dark Hills," the sunset huvers like the sound of golden horns.

2. The speaker imagines the last of days fading, and all wars being dun.

3. The speaker in "Solar" pays tribute to the sun that shines high abuve.

4. The speaker is grateful for the burst uf heat that the sun is always giving out.

5. In "Incident in a Rose Garden," the gardener wishes to see his suns in California.

Challenge: The Word Bank word *scythe* comes from the Latin word *scindere*, meaning "to cut." Use a dictionary to help you determine the origins of other Word Bank words.

1. Which word comes from the Latin word *legere*, meaning "to select"? _____

2. Which word comes from the Latin word *gerere*, meaning "to bear or do"? _____

3. Which word comes from the Old English word *beacen*, meaning "beacon"? _____

4. Which word comes from the Middle English word *hoven*, meaning "to stay"? _____

5. Which word comes from the Latin word *pendere*, meaning "to weigh"? _____

6. Which word comes from the Latin word *continuare*, meaning "to join"? _____

"The Dark Hills" by Edwin Arlington Robinson (text page 876)
"Solar" by Philip Larkin (text page 877)
"Incident in a Rose Garden" by Donald Justice (text page 878)

Build Grammar Skills: Correct Use of *like* and *as*

The words *like* and *as* are often confused. Remember these rules:

- The word *like* is a preposition in a prepositional phrase. Use *like* before a noun or pronoun.

   Example: The child behaved *like* an adult.

- The word *as* may be a preposition, but *as*, *as if*, and *as though* are also subordinating conjunctions in a clause with a noun and a verb.

   Example: The child behaved *as* an adult would act.

- Do not use the word *like* to introduce a clause with a noun and verb.

   Wrong: It happened just <u>like</u> I described it.

   Right: It happened just <u>as</u> I described it.

A. Practice: Write the word in parentheses that completes each sentence correctly.

1. The sun sets (like, as) _____ the sound of golden horns.

2. You fade (like, as if) _____ the last of days were fading.

3. Our needs for the sun climb and return (like, as) _____ angels.

4. The sun shines (like, as) _____ a lion's face beams in the sky.

5. The gardener ran from Death (like, as) _____ any person might do.

6. The figure of Death looked just (like, as) _____ his picture.

B. Writing Application: Write sentences that follow the instructions below.

1. Write a sentence about dark hills that uses *as*, *as if*, or *as though*.

   _____

2. Write a sentence about dark hills that uses *like*.

   _____

3. Write a sentence about the sun that uses *as*, *as if*, or *as though*.

   _____

4. Write a sentence about the sun that uses *like*.

   _____

5. Write a sentence about death that uses *as*, *as if*, or *as though*.

   _____

6. Write a sentence about death that uses *like*.

   _____

"The Dark Hills" by Edwin Arlington Robinson (text page 876)
"Solar" by Philip Larkin (text page 877)
"Incident in a Rose Garden" by Donald Justice (text page 878)

Reading Strategy: Respond

Poetry is not a spectator sport. That is, poets do not wish for you merely to sit back and read their words. They want you to participate, or **respond**, to what they have written. When you read a poem, you should try to bring your own experiences to the words. Use your memory and senses to imagine what the poem describes. Listen to and feel the beat of the rhythm. Think about whether or not you agree with the poet's ideas. Let the poem inspire you to ask questions, and then answer them.

For example, in "Solar," the speaker envisions the sun as a "suspended lion face." This may set you to thinking about the color and shape of the sun. You might consider if the comparison of the sun and a lion's face works well for you. You might question what other animal's face may better describe the sun.

DIRECTIONS: In the web below, respond to each poem by recording your thoughts, feelings, and questions about the work. There are no "right" answers, since your response is based on your own special experiences, which are different from all other people's.

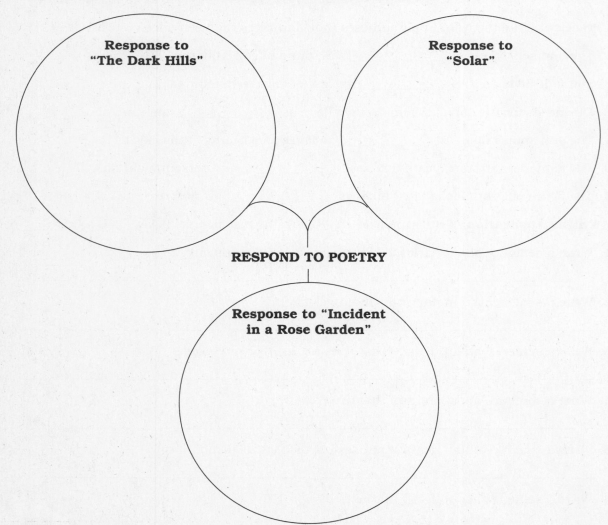

Response to
"The Dark Hills"

Response to
"Solar"

RESPOND TO POETRY

Response to "Incident
in a Rose Garden"

"The Dark Hills" by Edwin Arlington Robinson (text page 876)
"Solar" by Philip Larkin (text page 877)
"Incident in a Rose Garden" by Donald Justice (text page 878)

Literary Focus: Figurative Language

Poets frequently use **figurative language**—language not meant to be taken literally—in order to make their writing more vivid and colorful. Figurative language includes three main devices:

- A **simile** is a comparison of two unlike items that uses the word *like* or *as*. For example: *A meteor flies like a red-hot baseball.*

- A **metaphor** is a direct comparison between two unlike items, describing one as if it were the other, without using *like* or *as*. For example: *A meteor is a red-hot baseball.*

- **Personification** is a description of something nonhuman as if it were human. For example: *The meteors danced in the heavens.*

DIRECTIONS: Use the following chart to record examples of similes, metaphors, and personification in each of the three poems. One example is provided.

Poem	Passage	Figure of Speech	Compares What?
"The Dark Hills"	"horns that sang to rest old bones . . ."	personification	Horns are made to seem like a singer.
"The Dark Hills"			
"Solar"			
"Solar"			
"Incident in a Rose Garden"			
"Incident in a Rose Garden"			

Unit 9: Poetry

"Johnny Appleseed" by Rosemary Carr Benét (text page 895)

Build Vocabulary

Using Forms of *encumber*

A. DIRECTIONS: Each word below on the left is a form of the word *encumber*, meaning "to weigh down." Match each word with its definition. Write the letter of the definition on the line next to the word it defines.

____ 1. cumbersome   a. not weighed down by

____ 2. encumbrance   b. heavy, weighty

____ 3. unencumbered   c. a weight or burden

Now write an original sentence using each form of *encumber*.

4. encumber _____

5. cumbersome_____

6. encumbrance_____

7. unencumbered _____

Using the Word Bank

gnarled	ruddy	encumber
tendril	stalking	lair

B. DIRECTIONS: Write the Word Bank word that best matches each clue.

1. It's where you might find a bear. _____

2. It might describe an apple or a cheek. _____

3. It grows out of a plant. _____

4. It's how an old tree trunk might look. _____

5. It's what someone behind you may be doing. _____

6. It's what a heavy load will do to you. _____

Recognizing Synonyms

C. DIRECTIONS: For each related pair of words in CAPITAL LETTERS, choose the lettered pair that best expresses a *similar* relationship. Circle the letter of your choice.

1. RUDDY : RED ::
   a. tan : brown
   b. white : blue
   c. funny : joke
   d. runny : nose

2. LAIR : LION ::
   a. jungle : trees
   b. tiger : stripes
   c. nest : feathers
   d. cave : bat

3. TENDRIL : PLANT ::
   a. leaf : green
   b. branch : tree
   c. garden : flower
   d. stem : bottom

"Johnny Appleseed" by Rosemary Carr Benét (text page 895)

Build Spelling Skills: Confusing Words with *ia* and *ai*

Spelling Strategy   The Word Bank word *lair* is sometimes mistaken for the word *liar*.

- When spelling a word with the letter combination *ai* or *ia*, do not transpose the two letters and accidentally spell a different word.

Examples: lair/liar   dairy/diary   trail/trial   complaint/compliant

A. Practice: Write the word with *ai* or *ia* that matches each clue below. Spell the word correctly.

1. It's a path that hikers follow in the woods. _____

2. It's an event in court with a judge and jury. _____

3. It's a person who tells lies. _____

4. It's a home for a wild animal. _____

5. It's a private book in which people record their thoughts. _____

6. It's a place where butter and cheese are made. _____

7. It describes people who cooperate, or comply, with you. _____

8. It's a statement of unhappiness. _____

B. Practice: In each sentence, find a word with the letter combination *ai* or *ia* that is spelled incorrectly. Cross out the word and write the correct word above it.

1. Johnny Appleseed spent much of his life planting apple trees without compliant.

2. It would be interesting to discover a dairy in which Johnny recorded his experiences.

3. As Johnny walked the trial through the woods, he planted seeds along the way.

4. It was a difficult trail of Johnny's courage, but he passed with flying colors.

5. Even wild animals in their liar didn't dare interrupt Johnny in his work.

6. I would be a lair if I said that Johnny Appleseed was a poor role model for us today.

7. Johnny would rather work in an apple orchard than on a diary farm.

8. He was complaint with all the laws and broke none when he planted his seeds.

Challenge: The Word Bank word *stalking* could be tricky to spell because it has a silent *l*. Can you think of six more words that contain a silent *l*? Write your list on the lines provided. Then compare it to that of a classmate.

_____   _____   _____

_____   _____   _____

"Johnny Appleseed" by Rosemary Carr Benét (text page 895)

Build Grammar Skills: Unnecessary Commas

In your writing, you should avoid the use of **unnecessary commas**. Unless you are separating several items in a series or introductory or independent clauses, you do not need to use a comma.

Wrong: The apples were red, and green.   **Right:** The apples were red and green.

Right: The apples were shiny, red, and green. (commas used for items in a series)

Wrong: He walked along, and planted seeds.   **Right:** He walked along and planted seeds.

Right: He walked along, and he planted seeds. (commas used for two independent clauses)

A. Practice: Rewrite each of the following sentences, leaving out any unnecessary commas.

1. Jonathan Chapman, and Johnny Appleseed, were one and the same person.

   _____

2. Even when he was in his seventies, Johnny planted, and harvested.

   _____

3. He carried bags, and sacks, of appleseeds for planting.

   _____

4. Johnny knew, the roots, tendrils, and blossoms, of each plant.

   _____

5. As a result of his efforts, thousands, and thousands, of new trees grew annually.

   _____

6. Johnny was unafraid of any bear, or other wild animal that might roam the area.

   _____

7. Both children, and adults, now sing the praises of Johnny Appleseed.

   _____

8. As most everyone would agree, he is a hero, and a role model, for all the world.

   _____

B. Writing Application: Use each of the phrases below in a sentence. Use commas where necessary, but avoid using unnecessary commas.

1. woods and forests _____

2. a rake and a bag of seeds _____

3. difficult but worth the effort _____

4. took root and grew _____

5. looked at the results and smiled _____

Reading for Success: Strategies for Reading Folk Literature

Folk Literature is older than recorded history: Its tales, stories, legends, and myths have been passed down for many generations. Because these stories were often told orally, they often contain repetition (making them easier to remember) and dialect (specialized vocabulary and grammar of the region).

- **Understand cultural context.** You will better understand the actions and characters of a story if you know the culture from which it comes.

- **Recognize the storyteller's purpose.** Remember that these tales are traditional stories that people used to communicate shared beliefs and to explain their world. Try to identify the original storyteller's audience.

- **Predict.** Folk literature is predictable. Good characters and deeds are rewarded; bad characters are either banished or reformed This pattern makes it easy for you to predict the instructional message.

DIRECTIONS: Read the following tale, "Dixie, the Knight of the Silver Spurs" by M. A. Jagendorf, and use the reading strategies to increase your comprehension. In the margin, note where you understand cultural context, recognize the storyteller's purpose, and predict. Finally, write your response to the selection on the lines provided.

from "Dixie, the Knight of the Silver Spurs"
by M. A. Jagendorf

The following selection is a folk tale from the southern United States that takes place during the Civil War.

The armies of the North called him "Dixie" and Southerners called him "the Knight of the Silver Spurs," and when folks in Florida want to bring you a pleasant smile, they'll tell you grand tales about him. His real name was Captain John Dickison and, like the knights of olden days, he performed many daring deeds. Folks in Florida said he was better than any knight of any land.

He was captain of a small cavalry troop that brought no end of trouble to the Northern fighting men.

One night the captain came to a ball given by Federal officers. Before the pleasant evening had passed, he was off with eighteen horses, a dance band, an ambulance, and forty men. Could any knight of old beat that!

But the tale folks of the Golden Sand State like most to tell is how he and his cavalry band captured a ship of the deep blue sea. And this is how he did it.

Day and night he gave no rest to the Northern army that tried to stop supplies coming to the Southern fighting men. He was everywhere along the St. Johns River and its many offshoots of rivers nearby. He gave no rest to the soldiers on the land or on the water.

On a lucky day Dixie and his daredevils captured a Federal post at the mouth of the Oklawaha River, which made the Federals hopping mad. The commanding officer ordered two boats, the "Columbine"

Unit 10: The American Folk Tradition

and the gunboat "Ottawa," to capture Captain Dickison and his rebel band. The Captain learned of it and, hidden by the thick growth along the river, followed the two boats that were after him. When they reached a narrow part, his men opened fire. The boats answered, but the cavalry was getting the better of the fight.

The two captains of the vessels decided their boats were more important than victory over Dickison, so they separated to lead the fierce Captain off their track.

But you know success sharpens wits. Captain Dickison thought quickly and decided to follow the "Columbine," steaming southward. Hiding in the deep growth along the shore, this was a simple task. When both boat and cavalry reached Horse Landing where the river is very narrow, Dickison and his men opened fire. The boat tried to escape, but hit a sandbar. Dickison and his men kept up the attack fiercely, and soon the "Columbine" had to hoist the white flag of surrender.

Captain Dickison and his triumphant cavalrymen boarded the boat, took away all supplies useful to the Southern cause, removed the wounded prisoners, and burned the boat.

Thus it came to pass that a troop of cavalrymen commanded by a daring soldier conquered a vessel of the sea.

So proud and so grateful were the Southern folk of Florida for this heroic deed that the ladies of Orange Springs took all their silver treasures and heirlooms and melted them down to make a pair of silver spurs for Captain Dickison. And so he was called the Knight of the Silver Spurs.

The Union soldiers called him Dixie because he came upon them from Dixie Land, as the Southern states were sometimes called.

But, by whatever name, his is the fame.

"Johnny Appleseed" by Rosemary Carr Benét (text page 895)

Literary Focus: Oral Tradition

The **oral tradition** is the passing of stories, beliefs, and customs from generation to generation by word of mouth. Such stories include legends, folk tales, and ballads. After years of retelling, many of the stories were finally written down.

Stories in the oral tradition take on special qualities when you hear them or recite them, as opposed to merely reading them. For example, you might enjoy the rhythm or the rhyme of the lines. You may find favorite words or phrases in the stanzas. Anything about the story that you *enjoy* hearing is what makes the oral tradition so special.

DIRECTIONS: Read "Johnny Appleseed" aloud, or listen closely as a classmate reads it to you. Find a special element that appeals to you in each stanza, such as rhyme, rhythm, repetition, or a particular word or phrase. Use the chart below to record what you like most about each part of the story.

Stanzas	Elements I Enjoy Most
1 and 2	
3 and 4	
5 and 6	
7 and 8	
9 and 10	
11, 12, and 13	

"Coyote Steals the Sun and Moon" retold by Richard Erdoes and Alfonso Ortiz
(text page 902)
"The Spirit Chief Names the Animal People" by Mourning Dove (text page 905)

Build Vocabulary

Using the Suffix *-fy*

The suffix *-fy* means "to make." The suffix changes a noun or adjective into a verb.

Example: *pure + -fy = purify* ("to make pure")

A. DIRECTIONS: Match each word on the left with its definition on the right. Write the letter of the definition on the line next to the word it defines.

____ 1. horrify   a. to make larger

____ 2. classify   b. to make clear

____ 3. testify   c. to make false, tell a lie

____ 4. beautify   d. to make as one unit

____ 5. clarify   e. to give testimony

____ 6. falsify   f. to make beautiful

____ 7. unify   g. to cause a feeling or shock

____ 8. magnify   h. to put into groups or classes

Using the Word Bank

shriveled	pursuit	arouse	purify

B. DIRECTIONS: Write the Word Bank word that best completes each sentence.

1. The parents tried to _____ the sleepy child from his nap.

2. A raisin is a _____ grape that is usually seedless.

3. The man bought a filter in order to _____ the water from his faucet.

4. The criminal escaped, but the police were close in _____.

Recognizing Antonymns

C. DIRECTIONS: Circle the word that is most *opposite* in meaning to the word in CAPITAL LETTERS.

1. SHRIVELED: 2. PURSUIT: 3. AROUSE: 4. PURIFY:
   a. shrunken   a. surrender   a. wake   a. pure
   b. fat   b. chase   b. spend   b. light
   c. hot   c. dream   c. complete   c. soil
   d. cold   d. suit   d. deaden   d. heavy

"Coyote Steals the Sun and Moon" retold by Richard Erdoes and Alfonso Ortiz
-(text page 902)
"The Spirit Chief Names the Animal People" by Mourning Dove (text page 905)

Build Spelling Skills: Dropping the e or y When Adding -fy

Spelling Strategy   The Word Bank word *purify* is formed by adding the suffix *-fy* to the word *pure*. Notice how the word *pure* changes when the *-fy* ending is added.

• To add the suffix *-fy* to a word ending in *e* or *y*, change the *e* or *y* to *i* before adding *-fy*.

Examples: pure − e + i + fy = purify   beauty − y + i + fy = beautify

A. Practice: Change each adjective or noun in the left column into a verb by adding the suffix *-fy*. Write your new word on the line.

Adjective or Noun	Verb	Adjective or Noun	Verb
1. ample	_____	6. intense	_____
2. code	_____	7. mummy	_____
3. diverse	_____	8. note	_____
4. beauty	_____	9. verse	_____
5. false	_____	10. pure	_____

B. Practice: Complete each sentence below by changing the word in parentheses to a verb that ends in *-fy*. Write your new sentence on the line.

1. Coyote didn't want to (note) _____ the Kachinas that he and Eagle planned to take their sun and moon.

2. Coyote reasoned that the sun and moon would (ample) _____ his light and help him catch animals.

3. Instead of managing to (simple) _____ his life, Coyote complicated it by letting the sun and moon get away.

4. The Spirit Chief planned to (code) _____ all the animals by having a specific name assigned to each one.

5. Although Coyote didn't care for the name Imitator, it certainly did not (false) _____ the kind of character he was.

6. Complications began to (intense) _____ for Coyote after he overslept on the day when names were distributed.

Challenge: The Word Bank words *purify* and *pursuit* both start with the letters *pur*. How many other words can you think of that start with *pur*? Make a list on the lines provided, and later compare it with a classmate's.

_____   _____   _____

_____   _____   _____

Selection Support   **313**

Unit 10: The American
Folk Tradition

"Coyote Steals the Sun and Moon" retold by Richard Erdoes and Alfonso Ortiz
(text page 902)

"The Spirit Chief Names the Animal People" by Mourning Dove (text page 905)

Build Grammar Skills: Commas in Compound Sentences

A **compound sentence** is a sentence that contains two independent clauses. The clauses are joined by one of the coordinating conjunctions: *and, but, or, nor, for, yet.* When you write a compound sentence, use a **comma** before the coordinating conjunction in order to separate the two independent clauses.

COMMA

┌──────INDEPENDENT CLAUSE──────┐   ┌─INDEPENDENT CLAUSE─┐
Examples: Coyote wished to steal the sun and moon, and Eagle agreed to the plan.

Coyote and Eagle stole the items, but later the items escaped from them.

A. Practice: Rewrite each of the following sentences, inserting commas where they are needed.

1. Coyote was a poor hunter but Eagle was an exceptional one.

   _____

2. The two needed light for hunting so they stole the sun and the moon.

   _____

3. Coyote wanted to carry the items but Eagle refused his request several times.

   _____

4. Finally Coyote carried the box and sure enough the sun and moon escaped.

   _____

5. The Spirit Chief was giving out names and Coyote wished for a new one.

   _____

6. Coyote planned to show up early but the luckless character overslept.

   _____

7. Coyote had to keep his old name but the Spirit Chief also made him chief of all tribes.

   _____

B. Writing Application: Write each of the pairs of sentences below as a compound sentence. Use commas where necessary.

1. Coyote needed help with his hunting. The sun and moon could offer more light.

   _____

2. The box opened. The sun and moon escaped to the sky.

   _____

3. The world turned cold as a result. It was all Coyote's fault.

   _____

"Coyote Steals the Sun and Moon" retold by Richard Erdoes and Alfonso Ortiz
(text page 902)

"The Spirit Chief Names the Animal People" by Mourning Dove (text page 905)

Reading Strategy: Understand the Cultural Context

One way to appreciate a myth more fully is to **understand the cultural context** of the story. Pay close attention to details about the time and place of the myth, and the customs and beliefs of its characters. For example, in "Coyote Steals the Sun and Moon," the Kachinas perform sacred dances in which they imitate gods and the spirits of their ancestors. This detail helps you understand that the Zuñi culture that produced the myth strongly believed in the power of gods and in ancestors' spirits.

DIRECTIONS: Use the following chart to record details about the cultural context of the selections. Explain what each detail indicates about the culture that produced the story. One example is provided.

Selection	Detail	What It Shows
"Coyote Steals the Sun and Moon"	Kachinas dance to imitate gods and ancestors' spirits.	The Zuñi believed in the power of gods and ancestors' spirits.
"Coyote Steals the Sun and Moon"		
"Coyote Steals the Sun and Moon"		
"The Spirit Chief Names the Animal People"		
"The Spirit Chief Names the Animal People"		
"The Spirit Chief Names the Animal People"		

"Coyote Steals the Sun and Moon" retold by Richard Erdoes and Alfonso Ortiz
(text page 902)
"The Spirit Chief Names the Animal People" by Mourning Dove (text page 905)

Literary Focus: Myth

A **myth** is an ancient tale that has its roots in the beliefs of a particular group or nation. Myths often tell about the adventures of gods or great heroes who possess special powers. The common themes found in myths include subjects such as creation, the origin of the universe, the meaning of life and death, and occurrences in nature.

Often, a myth will attempt to explain a natural event, or explain why animals behave as they do. For example, "Coyote Steals the Sun and the Moon" offers an explanation as to why Coyote is such a poor hunter. It is because he does not have enough light to see clearly.

DIRECTIONS: Complete the chart below with details from each myth that explain natural events or an animal's behavior. One example is provided.

Myth	Explanation of a Natural Event	Explanation of an Animal's Behavior
"Coyote Steals the Sun and Moon"		Coyote is a poor hunter because he needs more light to see.
"Coyote Steals the Sun and Moon"		
"Coyote Steals the Sun and Moon"		
"The Spirit Chief Names the Animal People"		
"The Spirit Chief Names the Animal People"		

"Chicoria" by José Griego y Maestas and Rudolfo A. Anaya (text page 912)
"Brer Possum's Dilemma" by Jackie Torrence (text page 915)
"Why the Waves Have Whitecaps" by Zora Neale Hurston (text page 918)

Build Vocabulary

Using Synonyms

Many words in the English language are *synonyms*—words with similar meanings. For example, the words *small* and *tiny* are synonyms. Synonyms are helpful because they enable writers to avoid repeating the same word over and over.

A. DIRECTIONS: Choose the word that is a synonym for the underlined word in each sentence. Circle the letter of your choice.

1. The detective faced a <u>difficult</u> problem.
   a. simple   b. challenging   c. new   d. old

2. The <u>charitable</u> man gave away lots of money.
   a. selfish   b. confused   c. nervous   d. generous

3. We began to <u>categorize</u> the new books for the library.
   a. sort   b. stamp   c. read   d. unpack

4. The coffee machine is still not <u>operative</u>.
   a. present   b. large   c. working   d. cheap

Using the Word Bank

cordially	haughty	commenced	pitiful

B. DIRECTIONS: Write the Word Bank word that is a synonym for each word below.

1. began _____

2. sad _____

3. friendly _____

4. conceited _____

C. DIRECTIONS: Circle the word that is most *opposite* in meaning to the word in CAPITAL LETTERS.

1. CORDIALLY
   a. warmly
   b. nicely
   c. forgetful
   d. rudely
2. HAUGHTY
   a. humble
   b. quick
   c. slow
   d. evil

3. COMMENCED
   a. started
   b. ended
   c. watched
   d. wrote
4. PITIFUL
   a. sorrowful
   b. heavy
   c. caring
   d. proud

"Chicoria" by José Griego y Maestas and Rudolfo A. Anaya (text page 912)
"Brer Possum's Dilemma" by Jackie Torrence (text page 915)
"Why the Waves Have Whitecaps" by Zora Neale Hurston (text page 918)

Build Spelling Skills: The *aw* Sound Spelled *au, ou, o, a,* or *aw*

Spelling Strategy The Word Bank word *haughty* contains the *aw* sound spelled *au.*

• The *aw* sound in a word may be spelled *au, ou, o, a,* or *aw.*

Examples: <u>au</u>thor   br<u>ou</u>ght   t<u>o</u>ss   t<u>a</u>ll   l<u>aw</u>

A. Practice: Write a word with the *aw* sound that answers each clue. Put one letter in each blank.

1. opposite of large   ___ ___ ___ ___ ___

2. opposite of a win   ___ ___ ___ ___

3. people who watch a movie   ___ ___ ___ ___ ___ ___ ___ ___

4. past tense of *see*   ___ ___ ___

5. breathing dust may make you do this   ___ ___ ___ ___ ___

6. past tense of *think*   ___ ___ ___ ___ ___ ___

7. a child's toy that might walk or talk   ___ ___ ___ ___

8. a large place with many stores   ___ ___ ___ ___

9. clap hands for a performer   ___ ___ ___ ___ ___ ___ ___

10. create a picture by hand   ___ ___ ___ ___

B. Practice: In each sentence, find a word with the *aw* sound that is spelled wrong. Cross out the word and write the correct word above it.

1. In "Chicoria," the poet named Chicoria was brawght from New Mexico to compete with the California poet Gracia.

2. Chicoria sawt to sit at the master's dinner table.

3. Chicoria gawt the rancher to invite him after explaining how New Mexican goats nurse three kids at once.

4. Brer Possum had always thaught that snakes were dangerous and evil creatures.

5. He never should have stopped when he sau Brer Snake in trouble.

6. Nevertheless, Brer Possum helped free Brer Snake, hoping he wouldn't be cought and harmed by the snake.

7. The story tought the lesson that you shouldn't go looking for trouble if it doesn't come to you.

"Chicoria" by José Griego y Maestas and Rudolfo A. Anaya (text page 912)
"Brer Possum's Dilemma" by Jackie Torrence (text page 915)
"Why the Waves Have Whitecaps" by Zora Neale Hurston (text page 918)

Build Grammar Skills: Commas in a Series

When three or more words or phrases are listed together in a series, you use **commas** to separate them. You also use a comma before the final conjunction.

Example: The story's main characters are the ranch owner, Gracia, and Chicoria.

A. Practice: Write each of the following sentences, inserting commas where necessary to separate items in a series.

1. Chicoria was a poor unknown but talented poet from New Mexico.

   _____

2. When Chicoria spoke, the rancher sat listened and apologized.

   _____

3. Brer Possum was a friendly caring and generous creature.

   _____

4. Brer Snake appealed for help a first second and third time.

   _____

5. Brer Snake pleaded with convinced and finally tricked Brer Possum.

   _____

6. Mrs. Wind bragged that her children could walk fly swim sing talk and cry.

   _____

7. The proud powerful and clever Mrs. Water became annoyed with her boasts.

   _____

8. Mrs. Wind looked searched and called for her lost children.

   _____

B. Writing Application: Write sentences about the characters and events in the selections. Include the series of items below and use commas to separate them.

1. owners/workers/servants _____

   _____

2. looked/watched/listened _____

   _____

3. sneaky/mean/unpredictable _____

   _____

4. left/turned around/returned _____

   _____

"Chicoria" by José Griego y Maestas and Rudolfo A. Anaya (text page 912)
"Brer Possum's Dilemma" by Jackie Torrence (text page 915)
"Why the Waves Have Whitecaps" by Zora Neale Hurston (text page 918)

Reading Strategy: Recognize the Storyteller's Purpose

Storytellers tell stories for different reasons, or *purposes*. Sometimes a storyteller's purpose is to entertain or amuse the audience. Other times the purpose is to inform or educate people about a topic or tradition. Still other times the purpose may be to model a certain type of behavior, or to persuade the audience to accept a certain idea.

Sometimes a storyteller may have more than one purpose. For example, in "Chicoria," the storyteller entertains the audience by describing the bet that Chicoria makes. But at the same time, he teaches, models behavior, and explains as well.

DIRECTIONS: Complete the chart by supplying details about each story to illustrate the storyteller's purpose. One example is provided.

"Chicoria"	
Purpose	**Details from the Text**
to entertain	Chicoria makes a bet.

"Brer Possum's Dilemma"	
Purpose	**Details from the Text**

"Why the Waves Have Whitecaps"	
Purpose	**Details from the Text**

"Chicoria" by José Griego y Maestas and Rudolfo A. Anaya (text page 912)
"Brer Possum's Dilemma" by Jackie Torrence (text page 915)
"Why the Waves Have Whitecaps" by Zora Neale Hurston (text page 918)

Literary Focus: Folk Tales

A **folk tale** was originally composed orally and passed from generation to generation by word of mouth. There are many kinds of folk tales, including fables, legends, myths, and tall tales. Modern-day writers who retell folk tales try to capture the spirit of the original tales, so that the stories convey the same values and ideas.

Many folk tales have unusual characters. One reason the folk tale remains popular is because people enjoy telling about these entertaining individuals. For example, in "Chicoria," the title character is a clever person who is able to win a bet and win over an insensitive master at the same time.

DIRECTIONS: In the chart below, record details about a main character in each folk tale. Supply adjectives that best describe each character. Then give examples from the story to explain why the character is so unusual or entertaining. One example is provided.

Folk Tale	Character	Adjectives	Examples
"Chicoria"	Chicoria	talented, clever	He puts Gracia to shame with his poetry.
"Chicoria"			
"Brer Possum's Dilemma"			
"Brer Possum's Dilemma"			
"Why the Waves Have Whitecaps"			
"Why the Waves Have Whitecaps"			

from The Right Stuff by Tom Wolfe (text page 923)

Build Vocabulary

Tom Wolfe's book excerpt gives you an idea of how proud Americans in the 1960's felt about the astronauts who were beginning to explore the "New Frontier." In addition, the introduction to the book excerpt helps explain how America got involved in its "New Frontier" exploration, and what was expected of the astronauts who participated in the space program. How do the words in the box help to describe the space program and its challenges? What other words might you use to convey the idea of a new challenge for America and American explorers?

A. DIRECTIONS: Replace the italicized word or words in each sentence with the appropriate word from the box. Then write the new sentence on the line.

embark	frontier	tracts	rigorous	aerobatic

1. All astronauts were expected to undergo a *very difficult and strict* period of training before ever going into space.

   _____

   _____

2. The goal was to prepare astronauts to *begin a journey* on a space adventure that was adventurous but highly risky.

   _____

   _____

3. Even pilots with lots of *airplane stunt* experience had to start from scratch when learning how to fly a spaceship.

   _____

   _____

4. The astronauts' exploration of the *unexplored territory* in space was a historic step for the entire world.

   _____

   _____

5. Instead of conquering large *stretches* of land, the astronauts proved that stretches of outer space could be conquered by humans on Earth.

   _____

   _____

B. DIRECTIONS: Write two words you might use in a story about an astronaut. Then use each word in a sentence.

Word: _____

Sentence: _____

Word: _____

Sentence: _____

from The Right Stuff by Tom Wolfe (text page 923)

Connecting a Nonfiction Work to Social Studies

As a rule, nonfiction books do more than just report on specific people or events. Through their writing or reporting, authors of nonfiction also manage to convey the tone of the times about which they are writing. They give readers an idea of what people's thoughts, beliefs, and attitudes were at that time. When reading about a historical era, readers are able to compare and contrast that age with their own. They can think about ways that a nation's attitudes then, and its attitudes now, are similar or different.

DIRECTIONS: In the chart below, record details about the attitudes that people in the 1960's had toward each topic listed. Then describe the attitudes of people today on those same topics.

Topic	Attitudes in the 1960's	Attitudes Today
space exploration		
heroes and heroism		
the Presidency		
parades		
patriotism		

"Hammerman" by Adrien Stoutenburg (text page 934)
"John Henry" Traditional (text page 940)
"Paul Bunyan of the North Woods" by Carl Sandburg (text page 944)
"Pecos Bill: The Cyclone" by Harold W. Felton (text page 946)
"Davy Crockett's Dream" by Davy Crockett (text page 952)

Build Vocabulary

Using Forms of *skeptic*

The word *skeptic* is a noun meaning "a person who questions matters that are generally accepted." There are several other words that are forms of *skeptic*, including *skeptical*, *skeptically*, and *skepticism*.

A. DIRECTIONS: Complete each sentence with one of the following words:

skeptic   skeptical   skeptically   skepticism

1. Neither country agreed to sign the agreement because of _____ on both sides.

2. The _____ refused to believe that it would rain, despite the dark clouds.

3. The man viewed the stranger _____ as he told his hard-luck story.

4. Some people think it is wise to have a _____ view of the world.

Using the Word Bank

hefted	granite	commotion	usurped
invincible	futile	inexplicable	skeptics

B. DIRECTIONS: Write the Word Bank word that best matches each clue.

1. It's how a championship ball team might feel. _____

2. It's what an large accident might cause. _____

3. They're people who might not believe you. _____

4. It's what the weight lifter did in the gym. _____

5. It describes trying to stop a flood with a napkin. _____

6. It's a very hard rock. _____

7. It describes a mystery. _____

8. It's how the angry people got rid of their king. _____

"Hammerman" by Adrien Stoutenburg (text page 934)
"John Henry" Traditional (text page 940)
"Paul Bunyan of the North Woods" by Carl Sandburg (text page 944)
"Pecos Bill: The Cyclone" by Harold W. Felton (text page 946)
"Davy Crockett's Dream" by Davy Crockett (text page 952)

Build Spelling Skills: Multi-Syllable Words With *m* in the Middle

Spelling Strategy   The Word Bank word *commotion* has a double *m* in the middle of the word.

• If a multi-syllable word has the *m* sound in the middle, the sound is frequently spelled *mm*.

Examples: commotion   communicate

A. Practice: Supply the missing letter or letters in each word below. Then write the entire word.

1. co____itment _____

2. acco____odate _____

3. co____unication _____

4. co____ission _____

5. co____emorate _____

6. co____ittee _____

7. co____ander _____

8. co____encement _____

9. co____uter _____

10. co____unity _____

B. Practice: In each sentence, find a multi-syllable word with the *m* sound in the middle that is misspelled. Cross out the word and write the correct word above it.

1. John Henry was known for his power with a hamer.

2. John Henry was a comitted man who wouldn't give up once he took up a challenge.

3. The gramar in "John Henry" reflects a former African-American dialect.

4. Both "Hammerman" and "John Henry" comemorate the greatness of their hero.

5. According to legend, an earthquake resulted from the comotion of Paul Bunyan dancing.

6. Paul supposedly stopped the rain by swiming upward and turning it off.

7. One of the most famous comutes of all time was Pecos Bill's ride on a cyclone.

8. The entire comunity was amazed when Pecos Bill made the cyclone disintegrate.

9. In Davy Crockett's dream, a fellow called Oak Wing seemed to want to accomodate him.

10. Oak Wing was raming Davy with a pole to loosen him from a log, but in fact it was all just

    Davy's dream.

Challenge: The Word Bank word *usurped* begins with the *u* sound spelled *u*. Make a list of other words you know that start with the *u* sound spelled *u*. Write your words on the lines provided; then compare your list to classmates' lists.

_____ _____ _____ _____

Unit 10: The American Folk Tradition

"Hammerman" by Adrien Stoutenburg (text page 934)
"John Henry" Traditional (text page 940)
"Paul Bunyan of the North Woods" by Carl Sandburg (text page 944)
"Pecos Bill: The Cyclone" by Harold W. Felton (text page 946)
"Davy Crockett's Dream" by Davy Crockett (text page 952)

Build Grammar Skills: Variety in Sentence Beginnings

As a good writer, you should try to use **variety in your sentence beginnings.** Not all your sentences need to start the same way. For example, some sentences might begin with a noun or pronoun that is the subject of the sentence. Other sentences might begin with an adverb or adverb clauses. Still other sentences might start with a prepositional phrase.

Subject: John Henry was quite a powerful man.

Adverb: Ironically, his strength led to his downfall.

Adverb Clause: As the contest continued, John Henry tired.

Prepositional Phrase: In the end, John Henry won the contest but died.

A. Practice: Identify the underlined element that begins each sentence as either a *subject, adverb, adverb clause, or prepositional phrase.*

1. Southerners loved to tell stories about their hero, John Henry. _____

2. In John's mind, the best place to be was where the trains went. _____

3. When John heard about a contest against a machine, he signed up. _____

4. Sadly, John Henry died after winning the contest. _____

5. Paul Bunyan was famous for his great size and strength. _____

6. With his ox Babe, Paul cleared forest after forest. _____

7. Undoubtedly, Pecos Bill is one of our most colorful legendary figures. _____

8. After a cyclone threatened the area, Pecos Bill rode it away. _____

9. In a dream, Davy Crockett saw himself trapped in a log. _____

10. A fellow named Oak Wing began to ram Davy out of the log. _____

B. Writing Application: Rewrite each of the following sentences, using a different kind of sentence beginning.

1. John Henry raced the steam drill as everyone else looked on.

_____

2. To the surprise of many, John was able to beat the drill.

_____

3. An earthquake was once created when Paul Bunyan danced too hard.

_____

4. In one unbelievable story, two mosquitoes ate one of Paul's oxen.

_____

"Hammerman" by Adrien Stoutenburg (text page 934)
"John Henry" Traditional (text page 940)
"Paul Bunyan of the North Woods" by Carl Sandburg (text page 944)
"Pecos Bill: The Cyclone" by Harold W. Felton (text page 946)
"Davy Crockett's Dream" by Davy Crockett (text page 952)

Reading Strategy: Predict

As you read a tall tale, you may be able to **predict** future events by paying close attention to details about the main characters. Each trait that a character possesses can serve as a clue to something the character will do later in the story.

For example, in "Hammerman," John Henry says that he was born to swing a hammer in his hand. That comment indicates his trait of determination. Once you discover how determined John Henry is to use his hammer, you might predict that he will work as a builder of railroad tracks.

DIRECTIONS: Use the traits you learn about characters in the five selections to make predictions about what will happen to them. Record your predictions in the chart below. One example is provided.

Character	Trait	Prediction
John Henry	determination	He will build railroads.
Paul Bunyan		
Pecos Bill		
Davy Crockett		

Selection Support **327**

"Hammerman" by Adrien Stoutenburg (text page 934)

"John Henry" Traditional (text page 940)

"Paul Bunyan of the North Woods" by Carl Sandburg (text page 944)

"Pecos Bill: The Cyclone" by Harold W. Felton (text page 946)

"Davy Crockett's Dream" by Davy Crockett (text page 952)

Literary Focus: Tall Tales

A **tall tale** is a humorous story that presents exaggerated, impossible events in a matter-of-fact way. Many tall tales are associated with life on the American frontier. Although the stories themselves contain gross exaggerations, they often reveal aspects of settling the American West that are indeed real and true. For example, "Paul Bunyan of the North Woods" exaggerates the strength of its hero. However, the story also shows how lumberjacks undertook the task of clearing the West for future settlers and pioneers.

DIRECTIONS: In the chart below, record examples of exaggerations from each of the tall tales. Explain what each exaggeration reveals about real life at that time. One example is provided.

Tall Tale	Exaggeration	What It Reveals About Real Life
"Paul Bunyan of the North Woods"	The axmen's dance creates an earthquake.	Lumberjacks took time off to relax and celebrate.
"Hammerman"		
"John Henry"		
"Paul Bunyan of the North Woods"		
"Pecos Bill: The Cyclone"		
"Davy Crockett's Dream"		